# PRAISE
# WITCHCRAFT

MW00803911

"In this concise work, Craig Spencer approaches the origins and concepts of witchcraft from a unique angle, based upon his own local knowledge and language together with insightful research. This book will prove to be a constructive introduction to the concepts of the craft and equally a helpful study manual for the discerning student."

— Vikki Bramshaw, author of *'Craft of the Wise: A Practical Guide'* and *'New Forest Folklore, Traditions & Charms'*

"In this era of distractions and decontextualisation it is so important that we are reminded where the movements we belong to come from. Spencer's work asks us to celebrate the progenitors, and puts roots back in the soil of the past."

— Lee Morgan, author of *'A Deed Without a Name'*

"In his new book Witchcraft Unchained, Craig Spencer brings the mysteries of witchcraft into our modern times. This well researched book sheds light on magical ideas and practices that were once surrounded by shadows and whispers. It is here we learn about the origins of the modern craft and the magical practices of the witch. With this book you will take power from history and transform it into a workable craft for the 21st Century."

— Chris Allaun, author of *'The Black Book of Johnathan Knotbristle the Charmer'*

# WITCHCRAFT UNCHAINED

## Exploring the History & Traditions
of British Craft

# ABOUT THE AUTHOR

Living in the Northwest of England in the magical Lancashire County, I have long been surrounded by the occult. A holistic therapist, traditional witch, and avid bookworm, I love to explore both old and new areas of the Craft and work with them in new and creative ways.

Craig Spencer is a Lancashire-born Anglo-Italian witch who practices Traditional Lancashire Witchcraft. His academic background earned him a Bachelor of Science degree with honours from the University of Salford and a Postgraduate Certificate in Education from the University of Central Lancashire. He is an integrated therapist and Reiki teacher. In his downtime he enjoys reading, learning new languages (currently Mandarin "ni hao!"), and has a love for all things comedy and horror.

Other works by Craig Spencer include *Aradia: A Modern Guide to Charles Godfrey Leland's Gospel of the Witches* published by Llewellyn Worldwide.

Craig can be found on Instagram @WitchcraftUnchained and Twitter @CraigSpencer90.

# CONTENTS

# WITCHCRAFT UNCHAINED

## Exploring the History & Traditions of British Craft

## CRAIG SPENCER

Foreword by Ian Chambers
Author of *The Witch Compass*

Chicago, Illinois

First Edition.
First Printing, 2023.

Paperback ISBN: 978-1-959883-12-8
Library of Congress Control Number: 2023932946

Paperback cover design Wycke Malliway.
Special edition cover design by Wycke Malliway.
Typesetting by the talented Gianna Rini.
Edited by Becca Fleming.

Published by:
Crossed Crow Books, LLC
6934 N Glenwood Ave, Suite C
Chicago, IL 60626
www.crossedcrowbooks.com
@crossedcrowbooks

Printed in the United States of America.

*This book is dedicated to my great-grandparents, Joseph and Mary:*

*Joseph, who passed on to me his mischievous nature,
love of magic, the spirit world, and waistcoats.*

*Mary, who always called me Joe, for our shared love of nature,
her openness and warmth for everything and everyone, our weird
conversations about the afterlife and souls, and her iconic green gate—
held together by green paint and Witchcraft.*

# FOREWORD

**Witchcraft** is a noun that denotes the practice of a witch—it is what a witch does. From depictions of the late medieval witch, to post Gardnerian popular Wicca, the term witchcraft has accrued and exchanged an array of meanings—borrowing and absorbing simultaneously from folklore and memory, crass and derisory modern tropes, history and wider occult influences. Indeed, it is in regards to the latter that much of the modern interpretation has found itself for the better part of the last century, introducing the concept of pagan witchcraft as a religious movement that has spread from its humble beginnings in the British Isles.

To scale the heights for clarity, seeking elucidation above the gathering clouds of confusion and obfuscation to reach a precise definition, is often fraught with potential risk. Fools rush in where angels fear to tread, and it requires a good head and steady stride to step carefully and thoughtfully in attempting to steer such a diverse, open-source paradigm as modern witchcraft.

Nevertheless, the erudite and considered study affords a safe journey through the difficult and undulating terrain, measured with experience and understanding of the matter at hand. Much ink has been spilt in the representation of witchcraft as one definitive thing or another, rarely meeting with universal agreement. However, a good deal of the available material has been sometimes repetitious in the past, reproducing formulas around the popular forms of pagan Wicca since the latter half of the last century. Authors such as Scott

Cunningham arguably laid the foundation in the 1980s, with his thorough handbook on the practice and ideas of what has become the mainstream, popular movement of Wicca. Important to note, however, that not all Wiccans are witches and not all witches are Wiccans—an important and necessary distinction that *Witchcraft Unchained* observes and highlights as the reader is guided through the history of Wicca and witchcraft.

As the tide of popular currents continues to ebb and flow, the modern witchcraft movement has gained in maturity—a levelling out that provides the sobering mix of scholarly study and available research, together with the ecstatic, revelatory practice of the adventurous and intuitive modern witch. This marrying of honest and reasoned conversation with the experience of the practiced hand has produced some of the most informed literature and serious growth within the burgeoning movement.

To approach such a work, then, is not as easy a task as one might imagine, being bound on both sides with the furrows of differing and strongly held views and opinions. Indeed, as a lived tradition, witchcraft has never existed in a vacuum and shifting and evolving cultural convention and understanding must inevitably bear relevance. In fact, one might argue, the cultural witch is ever the rebellious spirit, the outcast, the shunned, the liminal figure on the perimeter edge of accepted society—thereby at the crush of the boundary and leading the push outward toward change. Transgressing social restrictions, we cast off cultural conditioning that restrains and confines, inhibits and controls, as we advance patterns of variation that are only available with the power thus obtained.

In *Witchcraft Unchained*, Craig Spencer has fearlessly approached the nuts and bolts of modern witchcraft, refusing to look away from where it comes from, whilst keeping a steadfast eye upon the present and future. "*There are few words in the English language that can be as empowering, offensive, and provocative as the word 'witch'*", writes Spencer, innately comprehending that it is from within this provocation that we may draw power. Any and all suggestion of hesitation signals an immediate and disastrous downfall, and Spencer navigates this adroitly.

Providing a refreshing and thoroughly relevant perspective, Craig Spencer observes the lay of the land as we find it—informed and self-aware. Indeed, within these pages we encounter necessary discourse upon such aspects as polarity and gender in magic, once again emphasising the power of the witch as keeper and transgressor of boundaries. Spencer doesn't turn away from difficult social discourse around issues such as polarity and inclusivity, and I am reminded of my own Alexandrian Wiccan initiators— the first a gay man and the second able to work polarity independent of gender. We are reminded, then, that it is incumbent upon traditions to not simply preserve and persevere, but also to remain consciously supple or else succumb to rigidity and shatter under the weight of time. Reflection and re-evaluation is a necessary part of growth, and *Witchcraft Unchained* represents a link in that ongoing process.

Ian Chambers,
Surrey Hills,
Martinmas 2022.

# INTRODUCTION

*Witch!* A word filled with a wide plethora of meanings, connotations, taboos, and social stereotypes. There are few words in the English language that are as empowering, offensive, and provocative as the word "witch." The reason for this is simple: "witch" means so many things to so many different types of people. It has only been seventy-two years since the repeal of the Witchcraft Act in 1951 and only seventy-four years since the Craft needed to remain hidden in plain sight in books such as Gerald Gardner's *High Magic's Aid* in 1949. Before the repeal of the Witchcraft Act, witches had no choice but to practise in secret. In response to this, witch and author Gerald Gardner was the genius mind who hid the Craft's teachings in his "fictional" work. *High Magic's Aid* remains a historic symbol of rebellion in Witchcraft. Not only did it defy the law of the time, but it also provided access to occult knowledge in a form that allowed devoted practitioners to practise outside of the public eye.

In the grand scheme of things, this isn't very long at all, yet so much of our history and practices have become skewed, and focus from their origins has been lost. Of course, I have no issue with natural evolution and progression; both are needed in all aspects of life if things are to remain healthy and productive. Although Witchcraft has evolved into broad and diverse branches over the decades, each and every aspect of the Craft is a product of the same

1

foundations; rooted in the history, magic, and culture of Britain. My hope is that this book will provide insights into the rich heritage that sparked the global Craft Revival and help restore some of that lost history to our ever-expanding community.

Those who are today called our *Craft Elders* are a unique group of people. Following the repeal of the Witchcraft Act in the UK, these brave people came out into the open and allowed the truth of Witchcraft to be known to the world. It is only by the sacrifice of these people, facing public abuse and backlash, that we now have the freedom as witches to be open about our practices. This eventually led to the legal protections against discrimination that many countries have today. Some may think it is unimportant to know who these people were, believing that they are outdated and irrelevant in today's Craft. We have a duty to remind them, politely, that they owe a lot to these "outdated" and "irrelevant" witches in history.

We need to know where we came from if we are to truly understand where we are going. Above the major temples of the Mysteries in days long since passed, the words "Know Thyself" were engraved. This was a reminder that part of the Mysteries, a large part, in fact, was about self-discovery and personal development. If we fail to learn from history, we are doomed to repeat it. It is in this sentiment that this book is formed; as a convenient place to access those key elements that make our Craft complete and allow personal empowerment and transformation to occur, not only for ourselves but for our community at large.

At the beginning of this introduction, I wrote that "There are few words in the English language that are as empowering, offensive, and provocative as the word 'witch.'" *Witchcraft Unchained* is a book of empowerment. Restoring the history of our practices will provide you with information that is quickly being lost to our community. Along the way, I will explore traditions and taboos that are considered provocative in our community in a way that puts the power back into our Craft, removing the chains of restraint that have been put onto a practice that should be as wild and free as the gods themselves.

# CHAPTER ONE

# WITCHES IN HISTORY

**Britain** is truly a magical place filled with standing stones, sacred springs, and ancient gods. For this reason, it is little wonder why Britain was the natural home of the global Craft Revival movement. After all, with so much history and magic woven into the very fabric of the landscape and culture, it was inevitable that something would rise to the surface and make its presence known—a presence that would grab hold of a nation and not let go.

Much has been published about the history of the Craft in Britain. Anyone who has been part of the Craft for even the shortest of time will know the general overview. I find that some aspects and angles of our history are often overlooked or otherwise interpreted with the biases of today, rather than from the perspective of the time the events occurred. It is with this in mind that I address the history of the Craft. I also intend to touch on cultural influences on the Craft's re-emergence, as this forms an important yet often ignored aspect that has directly contributed to the shaping of today's Craft.

## THE GODS AWAKEN

Growing up in a nation that is outwardly very Christian comes with an extraordinary amount of contradiction. Every child grows up with the magic of the land, from our history and folklore to the practices that aren't talked about and which have no name. During the period of the Second World War (WWII), Witchcraft was more relevant to Britain than it had been in a very long time. With so many legends about the protective spirits of the country, it would have been more bizarre if the people hadn't turned—or returned—to the Old Religion at this most desperate time; an action that would change the land forever. At the end of WWII, Nazi bombs had unearthed many hidden things. One of the most prominent things found is a fully intact temple dedicated to the god Bacchus, revealing itself in the heart of London. Despite having many bombs land directly on top of the temple complex, only very minor damage—consistent with its age—was found.[1] Was this the start of the old gods beginning to reawaken to the people? Hearing their calls and reaching out to reclaim a nation stolen by an invading god from long ago? I certainly believe so.

## PEOPLE OF THE REVIVAL

The Craft Revival movement would not have gone very far, nor been much of a movement, without the people involved. Regardless of whether our practices are similar to these people, their actions all contributed to giving us our freedom to embrace the Craft today. Note that there will, of course, be those whose names cannot appear here or in any book, as they had lived their entire lives without public notoriety. These unnamed and unknown individuals also contributed to the preservation of Craft lore and teachings and are no less important than the names to follow. The information presented below is brief. This is largely due to the fact that each has already been extensively written on. What is included below is intended to address the misinformation that is so often repeated concerning each individual. By restoring the historical facts about each person, it is my hope that more clarity about the global development of the Craft can be attained.

---

1    Bettany Hughes, *Bacchus Uncovered: Ancient God of Ecstasy*, produced by Sandstone Global Productions Ltd, First aired on BBC Four, April 11, 2018.

## CECIL WILLIAMSON
## (19TH SEPTEMBER 1909–9TH DECEMBER 1999)

One figure in Britain's Craft history who is almost universally written out is Cecil Williamson. Part of the tragedy of this, as you will see, lies in the fact that some of the events of Cecil's life are commonly misattributed to Gerald Gardner. In his youth, Williamson would have his first real encounter with the power of Witchcraft after he performed a spell, which he learned from a local witch, on the school bully. This seemingly simple act of magic resulted in serious injuries from a rather unfortunate skiing accident that prevented the bully from returning to school.[2]

Though this event was a prominent encounter with Witchcraft in Cecil's youth, this was not his first interaction with a witch. Cecil's first exposure to Witchcraft occurred when he came across a group of locals attacking an elderly woman who had been accused of bewitchment. Young Williamson jumped to the woman's defence, for which he was beaten by the angry mob before they dispersed.[3] I believe it was this act of kindness, much like a classic fairy tale, which set this young man on a lifelong path of magic. In the early 1930s, Williamson was recruited to play a part in an important MI6 Operation intended to take down the German forces during the war. Williamson was to use his occult background to work undercover, acting as a folklorist to obtain the names of every German military and government official with ties to the occult.[4] Williamson proved to be very good at his new job, and at the request of a family friend, Colonel Maltby, became a full-time employee for the secret services, where he formed the Witchcraft Research Centre.[5]

It was during his full-time employment that Williamson worked the Lammastide (August 1) rites against the German forces in 1940,

---

2    Steve Patterson, *Cecil Williamson's Book of Witchcraft: A Grimoire of the Museum of Witchcraft*. (Woodbury, MN: Llewellyn Publications, 2020), 123, 124.

3    Ibid. 122.

4    Ibid. 128, 154.

5    Ibid. 129, 194.

a ritual commonly misattributed to Gerald Gardner.[6] The government codename for the ritual was "Operation Mistletoe" and was attended by British occultists of all kinds, Canadian soldiers, and Amado Crowley, the son of the "Great Beast," Aleister Crowley.[7] Williamson himself was aware of Gardner's later claims to have been in attendance at this ritual, which Gardner said had taken place in the New Forest. Williamson stated that not only was Gardner not there, but also commented, "bless his heart, Gardner got the wrong forest." The actual events had taken place in Ashdown Forest, Sussex.[8]

When considered logically, Gardner would not have been able to partake in such a rite in any event. It has been said that he was able to organise this rite due to being part of the home guard; however, during wartime, the nation's borders were well protected. Someone like Gardner wouldn't be able to randomly organise a naked frolic in the woods for any old reason. MI6, on the other hand, could organise whatever they wanted. That's the benefit of being a secret service—who is going to ask questions? It wasn't just the D-Day ritual, Operation Mistletoe, that was wrongly attributed to Gardner instead of Williamson. The terms "Goddess of Life" and "God of Death and Resurrection" that are used to describe the gods of the witches of Britain were first recorded as the words of Williamson speaking generally of Witchcraft.[9] Williamson also coined the term "Book of Shadows," a term for a collection of texts on shadow lore held in the Museum of Witchcraft and Magic. He is also considered responsible for the phrase, "Drawing down the Moon." Gardner showed great interest in Williamson's *Book of Shadows* and used the title in place of the original name of his book, *Ye Bok of Ye Art Magical*. Gardner's borrowing of both of these terms is confirmed

---

6    Ibid. 131.

7    Maier Files, "Cecil Williamson another MI6 Dabbler in the Black Arts: Part 4—The Occult Adepts of British Intelligence, Cecil Williamson." Accessed September 10, 2020. https://www.maier-files.com/cecil-williamson-another-mi6-dabbler-in-the-black-arts/

8    Ibid.

9    Doreen Valiente, "Doreen Valiente: A Witch Speaks," In Pagan Dawn Beltane Edition 98, (London: Pagan Dawn, 1998), n.p.

in a letter between Williamson and Patricia Crowther, the longest serving Gardnerian Priestess.[10] The Museum of Witchcraft and Magic on the Isle of Man also owed its origins to Williamson, who was its owner and founder. Although it is true that the building was later sold to Gardner who opened a new museum on the site, Williamson was its originator and his legacy lives on at the museum's current location in Boscastle.[11]

## GERALD GARDNER
### (13TH JUNE 1884–12TH FEBRUARY 1964)

Often dubbed as the "Father of Modern Witchcraft," Gerald Gardner is a name that is deeply entwined within the history of Witchcraft. Born in Blundellsands, Lancashire, to a wealthy family, Gardner had a poor early start in life. Suffering from ill health for most of his life, Gardner spent much time reading and learning about other cultures, eventually sparking his keen interest in the occult. This interest led to Gardner spending much time abroad, with his most significant experience in Craft history beginning in 1938. Following their return from an extended stay in Cyprus, Gardner and his wife, Donna, set up residence in an apartment in London, however, the threat of the war would soon see them move for fear of being bombed.[12]

This move would alter the course of Gardner's life completely. Having friends in the New Forest area in Hampshire, the couple relocated to Highcliffe where Gerald quickly became known as an eccentric character wherein children would cross the road to avoid the presence of this strange figure.[13] It was around this same time that Gardner became a member of the local *Rosicrucian Order*, where he

---

10   Steve Patterson, *Cecil Williamson's Book of Witchcraft: A Grimoire of the Museum of Witchcraft*. (Woodbury, MN: Llewellyn Publications, 2020), 238.

11   Doreen Valiente, "Doreen Valiente: A Witch Speaks," In Pagan Dawn Beltane Edition 98, (London: Pagan Dawn, 1998), 11-12.

12   Michael Howard, *Modern Wicca*, (Woodbury, MN: Llewellyn Publications, 2009), n.p.

13   Philip Heselton, *Wiccan Roots: Gerald Gardner and the Modern Witchcraft Revival*, (Berkshire, UK: Capall Bann, 2000), 39.

was well-received as a member. Over time, Gardner would be invited to join an inner circle of the Order, an offer that he eagerly accepted. It was during his first meeting in this inner circle, at his initiation ceremony, that Gardner would first realise what he was becoming a member of.

At his initiation, in which he was bound and blindfolded while completely naked, he heard the word "Wicca" spoken during a portion of the ritual. As a Northerner, Gardner could only associate this word, which is rather unheard of in the South of England, with one thing—Witchcraft! It was at this point that he knew for the very first time that the inner circle of which he was being made a member was actually a witches' coven. Gardner took to being a witch with great enthusiasm, something that would stay with him for the rest of his life.

Following his initiation into the Craft in 1939, Gardner wrote his first book on Witchcraft, disguised as a novel titled *High Magic's Aid* in 1949. This was primarily done as a convenient way of putting rituals and theories concerning Witchcraft into print while the Witchcraft Act of 1735 was still in place, which restricted the sharing and publication of such information. Under this act, it was prohibited to make any statements claiming that witchcraft was real. Once the Witchcraft Act was repealed in 1951, Gardner went on to publicly promote religious Witchcraft to the masses. Gardner primarily carried out this promotion via press releases, TV interviews, and the release of two Witchcraft books: *Witchcraft Today* (1954) and *The Meaning of Witchcraft* (1959). This level of publicity was not well-received by others in the community who found the level of exposure potentially problematic. This would eventually lead to unnecessary divisions in the Craft community which are still present today.

Within the Witchcraft community, it has often been erroneously suggested that Gardner invented Witchcraft or the religion called "Wicca"; the latter of these points will be fully addressed in the next chapter. These suggestions seem to stem from a belief that there were no witches in Britain before Gardner, however, his own initiates have publicly stated that Gardner's first coven was founded with members who were already witches.[14] This should not really be a surprise to

---

14    Doreen Valiente, "Working with Gerald and Robert Cochrane, Magister," in *The Paganism Reader*, (London: Routledge, 2004), 223.

anyone. As already discussed, concerning Cecil Williamson's place in Craft history, there have always been plenty of witches about.

The concept of a Gardnerian tradition was completely alien to the Craft prior to 1965, only having been established after Gardner's death the year before in 1964.[15] It was the impact of his publicity and the opposing witches' attempts to separate themselves from the image he presented that led to the phrase "Gardnerian Tradition" becoming coined. The seeds of this tradition were inadvertently sown by a throw-away comment made in the March issue of *Pentagram* in 1965.[16]

*"I have experienced both of these versions; the former through my mother and my aunt, and the latter (rather too easily) through one of the many Gardnerian High Priestesses-who, I must emphasise, knew nothing at the time of my connections with the hereditary Craft. This has shown me just how great the gap is that exists, and the hard work that will be needed if we are to close it."*

Prior to this, in November 1964, one reader of *Pentagram Magazine* had written in to express a complaint shared by many witches: that Gardner's witches were the only ones being interviewed and it was limiting the public image of British Craft to the same "eight ladies and three to four men."[17]

## DOREEN VALIENTE
### (4TH JANUARY 1922–1ST SEPTEMBER 1999)

Doreen Valiente is possibly the most famous witch in Britain's history, perhaps even surpassing Gerald Gardner in reputation. The "Mother of Modern Witchcraft" seems to be the single figure for whom every witch from every path holds a deep fondness. This is only natural, as Valiente was one of the most vocal practitioners to

---

15    Janet Farrar and Gavin Bon*e, The Inner Mysteri*es, (Portland, OR: Acorn Guild Press, 2012), 14-15.

16    Taliesin, "Ancients" and "Moderns," in *Pentagram Issue March 1965* (UK: Pentagram, 1965).

17    "Before Gardner—What?" *Pentagram*, Nov. 1964.

cross the fabricated boundary of tradition and return to a "purer" form of Craft. Her most notable works of writing are *The Charge of the Goddess* and her re-working of the *Book of Shadows*.

Valiente was already an avid reader and enthusiast of the occult before she officially came to the witches' path. Reading about every related subject she could get her hands on, she quickly became a well-read and well-informed individual on the subject of magic and occult practices. On 29th July 1951, Valiente read an interesting newspaper article concerning Cecil Williamson. In this article, Williamson was calling for the covens of Britain to get involved with the Museum he had founded. At this time, he had already made arrangements for Gardner and his High Priestess, Dafo (Edith Rose Woodford-Grime), to conduct an opening ceremony.[18]

Although the article had caught her interest, Valiente would wait to act until 27th September 1952 when her curiosity finally got the better of her. It was then that another interview with Cecil Williamson would make a tabloid appearance. This time, Williamson provided details regarding the Old Religion of Witchcraft in Britain, including details of the God and Goddess, the sabbat dates and meanings, and the ritual he was part of against the Nazi forces in 1940. With her curiosity finally too much to contain, Valiente wrote a letter to Cecil Williamson to find out more about becoming a witch herself.[19]

Her written communications initially began with Williamson suggesting about six different covens which Valiente could connect with. However, her letters were passed to Gardner, who would later initiate her into the Craft himself. The initiation occurred the day before Midsummer of 1953, and the following day, Valiente, Gardner, and Dafo made a trip to Stonehenge to witness the Druids perform their seasonal rites.[20]

Though it may be controversial to say, I do not consider Doreen to be a Gardnerian witch. The term "Gardnerian" was applied to those who were "followers of Gardner" the year after he died. Valiente had already separated herself from being such a follower in 1957, years before the term was coined, a separation which was sparked by

---

18    Doreen Valiente, *The Rebirth of Witchcraft*, (London: Robert Hale, 2007), 11.

19    Ibid. 14-15.

20    Ibid. 40.

Gardner's publicity amongst other disagreements within the Coven.[21] In that respect, Valiente did not fit the criteria as a practitioner of the Gardnerian tradition, and it can hardly be applied to her work. I know of two covens personally—and a number of others, generally—that are down-line from Valiente following this split. None of them consider themselves to be Gardnerian. In fact, it has been said to me that, "We trace our lineage to Doreen [Valiente]. We're not Gardnerians, we're witches."

With this thought in mind, it can hardly surprise anyone that Valiente is still so universally celebrated. Without this hardened link to any one type of Witchcraft, Valiente and her legacy act as a cross-tradition touchstone to the very essence of the Craft without the limitations of tradition standing in the way. Her legacy is preserved and maintained by the work of the Doreen Valiente Foundation, which was founded by Doreen's last High Priest, John Belham-Payne, with whom she left many of her documents, magical artefacts, and writing.

## ROBERT COCHRANE
### (26TH JANUARY 1931–3RD JULY 1966)

A polarising and controversial though no-less relevant figure in Craft history is Roy Bowers, who is more commonly known by his pen name "Robert Cochrane." Founding the Clan of Tubal Cain in 1951 following the repeal of the Witchcraft Act, Cochrane wasted no time in embracing the new-found freedoms offered to observers and practitioners of the Craft. Unlike Gardner, Cochrane was reasonably "occult" with his practices in the truest sense of the word. When Doreen Valiente first encountered him and the Clan of Tubal Cain in 1964, it had been via a word-of-mouth recommendation by mutual friends that they should meet.[22] It is due to the strong occult nature of Cochrane's Craft that the only major details we have are from the two-year period (1964–1966) in which Valiente was an initiated member. Outside of this two-year period, little else has been made public other than details already confirmed by Doreen Valiente.

---

21    Ibid. 72.

22    Ibid. 117.

The work of the Clan of Tubal Cain—and of Cochrane himself—was not the same as that which Valiente had found with Gardner. It was for this reason that Valiente was grateful for being introduced to Cochrane's new ways of working. Some of these new ways included contact with the spirits of past Craft practitioners who were termed the "Hidden Company" by an unnamed American Tubal Cain Clan member.[23] Valiente remained with the Clan of Tubal Cain until early 1966, a few months before Cochrane's tragic death. Although often recounted as a suicide, evidence provided by Valiente indicates that his death was most likely an accident. For that reason, I will term his death as "death by misadventure." Cochrane had started to show signs of mental instability following his divorce and had continued to experiment with "potions" containing powerful hallucinogenic substances. These were used to test the worthiness of a person from the viewpoint of the gods.[24]

It was Valiente who first put forward the now popular theory that Cochrane had coined the term "Gardnerian" himself, with her belief being based simply upon the fact that he used it.[25] However, the evidence suggests otherwise, making Cecil Williamson the most likely originator. Furthermore, Valiente's testimony to its use by Cochrane at this time only indicates that the term had entered common usage, as its meaning was immediately understood. A commonly used term to describe Gardner's practices was bound to have been used by practically everyone at this time, making Cochrane's use of it hardly surprising.

Many question Cochrane's place within the history of British Witchcraft, mainly due to the fact that his Craft background has a huge question mark hanging over it, which is in no way unusual. Every founder of any branch of the Craft has at least one question mark hanging over their head in one way or another, a fact that should not diminish any practitioner's work. It is surprising that people will not accept the Clan of Tubal Cain as the foundation

---

23   Doreen Valiente, *The Rebirth of Witchcraft*, (London: Robert Hale, 2007), 127-128; Evan John Jones & Doreen Valiente quoted in Christopher Penczak, *The Mighty Dead*, (U.S.A. Copper Cauldron Publishing, LLC, 2013), 34.

24   Doreen Valiente, *The Rebirth of Witchcraft*, (London: Robert Hale, 2007), 135.

25   Ibid. 122

of the second Craft tradition in Britain (after Gardnerian). There is just as much legitimacy to Gardner as there is for Cochrane, therefore, it is difficult to understand the reasons for why it's considered unacceptable to place the Clan of Tubal Cain on the same historical timeline.

In the last few decades, there has been a rise in the teachings of Robert Cochrane. This is mainly via his surviving written records, known as *The Robert Cochrane Letters*. These letters formed a third of the American-formed 1734 Tradition and are freely available online. It was because of Cochrane's teaching, and of the 1734 Tradition that came after him, that Craft initiation could come directly from the spirits. This was a philosophy that deviated from the other Craft teachings of the day. Many believe that reading—and re-reading—the Cochrane Letters can trigger such a connection to the spirits and begin a personal journey into Witchcraft. For that reason, Cochrane is not only historically relevant but also relevant to the ever-growing and changing face of Witchcraft today.

## RAYMOND BUCKLAND
### (31ST AUGUST 1934–27TH SEPTEMBER 2017)

Born in London in 1934, no one could have known just how celebrated Raymond Buckland would become in the occult world. Following his move to America in 1962, Buckland came across Witchcraft for the first time. Deeply invested in entering the world of the witch, Buckland made the journey to Perth, Scotland, with his wife, Rosemary, to be initiated by Monique Wilson: Gardner's then-High Priestess. Raymond and Rosemary would then establish their own coven in America, effectively introducing the religion to the USA in 1964.[26]

It is worth noting here that Buckland cannot *technically* be credited with introducing Gardnerian Witchcraft to America as is so often claimed. As we have established, such a name or distinction from other forms of Witchcraft did not exist until the following year of 1965. Buckland should rightly be remembered as the public figure

---

26   George Knowles, "Raymond Buckland—3 June 2007" Accessed 07 September 2020. http://controverscial.com/Raymond%20Buckland.htm.

who brought Gardner's *teachings* to America. It wasn't long after such labels and separation started to filter into the Craft that Buckland found himself disassociating from what this part of the Craft was becoming.[27] In the early 1970s, he made the decision to reconstruct a form of Craft practice that was right for him. In 1973, he founded a tradition known as *Seax-Wica,* and the following year, the foundational materials for the tradition and how to establish your own coven were published.[28]

## ALEX AND MAXINE SANDERS
### (6TH JUNE 1926–30TH APRIL 1988), (30TH DECEMBER 1946–)

Alex Sanders is considered to be perhaps one of the most controversial figures in the history of the Craft Revival and based on anything written and recorded about him, it seems he would have been very pleased by this title. Born and raised in Manchester, UK, Alex claimed to have first been introduced to the world of Witchcraft by his maternal grandmother. She had moved to Manchester from her home in Wales when Alex was seven years old. This would lead, so he claimed, to him witnessing his grandmother performing a ritual and then initiating him into the Craft in order to keep him quiet about her practices. Of course, there have been strong cases made that this story is a total fabrication, as Alex claimed to have received material from his grandmother's Book of Shadows that she could not have possibly possessed; Doreen Valiente hadn't written them yet, according to Alex's timeline.

According to a now well-circulated letter written to Gerald Gardner by Pat Kopinski, Alex was first initiated into the Craft on 9th March 1964 by a witch known as Medea.[29] Anyone involved in the Craft, especially here in the UK, will be more than aware that this is where the very start of the controversy began. Much debate exists around the legitimacy of this initiation as Patricia Crowther

---

27    Raymond Buckland, Buckland's *Book of Saxon Witchcraft,* (Boston, MA: Red Wheeler/Weiser, LLC. 2005), n.p.

28    Ibid.

29    Letter quoted in Janet Farrar and Gavin Bone, *The Inner Mysteries,* (Portland, OR: Acorn Guild Press, Second Edition 2012), 16.

had denied Alex initiation, and Medea, one of Crowther's initiates, had gone against her wishes.

Under the strictest rules of the Craft, only an autonomous coven may make such a decision. However, any second-degree witch can initiate a new witch, so the rules in this instance are not as black and white as they first appear. Some argue that we do not know when, or if, Alex received his higher initiations. This is true, but as the saying goes: "Absence of evidence is not evidence of absence." Furthermore, the tradition that would later evolve from the work of Alex and Maxine Sanders—the Alexandrian tradition of Witchcraft—required only that Alex and Maxine were satisfied with their own abilities in the Craft.

Maxine Sanders was no stranger to Mystery traditions when she first entered the witches' Craft as she was previously an initiate of the Egyptian Mysteries.[30] Maxine was brought into much of the occult world from a very young age due to her mother's great interest in the subject and who brought Maxine along for many of her spiritual explorations.[31] Without a doubt, this allowed her to approach the Craft with a unique perspective and experience that wasn't shared by others entering the Circle for the first time. Soon, Maxine's experiences from her earlier years would draw her to the world of Witchcraft, something that she had initially found disturbing because her "studies (which included certain aspects of magic) had been imbued with a strong religious quality compatible with [her] Roman Catholic faith."[32]

Much like Gardner, neither of the Sanders' were trying to make a name for themselves by founding a tradition. As far as they were concerned, they were just witches. In Maxine's autobiography, *Fire Child: The Life & Magic of Maxine Sanders*, she explains that the term "Alexandrian" came into use when Stewart Farrar was finishing his book, *What Witches Do*. In her own words, she writes:

*"When the book was finally finished, Stewart came up with a problem: 'What do we call witches who follow your way of practising the Craft?'*

---

30   Maxine Sanders, *Fire Child: The Life & Magic of Maxine Sanders 'Witch Queen'*, (United Kingdom: Mandrake, 2007).

31   Ibid.

32   Ibid.

*We had no idea. To us, the Craft was just that, 'The Craft.' The answer was simple, and the Alexandrians came into being. Thank you, Stewart!*[33]

Far from trying to found a new tradition, the Sanders' demonstrated great dedication to their Craft with a very British attitude of "minding their own business and getting on with it." Considering how quickly they were both thrust into the media spotlight, their humility is very admirable. Not many witches today can find that balance of being in the public eye while also remaining occult. Among Alexandrians, Alex was recognised as the "King of the Witches" and Maxine held the title of "Witch Queen" until the age of thirty. It should be noted that the title Maxine held was not because of Alex, it was an initiatory title that she held in her own right.

In recent years, it has been wrongfully suggested that Alex and Maxine Sanders had issues with, and were unwilling to initiate, people with disabilities. This is not and never has been the case. If the student was serious, dedicated, and willing to put in the time, such things as disability never mattered, and for Maxine, they still don't.[34]

## SYBIL LEEK
### (22ND FEBRUARY 1917–26TH OCTOBER 1982)

Far more controversial a figure than the Sanders' was Sybil Leek. This utter icon of the British Craft movement caused much friction with her media presence, mainly due to the fact that her Craft deviated from the popular narrative. She was a traditional witch and very proud of the fact. Born in Stoke-On-Trent in the region of the New Forest, Leek claimed to have a Craft practice that could be traced back to 1134. With the release of her first book *Diary of a Witch* in 1969, Leek became known as "The World's Most Famous Witch" by the press. Following the repeal of the Witchcraft Act, Leek outed herself

---

33    Ibid.

34    "Maxine Sanders on Missing Digits & Disabilities—Oct '16" Maxine Sanders speaking, recorded by Sharon Day, video, 2:43, February 7, 2018, https://www. youtube.com/watch?v=_PPqG2SJ0HQ

as a witch, leading to a media storm upon her village. The residents did not like the sudden influx of cameramen and tourists coming to see the witch and quickly tried to shut it down by branding Leek a joke or a fraud.[35]

None of this resistance would stop Leek from becoming a notable witch, as she stood firm to her beliefs and position on the Craft throughout her life. One of the largest criticisms that she received from other witches in the media was that she was very much a proponent for the art of cursing. As many other witches claimed that "we don't do that sort of thing," Leek stood out as a momentous example of the fact that not all witches are Gardnerian. Of course, this opinion was not well received. One of Gardner's High Priestesses, Eleanor "Ray" Bone, voiced her dislike for Leek during a TV interview in America. The host challenged Bone to turn Leek into a toad, at which Bone remarked, "Why should I improve on nature?"[36]

It is worth noting that some have suggested that such an issue arose from the fact that Leek claimed to have a Craft origin that predated Gardner. This is not the case. Bone herself was first initiated into a tradition from Cumbria, England, in 1941 before becoming initiated into Gardnerian Craft. When Bone was no longer running her coven in London, she returned to Cumbria in the Northwest and resumed her practise of the Craft in which she had first been initiated …if she had ever stopped at all, that is.[37] There was never an issue of there being witches on other paths, it was the image that they chose to portray to the press that caused friction.

Authoring over twenty books in her lifetime, covering subjects such as Witchcraft, astrology, herbalism, exorcism, and cursing, Leek was a great source of information for people who could not access Witchcraft through a coven. Leek intended to make Witchcraft a lot easier to get involved with, and following the death of Gerald Gardner, she founded the Witchcraft Research Association. The job

---

35   "BBC Inside Out—Sybil Leek; White Witch." BBC, www.bbc.co.uk/insideout/south/series1/sybil-leek.shtml. Accessed 23 Dec. 2022.

36   Rosemary Ellen Guiley, *The Encyclopedia of Witches, Witchcraft and Wicca*, Third Edition, (United States: Facts on File, Incorporated, 2008), 32.

37   Ibid.

of the Association was to connect witches of every kind together with the understanding that sharing knowledge would help the Craft thrive. The Association was successful for a time, with great support from people such as Doreen Valiente and Robert Cochrane.[38]

Like Cecil Williamson, Leek also had a role during WWII in which she was called by the British Government to assist in their efforts by using her skills as an astrologer. Her role was not only to help plot tactical moves based upon astrology, but also to leak false astrological information to the Germans in order to misdirect the actions of the opposing side.[39]

### JANET AND STEWART FARRAR
### (24TH JUNE 1950–), (28TH JUNE 1916–7TH FEBRUARY 2000)

The Farrars are by far the most famous students of the Sanders' and are themselves well-respected authors, witches, and Craft Elders. Unlike the other figures discussed so far, the Farrars have a notably less complicated history in respect to clarity within the community. The history of their initiations into the Craft remain to be the one exception to their reputation for avoiding controversy. While it is well documented and undisputed that they were both initiated into the Sanders' coven, the dispute that often arises is in regards to their higher degrees of initiation and the founding of their own coven.

Janet and Stewart both received their second-degree initiation on 17th October 1970 at the Sanders' flat.[40] A few months later, the couple would hive, forming their own coven on 22nd December 1970.[41] There was a discussion between the Farrars and the Sanders' in early 1971 regarding the delay between their second- and third-degree initiations. A record dated 11th March 1971 shows that Maxine's reply was positive, stating that there was no need to worry about

---

38    Ibid. 69.

39    "BBC Inside Out—Sybil Leek; White Witch." *BBC*, www.bbc.co.uk/insideout/ south/series1/sybil-leek.shtml. Accessed 23 Dec. 2022.

40    Elizabeth Guerra & Janet Farrar, Stewart Farrar: *Writer on a Broomstick*, (Great Britain: Skylight Press, 2013), 103.

41    Ibid.

the delay and commented that the coven they had founded was "bloody marvellous."[42] It was indicated that they would be elevated to third-degree once Alex felt that the time was right.[43]

The right time must have been near, as by the next month, Janet and Stewart both received their third-degree initiation on 24th April 1971.[44] It has been commonly suggested that Janet and Stewart didn't receive their higher degree initiations and founded their coven while only at their first-degree. However, Maxine Sanders confirmed the details in an email to Elizabeth Guerra dated 23rd April 2007.[45] Maxine did admit that she could not remember the third initiation but made it clear that this wasn't to suggest that it didn't happen, only that it is difficult to remember as "…there were many initiates who passed through the Circle and went on to be teachers."[46]

### JANET FARRAR AND GAVIN BONE (19TH JANUARY 1964–)[47]

In the minds of many witches today, the work of Janet Farrar has been fossilised in time after the publication of *A Witches Bible*. Not only does this do a disservice to the wonderful work that Janet has produced since then, but it also denies Gavin his proper place in the ever-changing history of the Craft. Together, Janet and Gavin have produced some of the most beautiful, comprehensive, and timely works on the Craft. Every witch, regardless of their path, can benefit and find use in reading their works. Not only are the subjects that they address perfect for exploring the direction and future of the Craft, but they also build on a solid history base that strengthens the contribution of their work.

---

42   Ibid. 103-104.

43   Ibid.

44   Ibid. 104

45   Ibid.

46   Ibid.

47   Unless otherwise cited, all information comes from private correspondences between the author and Janet Farrar and Gavin Bone dated 11th September 2020–12th September 2020.

Of course, the forward movement of this couple's influence is not limited to their published works but to their Witchcraft as well. Despite rumours of homophobia that have been interpreted from twisting statements written in their books—primarily from *A Witches Bible*—the facts speak for themselves. The truth is that Janet, Stewart, and Gavin were very much inclusive due to the influence of, and friendship with, Doreen Valiente.

In the early 80s, when many Gardnerian and Alexandrian covens in the UK and US were denying initiation to gay seekers, these so-called "homophobes" were openly initiating gay people into the Craft. In the early 90s, their coven initiated their first transgender member. These facts were not celebrated as a big deal; it is coven business, after all. By the 2000s, their practical application of polarity had changed based on the work of Janet and Gavin following Stewart's death. These changes in thinking became the basis for training within their own coven and focused upon the energetic, or spiritual, level.

*"We've seen same-sex couples where there is no relationship of a sexual nature, raising as much energy as the traditional male/female concept of polarity. This is because we are teaching students to work on the spiritual level, and there is one thing that is undeniable. Our soul, our spirit has no gender. This has made our practices inclusive by nature."*

– Janet Farrar
in correspondence with the author,
dated 12th September 2020.

It is important to stress that this is not to suggest they have scrapped the concept of traditional male/female polarity altogether, simply that they use it only when "it is suitable for the individual."

It should also be noted that some are under the impression that Janet and Gavin founded a tradition called "Progressive Witchcraft," but this is not the case at all. The two make it very clear that any witch, regardless of path or tradition, can be progressive as it is fundamentally a mind-set. The nine tenets that outline Progressive Witchcraft can be found in their book *Progressive Witchcraft* which has since been republished as *The Inner Mysteries*. In that particular book, the very first of the nine tenets state that Progressive Witchcraft is not a tradition but outlines the evolving nature of Witchcraft presented in a "coherent magical and spiritual path for the next millennium."[48]

---

48    Janet Farrar and Gavin Bone, *The Inner Mysteries*, (Portland, OR: Acorn Guild Press, 2012), 41.

CHAPTER TWO

# TERMINOLOGY

**In** any practice that has such a long-standing history, the use of terminology is bound to be both abundant and significant. The Craft is no different. When there are so many broad and diverse expressions of one path, it is the common vocabulary that establishes unity. As time passed, many definitions of terminology have changed from their original meaning into something more contemporary. The same as anything else, terms and wording evolve; they are changed by people to suit their own practice or culture, creating a new meaning that better relates to how they practice their Craft. There is nothing wrong with linguistic evolution, but sometimes this can erase our history as it is acknowledged less and less in books and by communities. That is not to say that you shouldn't continue engaging with your own definition of these terms, that preference is yours. Instead, you are encouraged to acknowledge the history and origins of these terms and the original meanings behind them.

## THE CULTURAL ROOTS OF CRAFT TERMINOLOGY

Being born and raised in North-West England, I have a unique insight into the roots of these commonly used terms and phrases. Within the day-to-day conversations of the North-Western people of England, language is used that is interspersed with words from Anglo-Saxon (Old English), Middle English, Old Norse, Modern English, and occasionally, French. Basically, if a language was ever spoken here, then it has been retained to some degree or another. The Old Norse and Anglo-Saxon languages are by far the most commonly heard overall, and this should not come as a surprise to anyone.

Both Gardner and the Sanders' originally came from this part of the country. The following words and phrases would have been as commonplace to them as any other word in the English language. For a small country, England is extremely diverse due largely to the land originating as a tribal nation that eventually merged under a single figurehead (the British Monarch). A natural cultural divide exists to the present day. Referred to as the North-South divide, it is generally understood that people from the North don't fully understand people from the South and vice versa. Politics are usually blamed for this divide, but the truth is that the primary cause of the division is cultural.

When Gardner and the Sanders' moved from the North to the South, the best and most natural way to be discrete was to use words spoken only by Northerners. The culture of this language did not exist in the South, so many conversations could be safely held without anyone eavesdropping and being aware of what was actually being discussed. This was proven very convenient when it came to conversations about Witchcraft. What follows are some of the most common terms that exist in our wider community. These terms, *unless otherwise stated*, originate from the culture specific to the North of England and were largely brought forward due to the recognised primary founders of Revivalist Craft being raised within it.

## DEOSIL & WIDDERSHINS

*Widdershins* is the term used when magical work is done in an anti-clockwise direction. The word itself literally means "to go against" and is a variation of the local term *widdersinnis* ("against the way"). Many Witchcraft texts promote the idea that this is a direction used for evil workings, however, this is not the case. Locally, we know this as a direction used for or associated with the magic of Witchcraft. To say that this is a direction for evil workings is merely buying into the religious propaganda of a distant era and perpetuating a very outdated and superstitious notion.

*Deosil* is the term used for when witches work in a clockwise direction. In the Witchcraft community, there is sometimes confusion regarding the way it is spelled and where the spelling originates. This word's true spelling is *deasil*, taken from the words *dea* meaning "*right*" and *il* meaning "*direction.*" In this instance, the word *deasil* can be taken to mean "the correct way" or "moving towards the right."

In addition to the spelling of the word, there is also the question of pronunciation.

*A Witches Bible* by Janet and Stewart Farrar is frequently quoted regarding the pronunciation of this word. The English pronunciation of the word is *DEE-sil*. It is important to remember that the Farrars wrote *A Witches' Bible*[49] while living in Ireland and included the Irish Gaelic form of the word, *deiseal*, which is pronounced *Jesh'l*.[50]

It's important to note that due to the linguistic origins of these words, widdershins and deasil/deosil refer to the opposite directions as described here in the Southern Hemisphere.

## Besom

*Besom* is one of my favourite local expressions. The use of the word within the community today is *generally* used correctly. It is indeed a broom, but the reason that the broom was called a besom is why I love the expression so much. Haunting some of the lonely hills of Old Lancashire (current Lancashire and Greater Manchester) are a host of malevolent hill spirits known as *Besom*. These rather solitary creatures are very territorial and will cause great harm and misfortune to those who trespass on their property in a manner that they deem disrespectful. Taking the form of the stereotypical "witch," these spirits feed into the classic images of evil hags dancing at midnight to raise nefarious forces and who are often seen as silhouettes, flying on broomsticks from place to place. If you are one of the people unfortunate enough to live close to such a hill in this part of England, tradition says that you should beware. The Besom are able to send their malicious magic and enchantments into your home while you

---

49    Originally as separate works titled *Eight Sabbats for Witches'* and *The Witches' Way.*

50    Janet and Stewart Farrar, *A Witches Bible*, (Great Britain: The Crowood Press, Ltd. 2017), 38.

sleep, serving as a punishment for humans having built on their land…but there is hope!

Local legend tells that this region's goddess created covenants with each and every type of being—human, animal, or spirit—that calls this part of Britain home. These covenants were sealed by the Goddess Herself and have evolved into the rules that many of us have come to know as *Occult Law*. With regards to the Besom, it was decided that if a home had a broom, bristles up, by their front door before bed, the power of the Besom could not enter or affect those who live there. With some of the older generations, you can occasionally hear the expression "nowty (naughty) Besom" being used to describe a woman who is ill-mannered, rude, or generally up to no good. This expression is used in a similar way to the term "witch" when it is used as an insult for poor or malicious behaviour.

This broom is sometimes called a *besom broom* (or "*besom broosh*" in the local dialect). Over time, people started just calling it a *besom* for short, therefore, the use of the words *broom* and *besom* became synonymous.

I sometimes call a broom a "besom" just because it's part of the regional dialect. Overall, I find it amusing when people outside the area talk about "jumping the besom" at their handfasting. This usually conjures a rather peculiar image in my mind, but perhaps that's just me.

## SPELL

The word *spell* is often equated with the word *spelling*. For this reason, many authors will tell you that is why both spoken and written words are used in spell-work, however, this is not accurate. The word *spell* comes from the Anglo-Saxon word *spel*, meaning "narration," or "to narrate." When we work a *magic* spell, that is exactly what we are doing—magically narrating life. When we cast a spell, particularly in a magic Circle, we slip between the worlds to become a narrator with the power to shape reality.

Take, for example, the action of binding a harmful person. First, you take a poppet to represent the target, then you specifically name and declare that the poppet *actually is the target*. From there, you take a black cord and wrap it around the poppet while muttering your words of restraint against the person. You literally speak a narrative whereby the person can no longer carry out their harmful actions. This is a narration. You have narrated a facet of the person's life *magically* in order to bring about a specific result.

## JINX

A charm or a spell; the word comes from the Latin *iynx*, which evolved into *jynx* and doesn't specifically relate to harmful magic. The term was also applied to the wryneck bird due to the fact that it was often used in ancient Witchcraft and divination practices. Growing up in Lancashire, the term *wryneck*—although indeed a bird species—has another meaning. When people speak of *wryneck* in a magical sense, they are talking about any and all types of mischievous or malevolent spirits. Perhaps the word *jinx* became associated with this type of magic in English-speaking cultures because these particular wrynecks were being employed to work against the practitioners' enemies.

## HEX

Owing its roots to the old Germanic regions, a *hex* is any act of Witchcraft. The practice of Witchcraft was called *hexen* and the practitioners themselves were called *hexe*. Many witches today tend to draw on terminology from other practices such as hoodoo; an example is calling the small magical bags that witches make *mojo bags* instead of *hex bags*. When I was young, I remember these items being called *hex bags* because they were "hexed" (bewitched) by the art of Witchcraft. I, as do many others, still use the term today even if it confuses people. I feel it is important to not lose our own terms.

## CURSE

*Curse* owes its origin to the Old English word *cursian*, meaning "to wish evil to"; in short, it means exactly what you may think it means. A curse is understood to be magical or otherworldly forces or intelligences being used to work harm upon another person, place, or situation.

## COVEN

This is one of the few terms that is most recognisable regardless of whether an individual is on the witches' path or not. A coven is a gathering of witches—usually in the context of spell-work or worship—led by one or two experienced practitioners. A coven is a private group in which training in the Craft is made available, a definition which is as true today as it was in the medieval period. The earliest account of the term in Great Britain comes from the confessions of Isobel Gowdie, Scotland's Witch-Queen. It was she who specified the maximum number of thirteen and a minimum of three members per coven. Without this account—and those in witch-hunting manuals—it is highly possible that the persecutions would have completely eradicated the notion of witches working in groups at all.

The word *coven* evolved from the Latin word *convenire* meaning "covenant." As members of a coven are generally working within a context of worship, the covenant that they are entering is with the coven's specifically chosen deities. This relationship between a coven and its deities of choice helped drive the narrative that witches worship the devil, a misconception held both historically and today.

## COVENSTEAD

It has been previously established that the word *coven* derives from the word *covenant*. The word *stead* means "house" or "place," therefore, the word *covenstead* literally means a "house/place of the covenant." A covenstead is the location at which a coven meets to carry out their ritual and magical activities. Today, this is usually a secluded place in nature or at the home of one of the coven leaders. The location of the covenstead—and the times of the gatherings—are usually a closely guarded secret, known only to members of the coven itself. Historically, this would have been for the purpose of ensuring the safety of coven members and their loved ones.

## BOOK OF WAYS

The *Book of Ways* is a generic term used to describe any witch's personal working book. This personal record holds the rituals, spells, lore, and teachings that are important to its owner's path. The most well-known is the *Book of Shadows*, a text that originated with Gerald Gardner. Anyone who owns a copy of this specific text may rightly call their own book a "Book of Shadows." The *Book of Shadows* is just one of many examples of a Book of Ways and represents one of numerous different teachings. It is very common among British witches to give a specific name to their Book of Ways—this should be something personal to you and your practice. An historical example includes a text called *The Devil's Plantation* and was owned by a witch from Cambridgeshire in the nineteenth century.[51] My own family's book is called *The Skeleton Book*; a name which evolved out of the fact that it is often described as containing the "bare bones" of our particular Craft. *The Witches Qabalistic Tree* and the rituals that are presented in later chapters are adapted from my personal *Skeleton Book*.

## BLACK & WHITE MAGIC

When it comes to discussing Black and White Magic, note that these phrases are not related to race, but rather to a skill set and a set of magical practices. The terms *Black* and *White* have been used in Britain as early as 1387 to reference practices that occur at night and day, respectively.[52] When I was growing up, the terms *Black* and *White Magic*, as well as *Black and White Witches*, were understood in this sense. When considering common narratives and accounts of Witchcraft, you may have images of people visiting enchanted cottages to have their sicknesses charmed away and others of midnight gatherings under the full moon. Both of these images tell

---

51    Nigel G. Pearson, *The Devils Plantation*, (London: Troy Books Publishing, 2016), 11.

52    Iona Opie and Peter Opie, *The Oxford Dictionary of Nursery Rhymes, 2nd ed.* (Oxford: Oxford University Press, 1997), 357-60.

us something that we already know about magic—sometimes, it's better done during the day, and other times, at night.

I don't personally "colour" my Craft, however, there is nothing wrong with using the terms as they were intended. Of course, magic can be performed whenever it is needed, but the history of daylight and night-time hours is still something we *can* honour. It should also be stressed that this has nothing to do with ethics. A White Witch, for example, may practise love charms—this could easily be a charm to compel someone to fall for their client against their will while it may be the Black Witch who removes such a bewitchment from someone and restores their free will.

## LEFT-HAND & RIGHT-HAND PATH

The terms *left-hand and right-hand path* have become very popular within a wide range of magical systems and practices. As such, the terms have developed a number of different meanings depending on the path that is being followed. Within such practices, the terms are usually used to mean that (in very over-simplified terms) left corresponds to bad, and right, to good. In Craft, it is said that a witch should be able to work with both of their hands. As we have already discussed in Black and White Magic, the use of two complementary opposites is not seen as a battle between good and evil. Just as the Circle can be cast either clockwise or anti-clockwise, so too can our Witchcraft follow a left-handed or right-handed path.

In brief, a simple breakdown of how these paths are used in Witchcraft:

**Left:** Magical, feminine, the Moon, Goddess energy.
**Right:** Mystical, masculine, the Sun, God energy.

When we work magic, we are walking the left-hand path and when we are working in a mystical or religious context (such as a sabbat rite), we are walking the right-hand path. This is the main reason why those in traditional Craft say that they walk a crooked path—because the person is constantly alternating between the left and the right at any given moment. Some practitioners today solely view their Craft as a magical system without any religious context; for those, it could be said that they are walking a left-handed path of Witchcraft. Those who want to engage with the religious aspects—without necessarily using any spellcraft—could say they walk a purely right-handed path.

## WICCA

The word *Wicca* has a long history that, over time, has been taken out of its original context. What follows is a breakdown of the history of the word from its earliest use in Britain to the time of the Craft Revival. While it is up to the practitioner to decide for themselves how the word "Wicca" is used in their practice, it is important to remember that historical definitions are not rewritten as a word develops new meanings. The word is still actively used in language today and is often used to describe a rich and living culture of magical practitioners, specifically my own culture in this part of the UK.

The term *Wicca* is effectively Old English for "witch," and is drawn from the word "Wiccecræft" (Witchcraft). As the Craft was mostly perceived to be a woman's practice, it was the feminine form of the Saxon word, *Wicce,* that was used in Witchcraft. The word we most easily recognise today—Wicca—signifies a male practitioner. When the Saxon language blended with that of the native Britons, a new language was created: Anglo-Saxon. The gendering of words in this new language was not popular and quickly fell out of use, despite both forms surviving within the newly created language.[53]

By 1601, the prominence of using either form, particularly the previously masculine *Wicca,* to apply to people of all genders had become so popular that men started being referred to as a "male-witch" or a "he-witch" to make the distinction more apparent.[54] This lack of gendering continues to the present day and remains a popular term, interchangeable with the word "witch" in many English-speaking countries.

---

53    Iona Opie and Peter Opie, *The Oxford Dictionary of Nursery Rhymes, 2nd ed.* (Oxford: Oxford University Press, 1997), 35; The Encyclopaedia Britannica (University Press, 1911), 755.

54    "Witch." *Etymonline,* www.etymonline.com/word/witch. Accessed 4 Sep. 2020.

## From Wicca to Witch

*Wicca* owes its origins to the compounding of the Anglo-Saxon words *vitka* and *weik*. *Vitka* began as the word *vita*, which was the Anglo-Saxon word for "*know*," which later evolved into *vitka*, their word for "*bewitch*."[55] *Weik* was a term used concerning things connected with both religion and magic; the division between the two was very fluid.[56] *Vitka* and *weik* compounded into the word *Wicca* that we know and more readily recognise today.[57] The word *Wicca* would later blend with the Scottish-Gaelic word for witch—*weche*—creating the new hybrid words *wiccha* (pronounced *witch-a*) and *wicche* (pronounced *witch-e*) during the development of Middle English.[58]

Today, the exact definition and distinction between *Wicca* and *Witchcraft* is as diverse and varied as those who practice the Craft. For some, these terms are distinct and separate, referring to similar yet separate practices. For others, these terms are highly interchangeable and refer to the same practice, regardless of the various expressions that practice may take. While personal feelings, opinions, and social changes all contribute to the evolution of terminology, history is the one constant. Therefore, the best way to look for a working definition of what Wicca/Witchcraft is should begin with a look at what Wicca/Witchcraft has been defined as in the past.

### OAK, ASH, AND THORN:
### THE TREE PRIESTHOOD OF BRITAIN

The phrase *Oak, Ash, and Thorn* is known to many witches from a variety of sources as a reference to the *Tree Priesthood of Britain*. It is, in short, any mystical priesthood that has existed in Britain and is associated with a tree.

---

55    Edited by George Laurence Gomme, F.S.A. *The Gentleman's Library Magazine: Popular Superstitions*, (London: Elliot Stock, 1884), 225.

56    Doreen Valiente, *The Rebirth of Witchcraft*, (London: Robert Hale, 2007), 81.

57    Edited by George Laurence Gomme, F.S.A. *The Gentleman's Library Magazine: Popular Superstitions*, (London: Elliot Stock, 1884), 225.

58    John Jamieson, D.D. *Etymological Dictionary of the Scottish Language*, (Edinburgh: Albernethy & Walker, 1818), n.p.

The first tree is for the Druids; they are associated with the oak tree from which they get their name. *Druid* is a compound word deriving from *Duir,* meaning "oak," and *Id,* "to know." In essence, a Druid is one who knows the teachings of the oak; the teachings that the oak tree represents for this particular priesthood. *Ash,* in this context, is in reference to the mountain ash or rowan tree. In the North, the tree is called by its Old English name *wicca* or *wicca rode* (*wiccan* is the plural).[59] In Modern English, we call it the *witches' tree.* It is due to this association between the practitioners and the rod that is used in the North where the word *Wicca* is used to describe a witch. It is the tree that symbolises the tradition and the process of initiation that is undertaken.

South of the border, we find practitioners who have been dubbed the *Thorn Witches.* These witches are connected to the hawthorn (also known as the whitethorn) and the blackthorn. Both woods feature in their Craft and represent the white and black aspects of the crooked path. The most famous Thorn Witch practitioners known today are of Cornwall and the surrounding area. The best way to spot a Thorn Witch is the inclusion of a staff in their Craft known as a *blasting rod* (or something similar). This rod is made of blackthorn and is an important tool in their Craft, just as the rod is important to the Wicca in the North. Some Thorn Witches use rods, and some Wicca use whitethorn and blackthorn in their Craft, but despite this apparent overlap, it is the central tool that makes the distinction.

When Gerald Gardner first launched his own brand of Witchcraft, it was initially shunned by other witches and later labelled *Gardnerian Witchcraft.* This was done in order to make a public distinction between the Tree Priesthood of Britain and what Gardner was promoting. Gardner had knowledge of the Tree Priesthood of Britain and respected it enough to distinguish his Craft from theirs, however, to a foreign audience, the distinction was too subtle. Gardner first branded what he practised as *Wica.* The single *C* makes all the difference: where *wicca* means "mountain ash/rowan," *wica* means "witch-hazel." Gardner was effectively associating his practice to a type of tree, just as every other

---

59    Rowan is also sometimes called *witche* and the spelling of Wicca can also be *Wicka* or *Wikka* depending on the different parts of the region. They are all the same word as "Wicca."

witch/magical practice has done before him. When Christianity came to Britain, the priesthood sought to legitimise their practices by associating themselves with the yew tree, as a tree was needed to "sponsor" or uphold a valid priest line. As the yew is known both as the tree of death and the tree of new life, it represents the mysteries of the Church and Her priesthood perfectly. Many old Churches across Britain still have the yew growing on their grounds, especially in those that have a graveyard.

As magical practitioners are represented by a tree, many Modern Gardnerian and Alexandrian Initiates wouldn't describe themselves as *Wicca*. The Modern practice of *Neo-Wicca* should rightly be known as *Neo-Wica*, as its origins sprang from what was made public by Gerald Gardner. Hopefully, we can see a recognition of the three ancient Tree Priesthoods of Great Britain on a more international scale. If this is achieved and some terminology is restored by this chapter, then that communication and recognition of the diverse paths and branches of Witchcraft that exist today would be far more harmonious.

## HEDGE WITCH

The term *Hedge Witch* is the historical form of what we today call a *Solitary Witch*. The word *hedge* has its roots in the notion of a solitary practitioner or someone unaffiliated with an organisation. The term was most popular in the seventeenth century and gave us terms like *hedge-priest* and *hedge-marriage*, denoting those things that existed outside of an organisation; usually the Christian Church.[60] Solitary practitioners are very commonplace in today's Craft, so it is only natural that the term *Hedge Witch* should be given its fair position here in this list of terminology. The term itself was first brought back into popular use for witches by author Rae Beth in her 1990 book *Hedge*

---

60    John Stephen Farmer, William Ernest Henley, *Slang and Its Analogues Past and Present: A Dictionary, Historical and Comparative, of the Heterodox Speech of All Classes of Society for More Than Three Hundred Years.* (United Kingdom: subscribers only, 1890), 295.

*Witch: A Guide to Solitary Witchcraft.* It is true that the modern usage of the term *Hedge Witch* to denote a more shamanistic Craft is possible, but the shamanistic aspects are not what makes an individual a Hedge Witch. The shamanic aspects of British Craft belong to the realm and magical practices of the Hag.

## Hag & Hag-Ridden

The word *hag* comes from an Old English word for "prophetess"—*hægtesse.* This hag, or prophetess, acted as a bridge or access point between a community and the Goddess. The term *haetnesse* (goddess) is directly related to the word *hægtesse* and was used to indicate deities known to have cults that included oracular possession, such as the Cult of Diana.[61] The word *hag* itself derived from the Old English word *haga* (connected to hawthorn) which was related to the Old Norse word *tunriða* (literally *hedge-rider*). The hawthorn is related to this "hedge," meaning the spiritual divide between the physical and the spiritual worlds. The shamanic or mediumistic aspect of the hag was therefore someone who bridged that divide or "rides the hedge."[62] The phrase for the hag becoming possessed by the deity in question, was "being hag-ridden." In the same way that Vodou uses the term *ridden* to describe trance-possession by the Lwa (Vodou spirits), the term is also used in a Witchcraft context to indicate the same state of being taken over by the spirit of a goddess.

Today, the term *Drawing Down the Moon* (DDM) is used to describe the same process, however, in older Craft traditional teachings, these terms are not comparable. DDM is used to describe rituals of drawing on the moon's power for certain spells or in some seasonal rites. When Gerald Gardner first began practicing Witchcraft, he used the term *Lifting the Veil* in place of *Hag-Riding* before replacing it with DDM. These terms wouldn't have originally been considered interchangeable, however, modern usage has since evolved to include DDM as a related practice.

---

61  "Hag." *Etymonline*, www.etymonline.com/search?q=hag. Accessed June 2, 2021.
62  Ibid.

## HAG STONES

*Hag,* as we have seen, refers to the prophetess. Belonging to the practices of the Thorn Witch, *hag* in this context also derives from the same root as *hawthorn.*[63] The term had no male variation and therefore indicates the power of the feminine as being necessary to this particular art. When it comes to the concept of *hag stones,* the same feminine powers hold sway. The feminine waters, pulled by the force of the feminine moon, beat on the rocks of the feminine earth to slowly form natural holes that run through the rocks. It is no surprise that these teachings come from the coastal regions of Britain where iconic hag stones are plentiful. When these stones, sometimes called *holey stones,* are held up to the left (feminine/Luna) eye, it is said that the viewer is able to see into the unseen realms.

## CIRCLE & COMPASS ROUND

A Circle, in a magical context, is designed to be a place between the worlds of the physical and spiritual. It acts as a neutral ground upon which certain types of magic are best suited. Within this neutral space, the forces called *fate* are more malleable, therefore, it is advantageous to work within a Circle when you need to turn a situation around. The main type of magic that is best worked within this type of space is the magic of polarity. Polarity magic is based upon the use of equal and opposing—yet complementary—forces to generate a surge of magical power. This method of power raising is sometimes described as *magical fertility,* as it works on the premise that two forces produce a third.

A *compass round,* in contrast, is less about being between worlds and more about affirming the fact that we are here. Just as an actual compass will show you where things are in relation to your current geographical position, a compass round will also be dependent upon your physical location. The compass awakens and draws in the virtue of the forces, gods, and spirits that are available at the site you are working. Some forces will be willing to travel as they are beckoned by the ritual that you are performing, but you are not likely to encounter anything that is truly alien to this space.

---

63    Ibid.

A compass has its own type of magic that is completely unrelated to magical polarity. The magic of the compass can be referred to as *magical friction*. Power raising in a compass is usually called *Treading the Mill*, with the mechanics of a millstone serving as an example for the way in which magical friction works. In polarity magic, two forces create a third using magical fertility; in magical friction, we grind down these forces in order to make something new. If polarity is creating forces via fertility, then friction is creating forces via breaking down. Just as a millstone uses friction to break down grain into flour, so too do we grind the power entering the compass to produce a new substance that can be harnessed to create magic.

## Housel

The *housel* is a ritual offering given to show thanks and gratitude to the gods and spirits that have been called upon to assist in a rite. Often associated with traditional Witchcraft alone, the housel is not confined to one set ritual. For example, the *Cakes and Wine* ritual used in Revivalist Craft is considered a housel. The word itself comes from the Old Norse word *húsl* (sacrifice, offering) and later became associated with the Eucharist in Old English.[64] The performance of the housel usually takes place toward the end of the ritual and contains both a food and drink offering. A housel can also be performed without any other ritual work being done. In this instance, it would be performed to show respect, pay a debt to a spirit for previous help, or build a relationship with a new spirit being or power. The housel can also be performed for the simple reason of making amends for an offensive action.

## Kerfan & Boline

*Kerfan* is the term for what is more popularly referred to as the *white-handled knife*. This knife is used to do all carving and cutting in a magic Circle or compass. The word itself comes from the old English *kerf* (carve), with the addition of the suffix *-an*, *kerfan* literally means

---

64    "Housel." *Etymonline*, www.dictionary.com/browse/housel. Accessed June 2, 2021.

"carving tool." As an added note, it is important that this knife should have a *white* handle—a kerfan's nickname, "white-handled knife," makes it clear that this is a necessary feature.

The *boline,* on the other hand, is a tool used to cut anything *outside* of the comfort of a magic Circle or compass. Usually taking the form of a blade with a white handle, the boline has a curved, almost moon-like shape, allowing it to effectively cut through herbs, branches and other materials. The word *boline* is derived from the Italian version of *The Key of Solomon* grimoire in which the sickle is called a *bolino.* The word was later anglicised as *boline* and has been used in Craft circles ever since. The word *boline* often has a number of pronunciations depending on heritage and tradition. As the word originates from Italian, the pronunciation of its anglicised form is *bo-leen.*

## ATHAME

When it comes to ritual tools, *athame* is one of the most recognisable words in the whole of the Craft. The athame is dubbed by many to be the true witches' weapon. Despite its instant recognition as the witches' working knife, not many know where the word came from or how it evolved into the word we know today. To explore that, it is important to first understand the function of this magical blade. The athame is never meant to be used as a physical knife; its power to cut is reserved purely for the realms of the spiritual. It is for this reason that the knife is said to hold the power to cause harm to spirits or, in some cases, even gods. The knife is effectively divorced from its conventional purpose so that it can become an instrument that is fully dedicated and aligned to the realms beyond the physical world.

The word itself was made most famous in *The Key of Solomon,* in which the knife has many different names depending on the translation of the text. Its earliest names are *adamos, adamcos,* and *athanus.*[65] These words derive from the word *adamantine,* which denotes a strong or robust metal, deriving its name from the Greek word *athantos,* meaning immortal—the prefix *a-,* meaning "without,"

---

65     "Key of Solomon Book II." *Esoteric Archive,* www.esotericarchives.com/solomon/ksol2.htm#chap8. Accessed June 7, 2021.

and the root *thantos,* meaning "death."[66] For this reason, it becomes clear that this knife was so named because it holds the power to harm those that are considered beyond the death of the physical world, i.e., spirit beings.

The name of the knife would evolve to *athana* and eventually become the French *arthamé*. Gerald Gardner most likely picked up this later incarnation of the word from Grillot de Givry's *Witchcraft, Magic and Alchemy* (1931), in which this word and many other typically "Gardnerian" concepts are readily found throughout. *Witchcraft, Magic and Alchemy* makes use of various historical records and accounts, and the arthame, although acknowledging *The Key of Solomon,* is almost universally accepted as the magical knife of a witch. In this text, the idea that a witch may harm an otherwise immortal being with this magical item is further compounded with commentary such as: "... grasping the arthame, or magic knife, with the point of which she [the witch] can instantly dissolve any of the evil spirits who should dare to attack her."[67]

The athame has become known as a magical tool that is often related to phallic symbolism. At the beginning of this section, it was mentioned that this is sometimes called the *true witches' weapon.* This tool is specifically referred to as a *weapon* and it is interesting to note that the root of the word *weapon* comes from the Old English *wæpen,* which means both "sword" and "penis."[68] This is a perfect example of how the past has been preserved in Craft traditions. The layering of cultural symbolism and nuance adds a depth to the Craft that deserves to be preserved.

## PENTAGRAM & PENTACLE

The pentagram is, of course, the five-pointed star design that is favoured by many witches the world over, past and present. Most witches' altars have a pentagram somewhere around the front-centre position.

---

66  "Athanasian." *Etymonline,* www.etymonline.com/word/Athanasian#etymonline_v_18011 Accessed June 7, 2021.

67  Grillot de Givry, *Witchcraft, Magic and Alchemy,* (London: George G. Harrap & Co. Ltd., 1931), 90.

68  "Weapon." *Etymonline,* www.etymonline.com/word/weapon#etymonline_v_4873. Accessed June 8, 2021.

The purpose of a pentagram on the altar is to act as an open doorway for the gods and spirits to enter the ritual space. Items are usually placed upon the pentagram during blessing or consecration in order to receive the power of the gods. When something is placed onto a pentagram, it is as if you are passing it into the otherworld, sending it directly into the hands of the gods or spirits being worked with. During ritual, the pentagrams are usually drawn at the cardinal directions to open similar doorways into the realms of the elemental powers. The pentagram is not solely limited to this doorway function: it can also be employed to draw in the power or energies of certain beings and send them on their way. It is from the "doorway" analogy that these functions work upon, opening the way for the power to flow or slamming the door shut in banishment.

The *pentacle,* on the other hand, is more than just a pentagram with a circle drawn around it. The word *pentagram* comes from the Greek words *penta* (five) and *gram* (drawn). The word *pentacle* does not originate from Greek, but the old French word *pendacol. Pendacol* literally means to "hang from the neck."[69] This is the reason why the old grimoires, themselves usually deriving from Old French, use the word *pentacle* to describe any amulet or talisman that is to be worn by a magician during a ritual.

## ROD, STANG, & STAFF

Modern traditional Witchcraft has boomed in popularity over the past ten years or so. Due to this popularity, many of the working tools associated with this path have also entered the community spotlight. One such tool is the *stang:* a forked staff that is often used as an altar and ritual focal point, usually decorated for seasonal rites. In contrast to this modern practice, the path of traditional Witchcraft uses a tool known as a *rod.* The rod can go by many names depending on the part of Britain that the practice comes from. All essentially mean a "rod," which is why it has such a broad and all-encompassing name. In

---

69    "Pentacle." *Etymonline,* www.etymonline.com/search?q=pentacle. Accessed June 2, 2021.

Cornwall, the rod is called a *gwelen,* and in Lancashire and Greater Manchester, it is called a *wünschelrute* (wish rod).

In the case of the rod, by whatever name it is known, the magical practice associated with it is initiatory based. This is the major difference between the stang and the rod: the stang is used regardless of whether an individual is initiated or not. The rod usually undergoes special ritual processes prior to being presented to a witch at the time of their initiation. It is this which makes someone part of their respective "Tree Priesthood," and in the case of the *wünschelrute,* what makes someone "of the Wicca."

The staff usually has a rounded top and is found among a diverse range of magical paths. This tool, similar to the rod, is used to call and direct various powers, virtue, and magical forces and allies to aid in the work. Like the stang, the staff is not bound to any particular initiatory traditional lines, though it is common among the Druids who employ them in much the same manner as a witch. Due to its similarity to both the stang and the rod, many feel that it is more practical to include a staff as a tool of their Craft. Others, following along traditional lines—whether initiatory or modern—will opt for the rod or stang, respectively.

None of these tools are better than the others, the difference is that one may be better suited to the magical system being operated within. The key is to know the distinction between the three and opt for the one that best aligns with your practice. It should be noted that those who work within the Revivalist Traditions already have a set number of working tools and are unlikely to use any of the above. However, if a Revivalist practitioner is inclined to do so, the staff and stang are the best options as they do not represent a specific tradition or line of initiation.

## FOUR POWERS OF THE MAGUS

The prominent French occultist Éliphas Lévi gave us much valued materials that are found in a vast multitude of magical writings and practices the world over (often without credit). One of the most famous examples is the occult maxim: *To Know, To Dare, To Will, and To Keep Silence.* Since Lévi gave us these words in the mid-1850s, many occultists, particularly witches, have attempted to decipher the meaning of the words—often with large variation and interpretation. However, the need for such a deciphering isn't necessary as Lévi tells us the exact meaning of these phrases, as presented here in his own words.[70]

**TO KNOW:** An intelligence illuminated by study.

**TO DARE:** An intrepidity which nothing can check.

**TO WILL:** A will which cannot be broken.

**TO KEEP SILENCE:** A prudence which nothing can corrupt, and nothing intoxicate.

These four qualities are considered necessary for any magical practitioner to embody if they are to have great success within their chosen path. The definitions given by Lévi are very reasonable and worth preserving because when all four of these qualities are brought into balance, the power that is unlocked is well worth the effort.

## CONJURE & CONJURER

When it comes to Witchcraft and magic, we rarely think of the concept of "exorcism." It is true that the stigma exists wherein Witchcraft is considered evil and demonic and that witches are going to end up like Linda Blair in *The Exorcist*; yet, Witchcraft has an intriguing history with exorcism that is often missed in books on the Craft. That is the work of the *conjurer*.

The word *conjure* is often seen today as a word for calling on spirits alone, but this is not the full story. A conjurer has the power to both call upon and expel spirits. Both powers are important to the work of a conjurer and thus they are effectively the "exorcists" of the Craft.

---

70    Éliphas Lévi Trans. A. E. Waite, *Transcendental Magic Part 1*, (England: Rider & Company, 1896 Digitised: Benjamin Rowe, 2001), 3.

The word *conjure* effectively means to bind by words or commands. Historically, this often involved binding and controlling a spirit being by use of incantation or recitation that included holy names.[71] A conjurer straddled the world of Witchcraft and Christianity in a rather unique way. Although conjurers were viewed—and often executed—as witches, they would often draw from Christian imagery and prayer to work their magic. For the conjurer, the God of the Church was just another god among many. Many conjurers would use charms that combined the powers of this new God with the old gods of the land.

In my hometown of Leigh, Lancashire, the most famous conjurer was Edmund Hartley, who in 1594 was called upon to cast out the malicious spirits that plagued the children of Nicholas Starkie. In short, after the conjurer was called, the Starkie family tried to cheat Hartley on the deal they had made. After evading this deal, the family later found that the children and some of the house staff became tormented by evil spirits once more. It can be said that the Starkie family was *repossessed*. Hartley would later be tried and executed by hanging outside of Lancaster Castle for the crime of drawing the magic Circle.

Surviving in the English language from a historical source is the phrase "put off." If someone compared something you were about to eat with something horrible, then you could say that they have "put you off" of eating it. The phrase itself actually relates to the conjurer who had the ability to "put on" or "put off," referring to both spells and spirits.

## HANDFASTING & OVER THE BRUSH

The most commonly discussed meaning of handfasting is marriage, or at least, the ceremony that formalises a committed relationship for witches. The term itself comes from the Old English word *handfæsten*, literally meaning to "promise your hand [in marriage]," and was used to describe an engagement: the proposal for marriage has been made, but the wedding itself has yet to happen. Many people today still use

---

71    "Conjure." *Etymonline*, www.etymonline.com/word/conjure#etymonline_v_18215. Accessed July 22, 2021.

the term by its original definition of engagement, so it is important to be mindful of this fact when discussing this topic with others.

The term used for the wedding itself is "living over the brush." In the old Lancashire dialect, this is also commonly known as "living o'er t'broosh" or "living tally." The word *broosh* (brush) derives from the old name for a broomstick—*broosh steighl*—which is jumped over by the couple on their wedding day. Because the use of these terms may differ depending on where a person's Craft is derived, it can be easy to misinterpret what someone is referring to. For this reason, it is generally advisable to specify the use of these terms, ensuring that everyone in the conversation is on the same page.

## Ley Lines & Corpse Roads

*Ley lines* are a set of straight lines of mystical power that flow through the earth. When these lines intersect, they create "power spots" upon which sacred sites were built and later occupied by Churches. The discovery of these lines and the maps of their flows and intersections came to us from the work of English author and amateur archaeologist Alfred Watkins. This discovery was made in 1921 following Watkin's observance of sacred sites and old Churches appearing to be perfectly aligned with each other. The name itself came about due to the fact that most places where the lines converged contain the word *Ley* in their names.

Corpse roads are routes of a different nature, though are no less mystical. Also called a *burial road, coffin road, lych way,* and *lyke way,* these roads weave through the landscape and were used as travelling routes for the burial of the dead. Over time, these roads were said to be haunted by a wide variety of spirits and were sometimes known as *fairy tracks.* A special type of fairy called a *corpse candle* was said to appear on these paths as an omen of imminent death. The corpse candle appeared as a ball of light that would travel the corpse road from the burial site to the home of the soon departed and back again. It was believed that the winding of these roads would prevent the dead from wandering home, therefore encouraging them to move on. Today, the signs of corpse roads still exist all over Britain and some modern funerals will still follow these ancient routes to the place of burial or the site of the funeral services.

## Familiar

The connection between a familiar spirit and the gods is commonly overlooked. This is primarily due to the fact that the term *familiar* has recently become attributed to almost anything—usually the family pet. So, what is meant by *a familiar*?

The origin of a familiar can be directly traced to the presence of Saxons in the early development of what would later become Britain.[72] The term *familiar* means "companion" and is directly related to the word *fylgja*, meaning "attendant spirit"—originating from the verb meaning "to accompany."[73] The familiar itself often presents independently in animal form but is in fact part of the witch's soul expressing itself as an often-externalised entity. The familiar is commonly seen in folklore as directly tied to the witch and when harm is sustained by one, a corresponding injury is found immediately upon the other.[74] If you are familiar with the TV series *His Dark Materials*, you will have seen this concept played out in the role of the daemon and their connection with their human counterpart.

Witches are not the first beings to be depicted as having such animal spirit companions. The gods of old were often, and still are, associated with a wide range of animals. Isis was associated with the bull by the Egyptians as much as Hecate was with black dogs or the Morrigan with corvids among their respective devotees. The bond that the gods shared with these animal spirit companions was viewed as the source, or at least the reason, for their powers and divine

---

72    Mystic Britain, "Witches and Demons", Produced by Blink Films, First aired: 29 April 2019.

73    Gabriel Turville-Petre, *Nine Norse Studies, Volume 5*, (Viking Society for Northern Research, University College London, 1972), 54-55.

74    Gemma Gary, *Silent as the Trees*, (London: Troy Books Publishing, 2017), 99-100.

status.[75] As time went on, the devotees of the Old Religion were attributed to such spirits, indicating a soul connection between the witch and a corresponding deity.[76] In this sense, it can be seen that the call to the Craft is inevitable. Some believed that this connection was essential and tied them to the divine, and if an offence was made on the part of the human, then the familiar, or *fylgia*, would abandon them.[77] Ultimately, the job of the familiar—regardless of the cultural name given to it—was to support the spiritual development of the person, usually guiding them to the appropriate gods.[78]

My own belief is not that the familiar abandons those who shut them out—I find that reconnection is possible. It is like when you need to shut out background chatter in order to hear the person you are talking to. We possess the ability to filter out what we want to hear and what we want to ignore, and this applies to spiritual presences as well. The familiar, being part of the soul, is not something that can get up and leave—it is part of who we are. I often compare the apparent independence of a familiar to your heart as it is a self-sustaining process. You don't tell it when to beat, when to speed up if you get scared, or to slow down when you are calm. It is independent of your conscious processes and yet is still part of you. Your familiar is the same, but as an object of your soul. Like your heart, it makes hundreds, if not thousands, of decisions on your behalf without your conscious intervention. It may well appear to be a separate entity, but it is as much a part of you as your heart.

---

75    Mystic Britain, "Witches and Demons", Produced by Blink Films, First aired: 29 April 2019.

76    Ibid.

77    Pollyanna Jones, "Understanding the Fylgjur of Norse Mythology," Accessed November 23, 2020. https://exemplore.com/magic/Understanding-the-Fylgjur.

78    Diana L. Paxson, *The Essential Guide to Possession, Depossession, and Divine Relationships,* (Weiser Books, 2015), 60-61.

# Chapter Three

# THE GODS

**When** it comes to the subject of working with deities, there is a wide range of opinions to explore. This is naturally due to the fact that there are so many deities a witch can build a relationship with—if indeed they do so at all. In most cases, information about many gods and goddesses is abundantly available in books and online. Meeting people in the community who have a devotional relationship with a specific deity is also an avenue for new insights.

One scenario for introduction to a deity, though less common, is when an individual hears a call from that deity presenting in an archetypal form instead of a more readily identifiable persona. When this happens, it is often to people who did not plan on building a relationship with a deity at all. After such a call, when their natural curiosity drives them to find out more, they are presented with a dead end. When a deity calls and there is no reliable information available on how to reach out and build a connection, it can be rather frustrating and often leaves people feeling like they have hit a wall in their spiritual growth and personal development.

The re-embracing of deity archetypes only seems natural in a community that embraces—either in whole or part—the practices and underpinning philosophies of British Craft. Regardless of which form of Craft is being used, the inner world patterns will cause a stirring on those planes and a response should be expected. As stated in an earlier chapter, the gods of Britain reached out and grabbed hold of the nation when the people returned to their rites and ways, therefore, the re-emergence of the divine archetype is not surprising. Prior to the influence of the Roman Empire, native Britons did not give faces to their gods. That is to say that the British mind-set was to see deities *as* the thunder, rivers, trees, and earth, rather than just the beings that ruled over them. This tendency to make anthropo-morphic images of the gods came about from Roman syncretism and not from the natives themselves.[79] The goal of this following chapter is to reconsider this mind-set by exploring the major archetypes of the Triple Goddess and Dual God, address the interplay between the two, and guide you through the lesser-discussed aspect of Divine Fluidity. By exploring these three concepts and discussing the restric-tive thought patterns around them, you will be able to build more meaningful contact with the archetype—should they reach out to you and you wish to respond.

## RETHINKING THE MAIDEN, MOTHER, & CRONE

From the ancient world to archetypes in our collective consciousness, there have always been goddesses depicted in triple form. Powerful goddesses such as Hecate or Brigid have usually been represented as three women standing together, usually back to back, yet are interpreted to be the same goddess manifest in three distinct aspects. Until quite recently, the concept of the Goddess holding within herself a triple aspect has been a popular theological model. This triple archetype is usually referred to today as the Maiden, Mother, and Crone (MMC) and is believed by many to represent the different stages of the God-dess' own cycles and rhythms in the natural world.

Commonly symbolised by the triple phases of the moon, the Maiden is represented by the new moon and personifies youth, naivety, and sexuality. As the Mother, she is the full moon and personifies fertility, patience, and nurturing. Finally, the old moon represents the Crone, who personifies the Goddess' aspects of magic, wisdom, and death.

---

79     Elliot Rose, *A Razor for a Goat: A Discussion of Certain Problems in the History of Witchcraft and Diabolism*, (United Kingdom: University of Toronto Press, 1989), 58.

Although structured on truly ancient manifestations of the Goddess the world over, the MMC terminology, as it is most commonly thought of today, was first expressed in the 1948 work *The White Goddess* by the British poet Robert Graves. Despite the fact that *The White Goddess* has been a largely criticised work, especially regarding the interpretations of women, the model itself has taken root in our community. While the model in its current incarnation may be relatively modern, what it represents is of antiquity and should not necessarily be overlooked.

## The Birth of the Triple Goddess

Chasing down the origins of the Triple Goddess is not an easy task. Although most consider her to be the interpretation found in *The White Goddess,* her origins far pre-date 1948. Robert Graves himself discusses this aspect of the Triple Goddess in two of his earlier works, *King James* (1946) and *Hercules, My Shipmate, or The Golden Fleece* (1944). Although Graves uses many different titles to describe the three aspects of the Triple Goddess, she was a distinctly present figure within his mind prior to *The White Goddess.*

Notorious occultist Aleister Crowley also discussed the Triple Goddess almost two decades before *The White Goddess* came into print. In 1929, Crowley wrote and published *Moonchild,* where he describes the three phases of the Triple Goddess as Maiden, Lover, and Crone. It is with Crowley that the last trace of the original Triple Goddess symbol is maintained: the manifestations of the Goddess as the new, half, and full moon.

The psychologist Sigmund Freud also expressed the importance of a Triple Goddess in his 1913 work *The Theme of the Three Caskets.* Here, Freud discusses how even goddesses such as Aphrodite contain within them the power of both creator and destroyer—he even goes so far as to recognise a correlation between her, Mother Earth, and the triform Artemis-Hecate.[80] A decade earlierin, the so-called Cambridge Ritualist Jane Ellen Harrison wrote of a similar Triple Goddess concept in her 1903book *Prolegomena to the Study of Greek Religion.*[81] Though it is important to state that Harrison specifically refers only to the Maiden and Mother aspects in her work, the triple nature of the feminine divine is affirmed throughout.

Casting our timeline back to the third century, we meet the Neoplatonic philosopher Porphyry (234–305 CE) who wrote about the aspects of the Triple Goddess in his work *On Images*. Although the triple moon symbolism used by Crowley (new, half, and full moon) is only partially hinted at here; it is a strong indication of the Triple Goddess being remembered in her three key aspects:

> *"But, again, the moon is Hecate, the symbol of her varying phases and of her power dependent on the phases. Wherefore her power appears in three forms, having as symbol of the new moon the figure in the white robe and golden sandals, and torches lighted: the basket, which she bears when she has mounted high, is the symbol of the cultivation of the crops, which she makes to grow up according to the increase of her light: and again the symbol of the full moon is the Goddess of the brazen sandals...And, again, the Fates are referred to her powers, Clotho to the generative, and Lachesis to the nutritive, and Atropos to the inexorable will of the deity."*[82]

Prior to Porphyry, Paulus Vergilius Maro (better known as *Virgil* or *Vergil*) wrote his classic book series, *Aeneid*, between 29–19 BCE. In the sixth book of this collection, entitled *Fate of Queen Dido*, Virgil, recording the stories of the classic myths of the day, makes reference to the Triple Goddess in a rather significant way. The most published (and shorter) rendering of his work simply contains the line: "...threefold Hecate, virgin Diana's triple form."

---

80    Sigmund Freud trans. James Strachey, *The Complete Psychological works of Sigmund Freud*, (London: The Hogarth Press, 1958), 299.

81    Jane Ellen Harrison, *Prolegomena to the study of Greek Religion*, (Cambridge: University Press, 1908), 257-321.

82    *On Images* by Porphyry Translated by Edwin Hamilton Gifford http://classics.mit.edu/Porphyry/images.html accessed 30 Jan 2020.

Later, commentary on Virgil's work from approximately 400 CE by Maurus Servius Honoratus (commonly known as *Servius*) provided two expanded versions of Virgil's description of the Triple Goddess. Preserved in the original Latin text are found the two passages:

*"Hecate, whose power is said to be threefold, from which come the three faces of the virgin Diana."*

And

*"The three faces of the virgin Diana are a repetition, indicating the Moon, Diana and Proserpina. When she is above the Earth she is the Moon, on Earth she is Diana and under the Earth, Proserpina. Some argue that she is three-fold because the Moon has three forms, as on the first night, on the following nights and on the fifteenth.*

*Some call the same Goddess Lucina, Diana and Hecate because they assign to one goddess the three powers of birth, growth and death. Some say that Lucina is the Goddess of birth, Diana of growth and Hecate of death. On account of this three-fold power they have imagined her as three-fold and three-form, and for that reason they built temples at the meeting of three roads."*[83]

These three stages of the moon are directly related to the three classic phases of the moon that made up the months used by the Romans. These three phases were the *Kalends* (new moon), the *Nones* (half-moon or first quarter), and the *Ides* (full moon).[84] These phases

83 Servius' Commentary on the Aeneid, 4.511 http://www.perseus.tufts.edu/hopper/text?doc=Perseus%3Atext%3A1999.02.0053%3Abook%3D4%3Acommline%3D511 Accessed 30 Jan. 2019.

84 Betty Rose Nagle, *Ovid's Fasti: Roman Holidays* (Indiana University Press, 1995), 29-30.

correspond to the Triple Goddess symbol which was preserved from the classic pre-Christian period to Crowley's publication of *Moonchild* in 1929. Although Robert Graves would change the imagery associated with the Triple Goddess to the full moon between the waxing and waning crescent phases—which we are familiar with today—it is true to say that religious thealogy (matters of the Divine Feminine) has evolved our understanding of this goddess over time. Therefore, the change in imagery does not have a substantial impact on her significance.

The birth of the Triple Goddess is demonstrably pre-Christian. She is a formidable power who has refused to be silenced throughout the centuries. By reaching out through poets, philosophers, researchers, occultists, and even psychologists, the Triple Goddess has been able to maintain her presence within the world. By surviving the end of her temple cults, the rise of Christianity, and the persecution of goddess worshipping witches, this mighty goddess has proven that true power never dies and the voice of the old gods is forever available to those who truly seek out their Mysteries.

## MOTHER, MAIDEN, AND CRONE AS ROLES OF THE GODDESS

Take a moment to clear your mind and forget everything that you associate with the Mother, Maiden, and Crone (MMC) model. Release the symbols and associations that you have built around this philosophy and explore the aspects of the Goddess given here as if it were the first time that you have ever heard the terms *Maiden, Mother,* and *Crone.* As some of these interpretations will not necessarily be expected by most readers, it is truly important to release all previous associations and attempt to find the Goddess again.

As already discussed, these archetypes are ancient concepts that continue to have an effect on witches today. Referring back to the passages written by Servius, it was made apparent that the three aspects of the Goddess are concerned with how we relate to her. She is not supposed to be a roadmap for our lives and phases, rather, her phases are about how she relates to us. Before breaking down each part, it is important to look at what that relationship means when using the original teachings of the Triple Goddess.

According to Servius' records, the Mother is the first aspect of the Goddess. When we are born, it is from the Mother: the start of creation and life comes from her as she is the Mother of all. The Maiden, according to ancient accounts, is related to the instinct to grow and become mature. This includes the sexual awakening that arises from maturity and our independence from the maternal figure of the Mother. The final figure of the Triple Goddess is the Crone. She is the keeper of death as well as the wisdom of age. Remember that a good death also means that a life was lived. Therefore, the Crone embodies the spirit of death as well as the experiences of long-lived years.

We sometimes hear the term *Dark Mother,* and its use has seen a resurgence in recent years. When we speak of the Dark Mother, we are acknowledging that the death of the Crone is the life of the Mother. When the cycle of the moon passes from the Crone phase, it transitions into the aspect of the Mother who brings with her new life. For many witches, this is the promise of rebirth wherein souls will be born again into a new body. The Goddess in her "dark" and mysterious death-face hides underneath the generative power of the Mother. The use of the term *Dark Mother* is our way of acknowledging that the Triple Goddess is truly one goddess presenting three aspects. Each contains the other without contradiction, and she and her cycles are infinite.

## MAIDEN

In its simplest definition, the word *maiden* means "woman." In relation to the Goddess, the Maiden is the feminine power of the divine. But why *maiden*? Why not just say *woman*? Simply put, "maiden" is generally used in reference to an unmarried woman. She is the free, independent aspect of the Goddess, feminine power in all of its potential. She is pure feminine power without compromise or apology. It is said that every woman that exists, has existed, or will exist is reflected in the aspect of the Maiden.

The term is also used when describing beginnings, such as in the "maiden voyage" of a ship. In this sense, the Maiden archetype can be seen as the "original woman" or as the creative power that began all things. In my previous book, *Aradia,* an example is found of a creation myth where the Goddess is the primary force of creation, not the God. She is also the divine initiator who guides witches along the path of the Mysteries, which are a form of beginning. Due to the sheer magnitude of power that this archetype possesses, it is appropriate to attribute both the full and dark phases of the lunar cycle to the Maiden.

At the full moon, it is believed that spiritual power is at its peak. While the Maiden archetype expresses the power of the Goddess as a pure force of feminine power, it stands to reason that this phase of the cycle would connect to her. In times long since passed, it was believed that the full moon indicated the time that the Goddess menstruated, leading to taboo practices becoming associated with this time of the month.[85] Many women also find that when practising Witchcraft, their menstrual cycle—if they indeed have one at all—becomes in sync with the timing of the lunar cycle.

The other side of this archetype is the dark moon. Here the Goddess represents the hidden, covert side of her feminine power. This part of the archetype does not menstruate and does not contain the elements that are held in the sparkling silver, flashy side of the full moon. Keep in mind that the Maiden is still feminine in this stage as she is pure and without dilution. Between these two phases, the Maiden archetype represents the full spectrum of female identity and experience. She is the essence of all that a woman is and can be, which is demonstrated by her cycle as ever-changing and fluid without compromising her inherent purity.

Her sign is:
- The half-moon (classical accounts).
- The waxing crescent (contemporary imagery).
- Full and dark (*Witchcraft Unchained*, revised imagery).

## MOTHER

What is a mother? It seems to be a simple question at its surface, and this oversimplification appears to be why so many are opposed to the MMC model. Of course, when people hear the word *mother*, they are likely to think of their own. This is why so many simply connect the word with fertility and childbearing. When a woman gives birth, it is said that she has "mothered a child," but this is not the only context in which *mother*

---

85    Janet and Stewart Farrar, *The Witches' Goddess*, (United Kingdom: David & Charles, 2012).

is used. How many people do you know who have someone in their life that they describe as being "like a mother" to them? They are not saying that they gave birth to them. They are speaking of a role that this person fulfils in their lives—an important and valuable role that they honour by attaching such a powerful title to it.

Adopted children can still tell you who their mother is. The lack of biology between an adopted child and their adoptive mother does not lessen the mother's position as a parent. Limiting the use of the word *mother* solely to an act of biology makes little sense. A female caregiver, generally in a hospital, is sometimes referred to as a *matron*, a word which derives from the Latin word *mater* (mother). This example strongly represents the Goddess, as her role as a Mother is of a spiritual nature; she is the divine life-giver whose essence and love maintain the universe.

In the lunar cycle, the Mother archetype is symbolised by the waxing phase of the moon—primarily the waxing crescent. It is in this phase that the moon is "becoming" and is in a state of generation, an action which perfectly reflects the life-giving and preserving aspects of the Goddess. In the *Charge of the Goddess*, written by the late Doreen Valiente, the Goddess in her Mother aspect states:

*"Nor do I demand aught in sacrifice; for behold, I am the Mother of all living, and my love is poured out upon the earth."*[86]

Her sign is:
- The new moon (classical accounts).
- The full moon (contemporary imagery).
- The waxing crescent (*Witchcraft Unchained*, revised imagery).

## CRONE

Like the term *Mother*, the Crone often suggests to some that the MMC model disempowers women as they get older, however, others are happy with—and indeed feel empowered by—embracing and connecting to this phase of the Goddess. As is found within the previous two archetypes, there are far more details about the Goddess

---

86    Janet Farrar and Gavin Bone, *Lifting the Veil: A Witches' Guide to Trance-Prophecy, Drawing Down the Moon, and Ecstatic Ritual,* (Acorn Guild Press, 2016), 299.

than common and superficial beliefs suggest, and when explored, these details are also far more interesting.

*Crone* is a term ultimately derived from the older English word *carrion*, a reference to decaying flesh (usually of animals), which in turn comes from *caro*, the Latin word for flesh. Just as the Mother is the life-giving and preserving aspect of the universe, the Crone archetype reflects the aspect of the Goddess that acts as the midwife of souls. Her role is to bring life to an end so that the cycle can be completed, and new life can be formed. Energy cannot be created or destroyed, only converted from one form to another, and it is the role of the Crone to be that method of conversion.

The African starfish flower represents this aspect of the Goddess perfectly. Also known as the carrion flower, the *Stapelia gigantea* releases the smell of rotting meat in order to attract pollinating flies. Here the flies are killed, but their lives are reprocessed and provide a renewed life to the flower, helping it reproduce. The Crone archetype, much like the waning cycle of the moon that represents her, is in control of the diminishing power of life; the destroyer and Queen of the Underworld.

Her sign is:
- The full moon (classical accounts).
- The waning crescent (contemporary imagery).
- The waning crescent (*Witchcraft Unchained*, revised imagery).

These cycles of the moon and the aspects of the Goddess are also reflective of the human condition. We are born, grow up, become old, and finally, we die. The Goddess, however, reflects a spiritual renewal found in death that is our promise of an afterlife. The Crone is not separate from the Maiden or the Mother because the ancient depictions of the Triple Goddess were not of women of different ages; they were the same divine woman, revealing her various roles within the lives of her people.

*"The sun is always the same, always itself, never in any sense 'becoming.' The moon, on the other hand, is a body which waxes, wanes and disappears, a body whose existence is subject to the universal law of becoming, of birth and death. The moon, like man,*

*has a career, involving tragedy, for its failing, like man's, ends in death. For three nights the starry sky is without a moon. But this 'death' is followed by a rebirth: the 'new moon.' The moon's going out, in 'death,' is never final.*

*... Its beginnings, and this ever-recurring cycle make the moon the heavenly body above all others concerned with the rhythms of life. It is not surprising, then, that it governs all those spheres of nature that fall under the law of recurring cycles: water, rain, plant life, fertility."*[87]

## MEMORIES OF THE GODDESS

### Mary, the Blessed Virgin

Remnants of this Goddess form can be found surviving within the theology of the Christian Church in the form of the Virgin Mary. Here, the Church reflects all three goddess aspects into their interpretations of the Blessed Virgin, as will be seen. Here we will discuss her Maiden, or Virgin, archetype.

Most people the world over are familiar with the concept of the Immaculate Conception, however, it is the notion of the perpetual virginity of Mary which depicts her as remaining pure and incorruptible in her femininity. The biggest clue that her virginity speaks of a more spiritual state is demonstrated in the Gospels themselves. Here we find that Mary was not a virgin in the sense that we think of today, as she not only consummated her marriage to Joseph but in fact had other children after the birth of Jesus.

*"...and she gave birth to her firstborn, a son. She wrapped him in cloths and placed him in a manger, because there was no guest room available for them."*

Luke 2:7

---

87  Mircea Eliade, *Patterns in Comparative Religion*, (U of Nebraska Press, 1996), 154.

*"But he did not consummate their marriage until she gave birth to a son. And he gave him the name Jesus."*

Matthew 1:25

*"Isn't this the carpenter's son? Isn't his mother's name Mary, and aren't his brothers James, Joseph, Simon and Judas? Aren't all his sisters with us? Where then did this man get all these things?"*

Matthew 13:55-56

*"For even his own brothers did not believe in him."*

John 7:5

Jesus himself is recorded as having used his family to illustrate a point in his teachings by equating strangers who follow the will of God as members of his own family.

*"And he looked round about on them which sat about him, and said, Behold my mother and my brethren!*

*For whosoever shall do the will of God, the same is my brother, and my sister, and mother."*

Mark 3:34-35

Within Jewish custom, it is normal for a mother to be considered tainted by birth and a period of adjustment is undertaken before a state of ritual or spiritual purification is again attained. In the narrative of Mary's birthing, however, this is not the case. Her perpetual virginity suggests that she is incapable of being impure in her own right which is the reason she was chosen to be the Mother of God.

In the scripture Luke 1:28, the Angel Gabriel addresses Mary in the following manner:

*"Hail, full of Grace, the Lord is with you."*

According to the Greek version of the same text, the context of this strange address is to be understood as *"hail, you who have been perfected in grace.*" This indicates that Mary was herself conceived in this state of purity and has no direct bearing on her future as the mother of Jesus.[88] In comparison, Mary is to the Church what the Maiden archetype is to witches. She is the central unblemished feminine figure within the religious tradition—pure and complete in her own right.

The Maiden archetype, having been equally represented by the full and dark moons, is also reflected within the teachings of the Church. The theological ideals and teachings surrounding Mary are balanced by Eve of the Old Testament. *Eve,* literally meaning "life," is the natural counterbalance on the spectrum of feminine power as expressed within that religious theology. Therefore, the sacred feminine figure shows remnants of an understanding that the Maiden archetype needs to have light and virginal aspects as well as a "fallen" aspect to represent two extremes, and by extension, every variation in between.

Witchcraft is no different.

## Mary, Mother of God

Within the Church, we find our Mother Goddess archetype reflected again in the Blessed Mother. This time, she appears in the rosary prayer "Hail Mary, Mother of God." Here, she is not simply the mother of Jesus, but of God in His totality. This is a powerful statement that speaks to her origin and connection as a Mother Goddess. It can be said that the doctrine of the early Church merged these attributes of the Goddess into the personage of Mary.

Among her many other titles is found the epithet *Mother of Angels*, and the same Grace that fills her is found within the Church—which is referred to as *Holy Mother Church*. Churches themselves house the presence of God as much as Mary housed the same essence within her womb. For this reason, the Church is referred to as *Her* with the capitalised "H" to balance with the *Him* that is attributed to God. The two are paralleled, indicating a holy and divine Mother archetype.

---

88    Mark I. Miravalle, *Introduction to Mary: The Heart of Marian Doctrine and Devotion* (Queenship Publishing, 2006), 65-66.

## Mary, Empress of Hell

To complete the section, it is only fitting to discuss the ways in which this aspect of our goddess has survived within the Church's Holy Mary. The Crone as the Goddess of the underworld and death is reflected within two key components of Mary's influence. The first is found in the *Hail Mary* prayer, "pray for us sinners now *and* at the hour of our death." This illustrates two facets of Mary's role as petitioned here. First, she is asked to pray for the person *now:* they are directly seeking her intervention in the situation at hand. Second, she is asked to pray at the hour of their death. She is being asked to intervene in death which indicates that it is Mary, and not Jesus, whom believers seek as the redemptive power at that moment. Despite what the Church's theology states, the proof is in the practice.

Mary also has a "Hell" or underworld aspect. One of her many and lesser known titles is *Empress of Hell*. This aspect of Mary reflects her power as a destroyer, mainly of demons, but also demonstrates that she has dominion over Hell.

> *"Not only is the most Blessed Virgin the queen of heaven and of all saints. She is also queen of hell and of all evil spirits. For she overcame them valiantly by her virtues. From the very beginning God foretold the victory and empire that our queen would one day gain over the serpent, when he announced to him that a woman would come into the world to conquer him: 'I will put enmity between you and this woman ... She will crush your head'* (Genesis 3:15). *And who could this woman, his enemy, be but Mary, who by her fair humility and holy life always conquered him and beat down his strength?*
>
> *As St. Bernard remarks, this proud spirit, in spite of himself, was beaten down and trampled underfoot by this most Blessed Virgin. Now, as a slave conquered in war, he is forced always to obey the commands of this queen: 'Beaten down and trampled*

*under the feet of Mary, the Devil endures a wretched slavery.'
And she bound him in such a way that this enemy cannot stir so
as to do even the least injury to any of those who go to her for
protection."*

St. Alphonsus Liguori, The Glories of Mary[89]

As the Triple Goddess of the Church, Mary has three distinct titles
of importance: *Queen of Heaven, Mistress of the World,* and *Empress
of Hell.*[90] Mary is clearly indicated as being far more than an average
woman as she holds positions that are truly divine. Although the
Church may suppress these truths, they are there for all to see. If
the Goddess in her triple form can be so well preserved in such
a patriarchal religion, then surely, as witches, we can restore the
Goddess to the position of reverence and respect that she deserves.

## THE THREE FATES

The three aspects of the Goddess are not only found reflected in her
lunar cycle—the concept of the three Fates also shows signs of a
goddess who presents herself as a triple-formed power. The Fates
represent birth, life, and death. In this model, the originating power
is honoured by birth, the human experience in its full spectrum of
potential is recognised by life, and the converting power is expressed
as death.

The three aspects of the feminine divine have permeated into
every culture and tradition across the world and across time. Whether
reflected as Fate or as a moon goddess, this divine expression has im-
pressed itself into the minds and cultures of humanity for millennia.
This begs the question: Why does the Goddess constantly pull us
back to this three-form expression of her presence and power?

---

89    Liguori, Alphonse. *The Glories of Mary.* 1868.

90    John Whiterig, *Christ Crucified and Other Meditations of a Durham Hermit,*
      (Gracewing Publishing, 1994), 119.

## Summary of The Triple Goddess

So, who is the Triple Goddess? She is the power of women, undiluted and unapologetic. Her full and dark aspects are capped with waxing and waning phases that highlight her important work in the rhythms of recurrence in nature and the universe. Yet, all flows back into her true essence as the Sacred Feminine. That is what the MMC model represents. That is who the Triple Goddess truly is.

# WE ARE NOT THE GODS

For many, the notion that *we are not the gods* is easily accepted. After all, who other than cult leaders command people to dedicate a whole religious movement around them? That being said, there is an apparent struggle for some to accept that we are not the gods. This is most apparent in the opposition to the MMC model, as many practitioners argue that the model does not represent them and who they are. It is the interpretation that the gods *need* to represent us that appears to be the source of the disconnect.

Why should the gods have to be relatable to us?

Why should they have to be perfect carbon copies of our lives?

What makes us so great that the oldest powers in the universe should change to meet our expectations?

The gods are what they are, regardless of whether their myth cycles or representations mirror our own personalities. Why should that matter at all? Do you know of any Christians who demand that their child be conceived by Immaculate Conception? It just does not happen because these worshippers understand that they are not their god. They are human beings who have their own lives, stories, and experiences.

Consider the multitude of different ethnic backgrounds, religions, sexualities, and all other varieties of people in the world. Do we as witches, or as human beings, choose not to be around someone because they are not exactly like us? This should not be the case! Life would be very boring if everyone were the same. In fact, there would be no witches at all if people didn't answer their call of distinction from everyone else, so why discard these aspects of the Goddess?

## From Triple Goddess to Dual God

How do men relate to the model of the God? The question is rarely (if ever) asked by practitioners of the Craft—but it is important, as men make up a large part of this ever-growing community. Though not commonly perceived as a "triple god," the God does contain within his essence a triplicate. Unlike the Goddess, his powers are usually expressed as two separate poles without an archetype uniting the two. Therefore, the God is usually seen as a dual, or double aspect god. In this section, the God will be discussed in his three key aspects while also exploring the reasons for why he is more commonly considered to be solely of a dual nature. Just as re-exploring the Goddess required a clear and open mind, it is suggested that the following expressions of the God be approached in the same way.

### HORNED GOD

By far the most popular expression of the God that is found within our community is that of the Horned God. It is not surprising that this archetype of the Divine Masculine is so popular. Just as the Goddess has maintained her triple identity in our cultural, mythological, and psychological lives, so too has the God maintained his horned image since prehistory.

The earliest depictions of the Horned God are found as cave drawings and are accepted as magical acts—or petitions of worship for divine intervention—to ensure success in aspects of life necessary for human survival.[91] From images of hunting to those illustrating success in combat, the presence of the God as a necessary aspect of human existence has long been associated with his horned manifestation. There are no signs of this going away.

In the community of the Craft, the Horned God is perhaps the most beloved of all expressions of the Divine Masculine. As a community that covers diverse traditions and systems of practice, it is hugely significant that this expression, above all others, is still as relevent to our lives as it was when our ancestors were still in caves,

---

91    Doreen Valiente, *An ABC of Witchcraft Past and Present* (Phoenix Publishing Inc. 1986), 181-182.

discovering the first fire. The long and sustained relationship that humanity has with this archetypal image truly speaks to the essential nature and power of the Horned God.

## Why Horns?

Horns initially seem to be an odd attribute to so strongly associate with a divine being. It has long been believed that horns represent divine power and have been worn by a number of gods, emperors, and pharaohs alike.[92] For this very reason, the famous sculpture of Moses by Michelangelo depicts him with horns, demonstrating the fact that he was touched by God. The idea that Moses had horns is found in both the Hebrew texts and in the original Greek and Vulgate Latin forms of the Bible.[93] Within Samuel Mathers' *The Key of Solomon the King,* horns are an important, though subtle, symbol of divinity in the image of the First Pentacle of the Sun. In this image is the face of the Christian God depicted with horns.

Although in his personal notes Mathers claims that the image is that of the angel *Metatron*, the Latin text around the edge of the pentacle is deciphered as saying, "Behold His face and form by Whom all things were made, and Whom all creatures obey." This text makes it clear that the image is that of the "face and form" of

---

92   Ruth W. Mellinkoff, *The Horned Moses in Medieval Art and Thought* (Wipf and Stock Publishers, 1997), 1-9.

93   Thomas Römer, Trans. Liz Libbrecht, "The Horns of Moses. Setting the Bible in its Historical Context", https://books.openedition.org/cdf/3048?lang=en Accessed 03 Jan. 2020.

the Christian God. He, like so many of the pre-Christian divinities, has horns.[94]

This connection between horns and the divine led to the inevitable development of sympathetic ritual uses of horns that can be found woven into most cultures throughout history. The prominent use of drinking horns, horns as instruments to sound to spirits or gods, and even the use of powdered horns as a form of tribal medicine speaks to the profound importance that was placed on the archetype of a Horned God.

## THE DIVINE MASCULINE IN HUMAN AFFAIRS

No writing on the Horned God could be complete without mention of the Vikings. Although popular opinion imagines these prehistoric warrior people with horned helmets, the truth is that their helmets were not found to bare horns at all. The only legitimate use of horned helmets found among the Vikings was devoted only to religious or magical use, the most common being among the warrior group known as *Berserkers*.[95] The Berserkers, the root of our modern term *berserk*, were a band of warrior men who entered battle naked with only weapons, shields, and horned helmets. These warriors were possessed by the power of the Divine Masculine, causing them to enter a trance-like state of wild frenzy. This state prepared them for battle and provided them with the rage and determination for victory, leading to the popular image of Berserkers as powerful and bloodthirsty warriors.[96]

## WHO IS THE HORNED GOD?

The Horned God is the total embodiment of the Divine Masculine in all its potential. He is the unifying archetype of the two aspects of the Dual God, making him the obvious choice for the focus of veneration of the Divine Masculine from Prehistory to the modern day.

---

94    S. Liddell MacGregor Mathers, *The Key of Solomon the King* (Book Tree, 1999), 65.5-71.

95    Natmus, "Helmets," https://en.natmus.dk/historical-knowledge/denmark/pre-historic-period-until-1050-ad/the-viking-age/weapons/helmets/ Accessed 03 Feb. 2020.

96    Ibid.

## Sacrificial God

Within the archetype of the Horned God is the *Sacrificial God*. Although these two aspects may be perceived as separate, thereby implying a Triple God, they are in fact overlapping qualities. Just as the Goddess represents the essence of life in her mother aspect, so too does the God represent the process of life. Think of the Goddess as the catalyst of a process and the God as the unfolding of that process. In this light, the God is the process of life. Our God in his horned aspect encompasses all elements that are necessary to survival: hunting, combat, shelter, fire etc. It is within this role that he also acts as the Sacrificial God.

A common expression concerning the Horned God is that he is both the hunter and the hunted. This expression means that just as life requires us to eat (as the hunter), life also needs that which is to be eaten (the hunted). As the God is the process of life itself, he must actively embody that which sacrifices and that which is sacrificed. All life feeds on life, whether that is plant life or the life of other animals. Our Horned God is found within both, making him the horned hunter and the god who sacrifices the life which he embodies to sustain the hunter.

> *"The witches explain this duality by a ritual in which they invoke the Old God: 'Thou art the Opener of the Doorway of the Womb; and yet, because all things that are born must also die, that they may be renewed, therefore art thou Lord of the Gates of Death.'"*

Gerald Gardner, *The Meaning of Witchcraft*[97]

His symbol is the sign of Taurus.

## Taurus

The zodiac sign *Taurus* is the quintessential symbol of this aspect of the God. As the builder of the Celestial Powers, Taurus perfectly reflects the God's qualities of life, fertility, and survival. Ruled by the planet Venus, the sign of Taurus reflects the fact that love is the driving force

---

97    Gerald Gardner, *The Meaning of Witchcraft* (Red Wheel/Weiser, LLC, 2004), 150.

behind his power. It is due to this love that the hunter provides all that is necessary for survival, and it is this same love that causes him to become the hunted: the necessary sacrifice so that life may endure. As Taurus corresponds to the throat, it is difficult to avoid the deeper symbolism of both the hunter eating his prey and the slit throat of the ceremonial sacrifice reflected within the God's nature.

## Death and Resurrection

The opposite and complementary aspect of the Dual God is his role as Lord of Death and Resurrection. Just as the Goddess in her Crone aspect is the catalyst for the process of death (and transformation), the God himself is the active process of death. This is usually perceived as a gatekeeper role whereby he is the guardian of the threshold between worlds. It is the job of the Lord of Death and Resurrection to open the gates between the worlds so that the process of dying, grieving, and renewal of the soul can occur.

As so much of the God's nature in this aspect is intimately tied to life that exists after life, it can be difficult to pin down his patterns in directly relatable ways. In the earthly realm, the most closely related experience is the *death of initiation*. This process of a new beginning sparked by ending an old phase of life is the very experience of touching the mystery of the God in all his glory. Not only are we touched in that moment by his deathly hand, but we are also renewed by his life-giving power which begins (or initiates) a newly unfolding process in the path of our lives.

His symbol is the sign of Scorpio.

## Scorpio

The zodiac sign *Scorpio* is the best symbolic expression of the Death and Resurrection aspect of the God. No two words better encapsulate the essence of Scorpio than *sex* and *death*. Though these two words seem unrelated, within the sign of Scorpio is found the resolution of a paradox. The colloquial French expression *la petite mort* (the little death) is used to describe the experience of orgasm—or more specifically, the transcendental or ecstatic state of "otherness" that is experienced within the moment of orgasm.[98] The notion of sex and death being linked has long been held in our spiritual mind-sets. The fact that we can be immortalised within our descendants is a way in which mortal beings "cheat" death. A fact that is actively celebrated by the Gédé—the Vodou spirits of death.

The two aspects of the God, expressed as sex (or life) and death, are tied to the process of the human condition. When I was training in past life therapy and clinical hypnotherapy, one of my assignments called for a discussion on the link between fear and sexuality. Within this work, discussing the link between sexuality and death was inevitable. The following extract of my writing from that assignment perfectly expresses the interrelatedness of these two aspects of the God:

> *"The link between fear and sexuality, which could be further reduced to primal pain and pleasure, is linked in a manner not too dissimilar to the conscious and subconscious mind. When one instinct is dominant in its expression, the opposing or complementary opposite is suppressed or inhibited. When one needs to fight or flee, sex and intimacy provide no useful survival strategies and are therefore inhibited to allow the appropriate survival urges to take precedence. Likewise, in times of war, the rates of pregnancy and births tend to increase. In this instance, the fear instinct becomes inhibited or suppressed so that the instinct to reproduce takes a dominant position. This can be seen as a way of compensating for the potential loss of lives during a dangerous time and protecting the genetic line in case of invasion and the threat becomes a more personal issue."*

Doreen Valiente also supported the link between these two aspects of the God when recommending the design of markings for the athame based on illustrations found in *The Key of Solomon*:

> *"Now, Taurus and Scorpio are opposite in the Zodiac. When the Sun is in Taurus, May Eve occurs, the commencement of the summer half*

---

98    More details of this state can be found in the chapter Sacred Sexuality.

*of the year; and when the Sun is in Scorpio, Hallowe'en occurs, the commencement of the winter half of the year, according to our Celtic ancestors.*[99]

Their meanings, briefly, are as follows:

 *"The Horned God. Also the powers of fertility, May Eve, the 'light' half of the year...*

 *[Sign of Scorpio] Scorpio, sign of Death and the Beyond, the 'other side' of the God as Lord of the Underworld. Hallowe'en and the 'dark' half of the year.*[100]

## THE INTERPLAY OF THE GODDESS AND GOD

The nature of the Goddess is the essence, or catalyst, of an event, be it life or death, whereas the nature of the God is the actual movement and unfolding of that event. If she is the initial origin of a thing, then he is the action and development of it. This speaks to why the Goddess is considered a Triple Goddess and the God, a Dual God. The Goddess has roles of beginnings and endings, but she is only its initiator. The Goddess herself is an eternal power and so requires an aspect that is stable and unblemished: the Maiden.

The God, on the other hand, is her complementary opposite, therefore he must be "unstable" or ever-changing. Just as the seasons progress and change, as we grow up and grow old, so too does the God. Where the Goddess is immortal and spiritual, the God is mortal and physical. The God is the constant change and the rhythm of life and death. That is why his two aspects are parts of each other: they are interwoven within the same essence. The Goddess is unchanging in her power and the power of the God is found in ever-changing cycles.

---

99   Janet and Stewart Farrar, *A Witches' Bible*, (Hale, 2017), 254.
100  Ibid. 255.

## DIVINE FLUIDITY

Although the Goddess and God have their strong feminine and masculine energies respectively, they are in no way bound to these specific roles. The Goddess is generally accepted as the passive power due to her catalytic nature, while the God is accepted as active due to his embodiment in the unfolding or changing nature of an event. Despite these seemingly static qualities, they are more complex than they first appear.

Within the ancient world, there are numerous examples in which the Gods do not sit so neatly into these binary identities, thereby implying a divine fluidity within their nature. One of the classic examples is found within common expressions used in Roman prayers. It was commonplace for a priest, an actively initiated dedicant of a specific deity, to be unsure of their God's name or gender. To compensate for this, they would add safety clauses to their prayers such as: "whether you are a god or a goddess,"[101] or they would ask them to accept their prayers "by whatever name" they wished.[102] It can be argued that the Roman gods had many ritual titles or epithets which could contribute to the use of these clauses, however, it would be short-sighted to dismiss this evidence of divine fluidity as there is strong evidence that their gods were not static in their forms.

Aphrodite with a beard? Dionysus with breasts? Yes, these are classic depictions of the *assumed* entirely female and male divinities. Historian Professor Bettany Hughes, OBE, explored both of these examples in her BBC documentaries *Venus Uncovered: Ancient Goddess of Love* and *Bacchus Uncovered: Ancient God of Ecstasy.*[103] Although the language for *transgender* and *gender fluid* had not entered the vocabulary of the

---

101 Thomas Dudley Fosbroke, Dionysius Lardner, *A Treatise on the Arts, Manufactures, Manners, and Institutions of the Greeks and Romans, Volume 1* (Longman, Rees, Orme, Brown, Green & Longman, and John Taylor, 1833), 298.

102 Sarah Iles Johnston, *Religions of the Ancient World: A Guide,* (Harvard University Press, 2004), 366.

103 Bettany Hughes, Venus Uncovered: Ancient Goddess of Love, Produced by: Sandstone Global Productions Ltd, First aired on BBC Four: November 15, 2017; Bettany Hughes, Bacchus Uncovered: Ancient God of Ecstasy, Produced by: Sandstone Global Productions Ltd, First aired on BBC Four: April 11, 2018.

ancient world, it is still a powerful reoccurring theme within the divine to transcend gender or shapeshift their gendered form.

In part, this can be interpreted as the divine expressing to humanity that it is not confined to the anthropomorphic expression in which we assign them to. On the other hand, it could be inferred that some divinities express their mystery via the vehicle of bodily transformation or non-static expression. It is the latter of these that will be explored here.

Ovid, among a long list of other classical writers, describes the common theme of men and women exchanging clothing when sacrifice or worship was given to certain deities. Aphroditus, the male expression of Aphrodite, is a common example of this form of ritual practice.[104] A common depiction of Aphroditus is of the figure of the goddess Aphrodite lifting up her dress only to reveal an erect penis. This depiction of the deity is commonly believed to be a strong apotropaic gesture (that which averts evil) or a bringer of good fortune.[105] This provides a strong indication that breaking social norms of gender stereotypes was not only acceptable but perceived as a gateway to the mysteries of the divine in the ancient world.

In Skyros, Greece, the annual goat festival marks the start of spring. This ritual procession, in honour of Dionysus, demonstrates the God's divine fluidity. The *Ieros*, or ancient ones, are the performers in the procession. Men dress as the God in the form of a shepherd with goatskin masks hiding their faces. They are accompanied by veiled women who dance in imitation of the feminine aspect of Dionysus. These dances are performed both by women and men in drag.[106]

The goddess Athena is an excellent example of a deity who displays divine fluidity. Unlike those already discussed, Athena does not actually display an aspect that *isn't* in some way fluid. This is best seen in her dress, wherein she wears clothing typically worn by a goddess but that is underneath traditionally male armour. Her hymns also highlight this aspect of her nature. In the Orphic

---

104   Ovid, Brookes More, Ovid Volume 1, (M. Jones Company, 1978), 585.

105   Ann Olga Koloski-Ostrow, *Naked Truths: Women, Sexuality, and Gender in Classical Art and Archaeology* (Routledge, 2000), 230-231.

106   Bettany Hughes, Bacchus Uncovered: Ancient God of Ecstasy, Produced by: Sandstone Global Productions Ltd, First aired on BBC Four: April 11, 2018.

Hymns, she is described as "female and male" and in the Proclus' Hymns, she is described as "male-spirited, shield-bearing, of great strength, from a mighty sire."[107] It's interesting that the language of the day still acknowledges the fact that Athena isn't completely female despite the fact that female pronouns are always used when addressing her. This strongly suggests that the devotees and priesthood who were reciting these hymns felt that it was important to demonstrate their understanding of her nature despite the pronouns that she seems to favour.

Within some branches of British Craft, there is also a fluid or non-gendered element to divinity. The most popularly discussed of these is the concept of *Dryghten* (pronounced *dryk-ten*). This divine power is the one unknowable and unnameable presence from which it is believed that the God and Goddess manifested. To simplify the concept, consider the God and Goddess as the binary forms of divinity while Dryghten is above and beyond that binary.

The following prayer of blessing is used at the closing of ritual and was written by Doreen Valiente and made popular by its use in Patricia Crowther's book *Witch Blood! The Diary of a Witch High Priestess.*[108] Within this prayer, which uses the spelling *Dryghtyn*, is an explanation of the basic concept that the unknowable force is experienced via interaction with the God and Goddess. The gods themselves are then further made manifest through the four elemental powers.

### BLESSING PRAYER

*"In the name of Dryghtyn, the Ancient Providence,*
*Who was from the beginning and is for eternity,*
*Male and Female, the Original Source of all things;*
*All-knowing, all-pervading, all-powerful;*
*Changeless, eternal.*

---

107   Theoi, "Orphic Hymns", https://www.theoi.com/Text/OrphicHymns1.html#31 accessed 21 May, 2021; Radek Chlup, *Proclus: An Introduction*, (United Kingdom: Cambridge University Press, 2012), 192.

108   Patricia Crowther, *Witch Blood! The Diary of a Witch High Priestess*, (United States: House of Collectibles, 1974) n.p.

*In the name of the Lady of the Moon,*
*And the Lord of Death and Resurrection.*
*In the name of the Mighty Ones of the Four Quarters,*
*The Kings of the Elements.*
*Blessed be this place, and this time,*
*And they who are now with us."*

In many ways, the concept of this unknowable force is similar to the concept of the Tao in East Asian religion and spirituality. Dryghten represents something that cannot be known or fully understood, but rather something that can be experienced. A quotation from Doreen Valiente explains that:

*"[Witches] believe in a supreme Divine power which is the original source of all things. Out of this Ancient Providence come the gods and goddesses, and the hierarchies of spirits in their many orders. The divinities of the witches, the 'Old Ones' are the primordial gods. They are the personifications of the forces of Life, Death and Resurrection. They are nameless, having countless names."[109]*

For the modern-day practitioner, this is an important aspect to consider. Many within our community discuss issues regarding the lack of inclusivity or the heteronormative stance of ritual in some traditions. Just as it was in the ancient world, there is far more opportunity for a coven worshipping Aphrodite and Dionysus (or other gender-fluctuating deities) to experience divine fluidity today. In many traditions, the unknowable aspects of divinity are specifically expressed through non-binary-specific rites—a symbolic action used to represent the unknown Mysteries. On the other hand, if a coven is dedicated to the work of deities whose expressions are not so readily fluid, then the methods used when working their rites will mirror this binary-specific structure. As above, so below. The two must reflect in order to be in harmony.

If you personally resonate with the ideas of divine fluidity, then it is ideal to build relationships with those types of deities, however, be

---

109 Doreen Valiente, *Where Witchcraft Lives Fourth Edition,* (UK: The Doreen Valiente Foundation in association with The Centre for Pagan Studies, 2014), 79.

mindful of the fact that we are not the gods and our self-expressions do not need to be found within them. Likewise, there is something to be said for building relationships with gods that are *unlike* ourselves. When we allow our practice to more deeply inform us of ourselves and those who are different from us, we can be led to a greater general understanding of the Craft on many levels. In this way, all is known and all is understood.

## RECONNECTING WITH THE DIVINE

For us to truly build a healthy connection to the Divine in all its various aspects (Goddess, God, and Divine Fluidity), it is important to first reconnect with these aspects in a healthy way. As we are not the gods, it is important to connect or reconnect with all of the aspects of the Divine regardless of who we are. Remember, there is much to be learned from gods who are different from us; just as much as there is to be learned from those who are like us.

For this journaling exercise, please consider each aspect of your life, things you enjoy, your personality, favourite season, colours, what music or film genres are you drawn to? The goal here is to find which deity aspect you are most naturally attuned to, as this will make reconnection an easier process by starting with the deity you are already naturally attuned to. The following is an example:

Imagine a person who loves the autumn and winter months, the sight of the stars twinkling in the night sky. They love the smell of the night air, the silence that descends on the land after dark, and enjoys the beauty of a graveyard when taking a leisurely stroll. This person most likely has a natural connection to the Goddess in her role as the Crone. This means that the best way for them to connect with the Sacred Feminine would be via a goddess who fulfils the role of death-bringer and otherworldly Queen.

Another example may be an individual who has a great fondness for the natural world, is a keen recycler and upcycler, and donates to conservation projects for animals and trees. They love to be around animals (sometimes more than people) and could spend hours taking in the beauty of the wildlife that surrounds them. As this individual is actively involved in the *process* of preserving and nurturing life on planet Earth, including that of the Earth itself, then they are most naturally attuned to the Horned God. This is because he is the active force of life and that which nurtures and guides it along its path.

Regardless of what your list of qualities provides, use this information to find creative ways of blending those qualities into your Craft as a way of inviting the archetype you are most aligned with into your work. Once you have opened the door to the deity in question, whether that be by a specific name or as the archetype in general, you may start to find that they become more present when you enjoy the day-to-day activities that they are aligned with. After having built your connection with the archetype or deity in question, take some time to see how you relate with the other divine archetypes.

Although the first aspect you identify with represents your strongest alignment, it is important to remember that the divine has other aspects and by getting to know them too, you build a stronger relationship with the divine as a whole. This in turn will strengthen your magical practice as your connections will become stronger. You may also find that your altar setup changes at certain times of the year as well as the type of magic that you are called to use. Embrace the natural unfolding of these changes as you establish new connections and keep notes of your progress and newfound guidance.

# CHAPTER FOUR

# EXPLORING THE SABBATS

Take any Witchcraft 101 book off a bookshelf and you will very quickly locate a section on the sabbats or the wheel of the year. This stresses that these are important events in the witches' practice and are given far more importance than the esbats. The word *sabbat* has its origins in the word *sabbath* or *shabbat*, owing to a common connection between witches and Judaism in the distant past. This correlation between the holy days of witches and Jews is most prominently highlighted in texts such as the 1575 publication of *A Dialogue of Witches.*[110] Here, Danaeus links Witchcraft and Judaism to such an extent that the author uses the phrase "Synagogue of Satan" as a description of the meeting site of a witches' gathering.

Dr. Margaret Alice Murray, in her controversial 1931 book *God of the Witches*, claims that:

> *"There were two classes of meetings, the Esbats which were specially for the covens, and the Sabbaths which were for the congregation as a whole.*
>
> *The Esbats … were for both religious and business purposes."*[111]

---

110 Lambertus Danaeus, 1575, "A Dialogue of Witches," n.d. accessed 09 Jan. 2020, https://quod.lib.umich.edu/e/eebo/A19798.0001.001/1:1?rgn=div1;view=full-text

111 Margaret Alice Murray, *God of the Witches* (Oxford University Press, 1970), 77.

What made Dr. Murray's work so controversial was that elements of her claims, though not necessarily without merit, showed signs of poor research and contradiction. The statement above is one such case. Initially, the esbat is the private meeting of the witches, yet in the aforementioned sentence, it is the one whereby the congregation would also be present for business purposes. Support for esbats becoming more public can be found in records of Italian Witchcraft. The so-called "Synagogue of Satan" (sabbats) was a closed event, yet the *Tregenda* (esbat) was open for business.

In my previous book, *Aradia*, I discussed this aspect of the Tregenda:

*"One of the oldest references to the Tregenda comes over five hundred years prior to the publication of the Gospel of the Witches. In 1354, Italian poet Jacopo Passavanti tells how the witches gathered with demons to work magic for others, including contacting their deceased relatives, while in the company of [H]Erodias and The goddess Diana...*

*Passavanti makes the claim that the meetings must be of public knowledge, to a certain extent, as it is said that some fraudulent people would attend the meetings pretending to be witches so that they could con people seeking the witches' aid. Specifically it is indicated that these con artists or fake witches would trick people into believing that they were receiving genuine readings, messages, or spell work.*

*So what was the Tregenda of the witches of Italy? It was a popular and well-known event where witches would gather not only to worship the Goddess, but also to provide assistance and service to those individuals who needed the benefit of their magical education."[112]*

These accounts support the concept that the sabbats were intended to be private and closed ritual events in the witches' calendar. Unlike

---

112 Jacopo Passavanti, Filippo Polidori, *Lo specchio della vera penitenza*. (Firenze: Poligrafia italiana, 1354); Craig Spencer, Aradia (Llewellyn Worldwide Ltd. 2020), 22-23.

the esbats, covered in the next chapter, the sabbats held a significance for witches that was not meant for public display. Tradition tells us that sabbats are times of the year when magic is not supposed to be worked, with the exception of an emergency, which provides explanation to why they are private events/gatherings.

When these facts are taken into account, the natural question remains: At the sabbats, what are witches using the power for if not magic? To find the answer behind this mystery, it is important to establish the background of these key times of year. From the Jewish parallel, prominent in our history until very recently, it can be deduced that sabbats are meant as times of rest. As our Holy days, from which the word *holiday* derives, we usually interpret these as dates in the calendar when people have time off from work. The world seems to slow down and time out is taken, but are we as witches just supposed to put our feet up and rest at these times of year? No, there is important work to be done. Just as the Jewish people, with whom our rites have been historically linked, have important ceremonies to do on their days, witches do as well. So, why do witches celebrate the sabbats?

## SABBATS AND WHY WITCHES DO WHAT WE DO

It seems like an odd question to ask why we celebrate, but it is important to talk about. Many will be honest and say that it's simply because that is what witches do. This is very true, but the actual rationale of *why* we celebrate or mark these times of year isn't always explained. Part of this lack of discussion comes from a lack of understanding the traditional reasons for the rites.

> *"What is in the modern witches' minds as they celebrate these festivals? I doubt if many would give the naive answer of one lady when she was asked why she performed her rites: 'Because the sun wouldn't rise in the morning if I didn't'."*

> – Stewart Farrar in *What Witches Do*,
> Chapter Seven: The Seasonal Festivals[113]

---

113 Stewart Farrar, *What Witches Do*, (David & Charles fw media, 2012).

The late Stewart Farrar raises an interesting discussion point within this brief passage. Will the sun not come up if we don't celebrate? I am going to suggest that maybe it would not. Yes, seriously! Please bear with me a moment and I will explain.

When we work magic, we work. We are doing something to cause change in our lives and in the lives of those around us. When we come to the sabbats, most traditions say that unless it is an emergency, magical work should not be done at these times. Why? Because the power of our rites is needed. But where? Gerald Gardner gave us a hint to the answer:

> *"Our gods are not all-powerful, they need our aid. They desire good to us, fertility for man, beast and crops, but they need our help to bring it about; and by our dances and other means they get that help."*

> – Gerald Gardner in *Witchcraft Today*,
> Chapter Thirteen: Recapitulation[114]

This is not a new line of thinking. We have more than enough evidence to show that our ancient counterparts held similar views.[115] So what do the gods do with this power? Tradition tells us that the gods use this power to keep life going; keeping the crops growing and the cycles of life in their natural rhythm. Without this power, the world moves from balance into chaos. I know that the idea of the sun going out in the absence of celebration is a stretch, but the underpinning concept holds some value.

It has long been believed that witches hold sway over the happenings of the natural world and this is only the next logical step in that conclusion. A famous example of this widely held and time honoured belief states:

> *"If I command the moon, it will come down; and if I wish to withhold the day, night will linger over my head; and again, if*

---

114 Gerald B. Gardner, *Witchcraft Today* (New York: The Citadel Press, 2004), 140.
115 "Heka," Encyclopaedia Britannica, n.d., accessed Jan 10, 2020, https://www.britannica.com/topic/heka.

*I wish to embark on the sea, I need no ship, and if I wish to fly through the air, I am free from my weight."*

–Thomas Love Peacock in *Rhododaphne*
or *The Thessalian Spell: A Poem*[116]

You may be wondering if this is an outdated belief and whether it has any relevance today. Just look outside. The state of the environment, climate change, and extinction rates are at an all-time high. How many of us *are* raising power to help keep the world turning at these times of the year?

Is the world in bad shape because we are not raising power?

Is the world like it is because we stopped thinking about our sacred relationship to the Earth and are therefore neglecting it?

It is possible that the two are linked. I am *not suggesting* that without witches the sun would go out, so what does all of this have to do with the sun rising? An appropriate term to describe this is along the lines of: "If a tree falls in the forest and there's nobody around to hear, does it make a sound?" Yes, the sun will rise, but will we be here to see it? It's definitely food for thought.

In recent years, I have also found that fiction, especially TV, has started to do a great job at representing some of our core traditional concepts. This quote from *American Horror Story: Apocalypse* (Season 8, Episode 10) best encapsulates the concept of the sabbats' sacred work:

*"Darling, it seems Daddy didn't tell you the most important rule of bringing on the apocalypse. If you want to finish the job, the thing you have to do first is get rid of all the witches."*

– Myrtle Snow to Michael Langdon[117]

---

116 Thomas Love Peacock, *Rhododaphne, or The Thessalian spell: a poem*, (Philadelphia: M. Carey & Son, 1818).

117 "Apocalypse Then." *American Horror Story*, episode 10, season 8, written by Ryan Murphy & Brad Falchuk, directed by Bradley Buecker, first aired 14 November 2018.

## FORTY-TWO NEGATIVE CONFESSIONS

When it comes to the sabbats, I was reminded of one of my favourite concepts of the Egyptian afterlife rites—The Forty-Two Negative Confessions (of Ma'at). Many may be familiar with the concept of a human having their heart weighed against the magical feather of Ma'at to determine whether they are "pure" enough for entry into the afterlife. Some may be familiar with images of Osiris and Thoth presiding over the judgement, but many may not have noticed that in illustrations of this mythic scene, there are also forty-two gods watching in judgement over the newly deceased soul.

Within Spell 125 in the *Book of Coming Forth by Day*, usually known as the *Egyptian Book of the Dead*, each of these forty-two gods is directly named followed by a statement of something which the soul had *not* done to offend that god in their lifetime. Contrary to popular belief, the *Book of Coming Forth by Day* was never a standardised document, but one which was made specifically for each individual. Therefore, the negative confessions in Spell 125 were always written for the individual whose soul was expected to pronounce them in the afterlife.[118]

Like the suggestion that witches work their power at the sabbats to maintain the order and balance of the universe, the Ancient Egyptians also considered holy celebration in this way. As Ma'at is more the underpinning force of harmony and balance (natural law) than a goddess in the traditional sense; the negative confessions act as statements about how the soul has not disturbed this balance. The scales that weigh their heart against Ma'at, symbolised as a feather, demonstrates to what extent they have harmed the universe with their actions or inactions. As a feather is fragile, so is Ma'at. Just as the Egyptian people were expected to maintain order, so are witches expected to do the same today.

*"Stars, planets and seasons, rivers, plants and animals are all ultimately in harmony with Ma'at.*

---

118 "The Negative Confession," Joshua J. Marks, Ancient History Encyclopaedia, 2017, accessed Jan 10, 2020, https://www.ancient.eu/The_Negative_Confession/

*Ma'at must constantly be renewed and re-established in the face of the cosmological and moral tendencies toward disorder. Ma'at does not simply belong to the metaphysical realm, she is also present in the moral dimension of human decisions and actions. It is the disordered human soul that does wrong.*[119]

This view, as written by author Jeremy Naydler, that human action holds sway over the balance of the universe is possibly more relevant to us today than at any other time in the history of humanity. It seems strange to think that despite the lack of medical care and hygiene alone in the ancient world, humanity still managed to survive long enough to keep the species, and the world, going. Yet today the whole world seems to be going topsy-turvy every time a new headline hits the news.

When Gerald Gardner said that our gods *need* our aid, he wasn't wrong.

*"Ma'at, then, is a goddess whose existence would appear to consist of a perpetual giving of her substance in order that the divine powers can continue to function in an orderly and harmonious way."*[120]

Just as Ma'at is the personification of the rules that keep cosmic balance, her male counterpart, Heka, is the force behind the universe. Heka is sometimes translated as magic, but more correctly represents the power to move the universe in harmony with Ma'at to cause change. Therefore, Heka was important to the order of things and was the power that flowed through the Priest-Magician and the gods; thereby giving them their power.

This work of magic was most important at seasonal rites where it "… could be summoned up during the observance of religious ritual, and that its chief function was the preservation of the natural world order."[121] This supports the continuation of the need for power in the sabbat rites of witches, past and present.

---

119 Jeremy Naydler, *Temple of the Cosmos: The Ancient Egyptian Experience of the Sacred* (Inner Traditions, 1996), 94-95.

120 Ibid. 94.

121 "Heka," Encyclopaedia Britannica, n.d., accessed Jan 10, 2020, https://www.britannica.com/topic/heka.

## RAISING POWER

Occult law states that "The first thing that magic changes is the self." Nothing could be truer when it comes to raising power. Although this occult law holds a number of meanings—all of which are simultaneously true—within the context of raising power, it is the first "rule" that any witch should know.

Simply put, this law indicates that the witches' power originates from within themselves. It is true that we are capable of tapping into other forces of nature, however it is not the source of our power. *We are the source of our power.* Personal power is raised using a wide variety of methods, some of which are unique to specific traditions, while others are present in one form or another across all branches of the Craft.

Regardless of the method applied, *the first thing that magic changes is the self.* In this context, magic changes us by the very nature that it is accessed. To tap into our personal power, we need to shift our consciousness and enter a state where our power is more readily available and in which the natural world becomes more compliant to our use of that power.

By changing consciousness, we allow ourselves to be changed by our magic. Change is not a bad thing here: many may see this as a loss of control and will struggle to let go of ego, however, it is important to remember that ego (our day-to-day self) has no place in our magical working. It is the part of us that is dedicated to the work of the Craft—the part that first heard the call of the old gods—which must be allowed to reign supreme in this moment. When we allow our ego to step back and shift consciousness, then our power is released; in fact, it practically pours out. Like any aspect of ourselves, our power wants to be accessed, and without this release we repress a part of ourselves that is actively calling out.

### THE NATURE OF OUR POWER

Have you ever been asked to sum up what magic is to you, especially by someone who is not a witch? It's strange if you really think about it, isn't it? Magic is something that we understand even from a small age. We know it when we see it and we know exactly what it isn't, however, putting it into a simple statement never seems to fully capture the essence of the magic—pun unintended!

Many occultists have attempted to create an adequate definition for this power that we call "magic." Some of these definitions are very popular in our community, but are they really any good? If I am asked to define magic, I would say that *"Magic is Mystery."*

The reason is simple. The Mysteries are those things that we can understand, but that can never truly be put into words because in order to be discovered, they must be experienced. Although I am capable of intellectually knowing things, there are some that I will never know the *mystery* of. When I taught human anatomy and pathology at Wigan & Leigh College, I covered the topic of pregnancy. Although my all-female class, many of whom were mothers themselves, felt that I was excellent at my job, I know that I cannot truly understand the process of pregnancy, as it is something that I can only know from an outside perspective.

It is the same with magic. The armchair occultist will know lots of rituals, important dates, and the names of significant occultists, but that does not mean that they have touched any of the Mysteries of the occult world that they dedicate so much of their lives to. It is with that said that I provide the following methods of raising power for you to incorporate into your Craft as you see fit. Remember, *Magic is Mystery*. It needs to be explored in order to be known; and never forget that *the Mysteries* are always found within and *the first thing that magic changes is the self*.

## DRUMMING

Drums have been, and still are, used by people of many cultures from across the globe. From tribal or shamanistic rhythms to the ecstatic and steady beat provided in the music of your favourite band, we all understand the effect that a good drumbeat can have on us. By literally finding your beat, you will notice a stirring within your body. This may cause you to want to move in a rather spontaneous or instinctive way. You may find that the drum calls up strong emotions for you. Whatever experience is brought forward by the drum is an expression of your personal power. Allow it to be freely released, for it is this free flow of power that gets things done.

Due to the ecstatic nature of drumming, it is the ability of allowing your ego to step aside that does the work. Don't try to overthink this process as it is an instinctual, not an intellectual process. With that said, it is important to align the initial drum beat to your intention. If you are raising power for a protection spell, you may want to find your war-like warrior beat; think fast, strong, steady (like a well organised army), and consistent. If you are working to draw love, then try and find a beat—or a combination of rhythms—that speak to the qualities that you are looking to draw. For a sabbat, the spring equinox for example, you may want to be gentle to start and drum more quietly; slowly waking up the Earth by gently drawing its awareness back from its deep resting state. Whatever your intention is, just find that initial beat and trust in yourself to allow the rest to happen.

## CHANTING

Vocalise your power. Our words are an expression of our internal reality released into the external world—which is why it is our primary form of communication. By finding a simple and concise way to express your desire, you can create a strong expression of your personal power.

Think about it like this: If magic works by changing our consciousness to release power, then by repeating a spoken word, phrase, or passage over and over (a chant), eventually that shift will result in a state detached from the self. In this state, the words become unimportant and lose meaning as we lose our conscious and cultural attachments to them. The chant can then only express our desire, emotions, and personal power. That is what makes the difference between just reading a spell and truly incanting words of power.

## DANCING

Reach ecstasy—it opens doors to power. Just like drumming, dancing is a method of externalising our desire and allowing our spirit to freely engage with ritual. By finding the rhythm of your body, regardless of if anyone else would consider it dancing, you can move and manipulate energy in an intuitive manner that can shape your reality.

You can find your dance rhythm the same way you did with your drum: strong or heavy energies could include fast, frenzied movements and stomping; whereas energy that needs a more delicate touch can be expressed by being light on your feet (or on your toes) and incorporating jumping.

Due to the nature of our work, most witch dances tend to move in circular directions, however, the process is not the point. Again, as with the drum, it is about allowing the power to take over and move you. As drums and dancing work from a similar angle of accessing power, they are commonly used together to not only help to draw out the emotions of the people present (drumming), but also to drive the movement of the power and give it better direction (dancing).

## Offerings

The law of the conservation of energy states that energy cannot be created or destroyed, it simply changes form. In short, something must become something else. This, for me, is what offerings are all about. Spirits do not generally eat and drink the things that are gifted to them unless manifesting through one of their devotees. It is the principle that the energy of the offering becomes something else for them to enjoy when ritualised as an expression of our devotion.

Though most may not see offerings as an expression of our personal power, I disagree. The reason the offering is made is because I want to show something, such as gratitude or devotion, to the spirit in question. It is infused with the emotional significance that I have given to it. That is what makes it an offering. The ritualising of the process further envelopes the offering with my own power so that by the end of the working, it becomes more about the energy added to the item than what the item was in the first place.

## Worship

Offerings are not the only way to provide spirits with the energy that we wish to give to them. The gods are worshipped as a form of offering. By raising power, as previously discussed, the very act feeds the gods. They want to help us; so when we care for them, they care for us. Time becomes the method of raising power in this instance—the time that we dedicate to our sacred work.

Think about babies, pets, or even potted plants: neglected life dies, and that which is loved thrives. By dedicating our time to them, we empower them. It should be noted though that there is a reason worship is tied to words like *faith* and *devotion*. Just like a normal relationship, if you choose to be faithful (say, to your partner), you do so because you care. You are not in the relationship, or shouldn't be, because you want something from the other person. It is the same with the gods: If we are faithful to them, it is because we care for them, and they care for us. They are not there just because we might want something—that is not how true devotion or faith works.

## Eco-Friendly Sabbats

*As Above, So Below*—the two worlds reflect one another. It is only logical to conclude that if we are doing the spiritual work, then the physical work also needs to be taken care of. An easy start can be reducing your carbon footprint. How many candles do you burn at your sabbat rites? How much incense are you using? Do you really need all of this to raise power? If it doesn't have a practical purpose, then it doesn't need to be there at all.

A few years ago, I actually stopped lighting or burning anything as part of my Witchcraft. I ultimately didn't need to, so I saw no reason to carry on. If the only thing that my candles and incense were doing was harming the world, can I truly say that I respect the natural world enough if I treat methods as sacrosanct that do it harm? Though I may have been part of rituals that use some incense or candles sparingly, it has become very rare in my personal practices, as an alternative that produces the same or more power is easily found (dancing, chanting, etc.).

Things to ponder:
- What elements of your rites cause more chaos than harmony?
- Do they need to be there at all?
- What could you use in their place?

# SABBAT THEMES

The themes of the sabbats are some of the most widely discussed and often misunderstood aspects of the annual celebrations. Many stem from uncertainty around the cultural history that has informed them. This in itself is usually the result of repeated versions of history that were believed to be accurate in earlier days but have since been disproven. This section will provide a brief overview of the sabbat themes so that you will be able to make an informed decision when designing rituals for your own personal celebrations.

## THE WHEEL OF THE YEAR

When it comes to the origins of the Wheel of the Year, many believe that it is an ancient concept, while others dismiss it as something too modern to be taken seriously. The truth of the matter, like many other aspects of Witchcraft, lies somewhere in between the two extremes. The Wheel, as we know it today, is the product of two spiritual paths: Witchcraft and Druidry.

Gerald Gardner and Ross Nichols—the founder of the Order of Bards, Ovates and Druids (OBOD) each celebrated four holidays in the beginning of this path. Gardner, the four fire festivals, and Nichols, the solstices and equinoxes. During a conversation between the two in a pub, they decided that each had something worth deeper exploration. They decided to merge their calendars, forming what we (witches) know now as the eight sabbats. It was not until approximately 1965 that the phrase *Wheel of the Year* would be coined to describe the cycle of these eight holidays. So the concept of the Wheel of the Year is quite modern, but the holidays that the wheel marks are most definitely ancient.

Many books today would have you believe that in ancient Britain, people would either celebrate the fire festivals or the solstices and equinoxes, but never all eight (until modern times). I personally find this hypothesis absurd. We know that the fire festivals were celebrated over all the kingdoms of Britain before Britain itself was ever united as a single Kingdom. It is also known that the cycle of the solstices and equinoxes were important due to the many landmarks that have been built around the nation that perfectly align with their annual cycles. Despite all eight being widely celebrated, we are expected to believe that not *one single person ever* celebrated all eight at any point in history until two men "made it up" in the 60s. It doesn't stand up to any reason whatsoever.

Is the wheel ancient? No. Are the holidays on the wheel entirely modern inventions? No. There is a blend of old and new in our celebrations and we shouldn't be apologetic about that fact. All religious expressions evolve and grow over time—it is a sign that they are healthy and have people who are actively engaging with them. It is important that while being honest about the wheel's history, we don't inadvertently throw out the history of these holidays in the process. Everything evolves and grows—progress isn't a bad thing, nor is preserving our history. Traditions keep us connected to those who walked the path before us and allow us to hold the door open for those who will find their way here after we are long gone.

## SAMHAIN/HALLOWEEN:

Samhain (the "mh" together make a "wh" sound—as in *when*) is by far most witches' favourite sabbat of all—I know it's mine. This is mostly credited to the fact that it is the one time of the year when we are expected to be open about the spirit world. We also get to embrace such things as Witchcraft and unusual décor around our homes without anyone batting an eyelid. In short, it is the time of the year in which our oddities become normal. I celebrate the holiday by using both names: Halloween and Samhain. The first name, Halloween, is for the daylight hours of October 31st, and when the sun sets, *then* it is Samhain—until the sun sets on November 1st.

This was the final harvest of the year when animals were slaughtered to prepare for the harsh winter months ahead. At Samhain, it would have been impossible to ignore the amount of death that was involved which would understandably cause people to wonder if they themselves would be able to survive. Where were they supposed to turn for help? At this time of the year, it was understood that the veil between the worlds of the living and the dead was at its thinnest.

Because of this, many would feed their ancestral dead during this time to gain their favour and receive spiritual protection, asking for help to survive the winter months.

Also celebrated as a New Year's Day, people would gather a flame from the *Teanlay fire* (a bonfire) lit to rekindle the hearth fire in their own homes, adding new blessings to the household for the New Year. In my own part of the world, the act of relighting a new fire in the home has survived at our modern New Year's celebrations, showing that old traditions really do die hard. The act of venerating the dead at this time has also become echoed in the practices of the Church who moved their original celebration from May 13th (instituted in 609 CE) to November 1st in 835 CE.[122]

As well as feeding my own ancestral dead at this time of year, I also prepare a special water to be used later in the coming year at Imbolc—known as *Living and Dead Water*. It is a local custom where the waters gathered from a place in which both the living and the dead cross have attributes of powerful healing, cleansing, and protective powers. I usually place a glass bottle filled with water at the base of the altar to my ancestors. As the altar space acts as a threshold between my interaction with them—the dead—and their interaction with me—the living—it creates the necessary "traffic" to empower the water with these unique qualities. At sunset on November 1st, the veil is no longer as thin as it was, and the spirits have returned to their proper side. This is enforced by a hoard of spirits called the *Wild Hunt,* who round up all the wandering dead and ensure that they are back before the last rays of sun disappear.

In my locale, the Wild Hunt is accompanied by otherworldly white spectral dogs called *Gabble Ratchets.* These dogs are often associated with death and their appearance at other times of the year signals that someone is soon to die. At Samhain in particular, the Gabble Ratchet can be seen hovering over the rooftops of homes in which someone inside will not see another Samhain. The identity of the resident is clear, as the spectral hound will assume the face of the person who is fated to die—but don't go looking for them yourself without magical protection, for it is said that "catching their gaze thrice" is fatal.

---

122  Hugh Chisholm, "All Saints, Festival of," *Encyclopædia Britannica—11th ed.*, (Cambridge University Press, 1911) n.p.

## YULE/WINTER SOLSTICE:

The winter solstice is the time that the sun "dies," indicated by the word solstice (*sol* meaning "sun," and *stitium* meaning "stop"). The sun no longer declines or rises any further from our perspective on Earth. The sun occupies the same degree in the sky for three days before rising slightly on or around December 24th. This slight rising indicates the sun's rebirth or resurrection and the promise that the coldest times have passed, and warmer weather is to come. It is during our rites that we acknowledge the death phase of the sun. We raise power with our rites at this time to encourage the resurrection of the sun's life; ensuring that the light will not fade and leave us in the darkness and merciless cold. With the sun's rising, all of nature will be warmed and revived under the power of its light.

This time of year is not only about the sun, though it is important. The Goddess in the form of the Cailleach/Gentle Annie also plays her part in the traditions of Yuletide. The Cailleach (literally "Old Woman") rules the winter half of the year from Samhain to Beltane, while the goddess Brigid (known in parts of England as *Brigantia*) is seen by some as the other form of the Cailleach and rules the summer months from Beltane to Samhain.[123]

Either of these two themes (or both simultaneously) can feed into your seasonal celebrations. The burning of the yule log, traditionally collected by the oldest male in the household, can be symbolic of reintroducing the warmth of the sun to the earth as an act of sympathetic magic. Your Yule log can also be lit to rekindle the fires of Brigid, thus transforming the Cailleach back into her younger and warmer self and, by extension, doing the same for the land. Don't worry if you do not have or want an open fire or outdoor bonfire—you can easily adapt this. I know witches who have one log that they reuse each year. The log has been drilled into, creating space so that three or four tea lights can be placed inside. These candles are replaced each year while the log is retained as part of their solstice tradition.

---

123     Florence Marian McNeill, (1959). *The Silver Bough, Vol.2: A Calendar of Scottish National Festivals, Candlemas to Harvest Home*, (William MacLellan, 1959), 20–21.

Trees play an important role at this time of the year, also intended as an act of sympathetic magic. The evergreen is brought into the home to preserve the last piece of life that has survived, and if this can be protected until the solstice, then the sun will return. The tree itself is decorated with shiny ornaments to act as protective charms—malevolent and destructive spirits often get distracted by something shiny. Wooden soldiers are sometimes found among the ornaments too and the protective symbolism here should not go unnoticed. The fairy lights that are wrapped around the tree are in imitation of the fairy spirits that safeguard life and nature. The twinkling of the lights reminds us of the spiritual power that surrounds the tree and exactly what it is that we are seeking to protect by having one in our home. Regardless of whether your tree is real or artificial, the symbolism is exactly the same.

However you choose to celebrate in your own home, be sure to include the giving of gifts (either bought or handmade), good food, and good fun with the family. This time of year, we focus on the hope of nature's new life and growth. It is that spiritual hope that shines a bright light out to everyone during the holidays. Everyone seems a little nicer and more fun, and during this natural spirit of the season, is important to find time to celebrate.

## Witchcraft and SAD

Not many Witchcraft books speak about SAD (Seasonal Affective Disorder), and for witches who experience it as I do, this time of the year can also seem tough, like a disconnect from the spirit of the season. So what should witches with SAD do to embrace the holiday spirit more?

I have long said and believed that as the winter starts to creep in, some humans are meant to naturally hibernate but are without an opportunity to do so. We have to carry on with our lives, jobs, etc., yet we still stuff our faces with comfort food as if we are trying to survive winter without actually leaving our homes. It seems like such a natural instinct that we have, yet have no way to truly go along with it. If I had the choice, I would not leave my home at all during winter. I like to wrap up warm, get mad cravings for nearly everything (regardless of whether it's in the house or not), and the sight of decorations before a certain point (Samhain) threatens to push me over the edge.

It's not *all* doom and gloom, though. I love the sight of the birds in the garden and the frost on the windows when I know I don't need to actually go anywhere. The upbeat vibe of holiday TV and the decorations, when I'm finally in the mood for them, add a certain warmth to the otherwise cold environment. Despite the down in my mood and the dragging feel of the season, I actually appreciate being a witch with SAD; I like to think that I am just that in tune with the cycles of nature. When the sun is losing its "life," or the Goddess walks around as the tired old woman waiting for her own regeneration, I can feel that part of me is going on that journey with them. At this time of year, more than ever, I am made aware of my connection to the divine.

At this moment, I am writing on 16th December 2020, and I am far more upbeat than I was at the start of the seasonal turn. I have watched LOTS of holiday films—which I usually don't (two or three max)—and the time has really seemed to fly by. The possibility that COVID-19 has a part to play is not lost on me. With the lockdowns in the UK, there really hasn't been as much need to leave the house at all, making this a year in which we have had to appreciate our natural inclination to hibernate. If you are like me, then it is important to keep that positive mind-set and find the silver lining to SAD. Do things that pick you up, even something small, which is itself connected to the season. Even if it is slightly less involved than people around you who do not experience SAD, you will still feel like you are part of the whole spirit of the season.

IMBOLC/CANDLEMAS:

Accounts of this holiday's earliest celebration have survived in obscure texts that were translated many centuries later. These texts are clear that the theme of this holiday was *ritual purification*, with specific attention given to the head, hands, and feet.[124] Coincidentally, these are all points of the pentagram as mapped on the human form.

---

124   Trans. Kenneth Jackson, Ed. Kuno Meyer, *Hibernica Minora*, (United Kingdom: Clarendon Press, 1894), Appendix pg. 49.

Although many books today will tell you that Imbolc means "in the belly" or "ewes' milk," the contemporaneous records of this holiday being themed around ritual purification indicate that the word actually comes from an old term meaning "to cleanse oneself."[125] These other supposed definitions likely developed their own Imbolc-based associations, as this is the time of year that ewes were giving birth and producing milk for their lambs. It should also be noted that the month of February, which begins alongside this holiday, gets its name from the word *februare*—a Latin term referring to purification ceremonies, named after the Roman god of purification, *Februus*.[126]

It is at this time of year that you can incorporate purification themes into your rites and celebration activities. My personal recommendation is to use the Living and Dead Water that you made during Samhain for your Imbolc activities. Adding some of this water to a bath can create a simple and convenient ritual purification process that can be done before starting your celebrations and raising power for the day. As Living and Dead Water doesn't contain any toxic chemicals, herbs, or essential oils, it is also a great tool to use for cleansing around your home. You can also use it to anoint your kids and pets as it doesn't contain anything that would be contraindicated to medicines and health conditions. It can also be used by lightly sprinkling it around the home, clearing out the old before raising power to welcome the new phase of the year.

VERNAL/SPRING EQUINOX:

The spring equinox signals the time in which the corn dollies of the September celebrations (see *autumn equinox*) are returned to the Earth so that the spirit of the Earth Mother can be renewed and bring life back to the land. Today, many have named this holiday *Ostara*, in a variety of spellings, and credit this association between holiday and goddess to either Gerald Gardner or Aiden Kelly. The

---

125 Brian Wright, *Brigid: Goddess, Druidess and Saint*, (United Kingdom: The History Press, 2011), 83.

126 William Ralston Balch, *The Complete Compendium of Universal Knowledge*, (United States: Franklin Square Bible House, 1891), 495.

earliest reference made between a goddess named *Ēostre* and the spring equinox originated with a monk called *Bede,* who wrote a text called *The Reckoning of Time* in 725 CE.

Many scholars have attempted to discredit Bede by implying that there is no evidence that such a goddess existed at all, never mind having been associated with this holiday. There is, in fact, evidence of such a goddess found on numerous inscriptions discovered in 1958 which can be dated to a few centuries before Bede—approximately 150–250 CE.[127] This, at the very least, goes some way to supporting Bede's claim, even if we cannot be certain of this goddess' original role. That said, I see no reason for witches today to discard what is now a multiple-millennia-old tradition over academic musings and disagreements. Ēostre, or Ostara, is here to stay.

As the corn doll is replanted at this time of the year, is it highly plausible that Ēostre represents the Corn Mother, whose life-force is protected over the winter months before being returned to the earth in the spring, thus restoring its life and fertile powers (see *autumn equinox*). If this is indeed correct, then it explains how this particular Goddess became so strongly associated with life and fertility within popular belief and folk customs. Bird's eggs and hares are products of this time of year. In the wilder parts of England, it is quite common to see the typical March hares "boxing" each other as part of their annual mating season. Often believed to be two males fighting, they are in fact a male and female carrying out a mating ritual. The male demonstrates his ability to fight and defend the female should she become pregnant and unable to defend herself. When the male has proven his strength, the two will usually dart off together across the landscape and out of sight.

Traditionally, eggs are dyed and rolled down hills as part of the annual *pace-egging*. Lancashire has a long-established tradition of pace-egging, and it is believed that the rolling of the egg symbolises the return of life to the land. A rather unusual custom also exists that states that if a pace egg cracks or breaks, then the shell must be crushed into powder or witches may steal them to use as boats—yes, boats ... I don't get it either!

---

127    Philip A. Shaw, *Pagan Goddesses in the Early Germanic World,* (United Kingdom: Bristol Classical Press, 2011), 52, 70-71.

In your own home, you can incorporate the corn dolly, pace-egging, or any other fertility symbols into your celebrations to encourage the life-force to return to the land. Although this holiday specifically focuses on land and animal fertility, it is no accident that chocolate—a natural aphrodisiac—is found moulded into the shape of eggs at this time of year. Be creative, but also remember to make it family and land-oriented so that the full themes of the sabbat are embraced as part of your celebratory rites.

## Beltane/May Day:

As a day historically associated with fertility and sexuality, Beltane is possibly the one time of the year in which we are actively encouraged to enjoy being human. The Maypole is the most prominent symbol of this holiday and is the image most people have in mind when thinking of this time of year. The pole itself is a phallic symbol of the woodland and solar god known as *Jack in the Green*. His name comes from a term used to indicate the beginning of fertility rites in the ancient world, *Iako*, and the old Celtic term for the sun, *griene*.[128] The Morris Dancers would act as his priests during this time and cry *"Iako!"* to indicate the start of this fertility festival and invoke the presence of the god upon the rites.[129]

Effectively, the god associated with the Maypole is both a woodland and solar god named *Jack/Iako of the Sun*. It is the connection that Jack has with both the sun and the woodlands that gives name to the so-called *Greenwoods Marriages*, in which people would go off into the woods to enjoy the pleasures of their own sexuality—it's not just about that of the gods, after all. It was for this reason that in the UK in 1644, Puritans pushed for legal action to be taken by Parliament to suppress the rites of the Maypole due to the fact that when the women of the village went into the woods, "not the least one of them comes home again a virgin."[130]

---

128    J. G. R. Forlong, *Rivers of Life: Volume 1*, (United Kingdom: Quaritch, 1883), 449-450.

129    Ibid. 449.

130    British Culture, British Customs and British Traditions: MAY DAY, Quoted at https://www.learnenglish.de/culture/mayday.html accessed 11/12/2020.

In your rituals, incorporate some of these themes into your rites. In my hometown, we have the annual *Crowning of the May Queen,* and a procession passes right by my house each year. I frequently read in Witchcraft books that this custom died out in Britain in the 1700s, however, this is not the case. To incorporate some of these themes into your own rites, you could organise a Maypole dance (even a small one). Crown your own May Queen—modern traditions like to crown an expectant mother to tap into the theme of the holiday, or call upon Jack in the Green to bless your rites and take the power that you raise as an offering.

If you decide to celebrate your own version of a Greenwood Marriage with your partner that could potentially lead to a pregnancy, then you may wish to extend the May Day rituals to the third of May. On the third day of May, it was common practice for men to tie a red thread around a woman's neck to ensure that any child conceived on May first would reach full term. This custom stems from the belief that witches could work maledictions on May third to prevent a pregnancy from reaching full term. The red thread, which must be tied by the potential father, would act as a magical protection from such a curse.[131]

Many take issue with Beltane tradition, claiming that it isn't inclusive of all sexualities because it focuses so heavily on fertility. As I have previously mentioned, the sabbats are about keeping the wheel turning. Right now, it is about the theme of fertility and sexual interaction *between* our God and Goddess. That doesn't mean that you can't celebrate your own sexuality at this time; that is what the Greenwood Marriage aspect of the celebration is for. If this is what you want to do, get into the rhythm of the season by releasing your own sexual expression during this time. Remember that consent is *always* necessary. The ritual aspects surrounding the relationship between the God and Goddess are always going to be more reflective of heterosexuality simply because that is how *their* love story plays out. That doesn't mean that is how *your* story has to go. People are just people at the end of the day, and on this day, we are celebrating love in all of its glory.

---

131   J. G. R. Forlong, *Rivers of Life: Volume I* (United Kingdom: Quaritch, 1883), 451.

## Summer Solstice:

Known around the world for its annual alignment with many British landmarks including Stonehenge, Lud's Church, and Avebury Circle, this holiday marks an unusual time in the calendar year. Not only are we celebrating the sun at its highest and therefore warmest point, we are also called to remember that from this day onward, the sun will not be as high, the days not as warm, and the wheel will soon begin to turn toward its phase of death.

Records show that at this time, a form of sympathetic or representational magic took place across Britain and the rest of Europe in the form of a straw wheel (set alight in non-British countries) that was rolled down a hill and into a body of water. This was done to represent the decline of the sun. This practice was believed to ensure that the village or town would be provided with all they would need in the bitter months to come.[132] Over time, other customs that existed for the same reason became more widely observed. The fields were scattered with the ashes of the Beltane fires to ensure that the village had all it would need and any remaining scorched wood from the Beltane fire was carried as a protective charm from Midsummer until spring.[133]

What most people have in mind when celebrating the solstice is the concept of the rising sun, but what is most important is the actual time in which the sun stands still (solstice) at midday. At home, you can use this timing as part of your celebration. Go outside if possible and "sun-worship," soaking up the sun's rays and giving thanks. You can also make a sun effigy that can be blessed and hung up in your home, so that you will always have happiness and warmth in your life. Each year, take it down and re-bless it, returning it to its usual place.

Within Revivalist Craft, the adoption of a passage from a Rudyard Kipling poem is often used in Beltane rites. The original poem speaks of the celebrations of Midsummer, so if you wish to incorporate this

---

132 Ronald Hutton, *Stations of the Sun: A History of the Ritual Year in Britain* (United Kingdom: OUP Oxford, 2001), n.p.

133 Janet and Stewart Farrar, *A Witches' Bible*, (Great Britain: The Crowood Press Ltd, 2017), 96.

verse in your own rites, it would be best suited to the holiday for which it was originally written.

## TREE SONG[134]

*"Oh, do not tell the Priest our plight,[135]*
*Or he would call it a sin;*
*But we have been out in the woods all night,*
*A-conjuring Summer in!*

*And we bring you news by word of mouth,*
*Good news for cattle and corn,[136]*
*Now is the Sun come up from the South,*
*With Oak, and Ash, and Thorn!"*

**Rudyard Kipling circa. 1200**

Another theme popularised from the work of Stewart Farrar is the mythic exchange between The Oak and Holly Kings. As was seen with the interaction between Brigid and the Cailleach at Beltane and Samhain, there also exists a similar exchange between two mythic figures, sometimes perceived as two sides of the same being, at the summer and winter solstices. In these myth cycles, the two kings often fight or compete to rule half of the year, with the Holly King in reign from Midsummer to Midwinter while the Oak King reigns from Midwinter to Midsummer. My favourite example of this myth is captured in the tale of *Sir Gawain and the Green Knight*. If you are unfamiliar with the tale, of which there are a number of versions with minor variation, here is the story in brief summary:

King Arthur and his knights are celebrating a winter holiday and having a great time. Suddenly, a knight who is completely green from head to toe and wearing a crown of holly bursts in on an equally

---

134  https://www.poetryloverspage.com/poets/kipling/tree_song.html accessed 17 December 2020.

135  In Revivalist Craft, the word "plight" is usually replaced with the word "Art."

136  In Revivalist Craft, the words "Good news for cattle and corn" are usually replaced with the words "For woman, cattle, and corn."

green horse. The knight makes a wager with the King that he has the right to take the knight's axe and give him one blow (in order to chop off his head) if in one year's time he is offered the same in return.

The King, favouring his odds, is about to accept the deal—what harm can a dead man do to him in a year's time? He is stopped by Sir Gawain. Gawain believes this must be a trick, so he takes the wager to ensure the King's life is not put at risk. Gawain takes the axe, and with one quick blow, knocks the Green Knight's head off. The people resume their celebrations, amused at the foolishness of the Green Knight. Then, the Knight's body stands up and collects his head from the floor. The head—still swinging in his hand by its hair—tells Sir Gawain the location of their meeting in one year's time.

When the time draws near, people try to talk Gawain out of going, but he is true to his word and sets off on his quest. On his way to the meeting place, Gawain faces a number of events that are shown to be tests of his worth. Upon his arrival, the Green Knight makes his blow and slightly catches the side of Gawain's neck with the axe, drawing a few drops of blood—that being what is owed for a minor failing on one of the tests.

This story reflects the cycle for a number of reasons:
- The Holly King must fall at the winter solstice.
- The Holly and Oak King (King Arthur) have an arranged appointment.
- What is done to one must be done to the other to maintain the cycle and balance.

In some versions of the tale, the axe itself is made of oak and belongs to Sir Gawain. It can be interpreted that King Arthur is the actual Oak King of the story and the Green Knight bearing his holly crown is, of course, the Holly King. The story determined that the meeting of the kings took place in one year's time, not at the six month-cycle turning point, which may explain why Gawain does not fall—it was not his time.

Interestingly, the place of their meeting is said to be Lud's Church in the Peak District, England, which has a natural alignment with the summer solstice sun. Many believe (myself included) that perhaps the tale echoes an older story where the meeting of this pair would take place during the time in which this cavern was fully illuminated by the summer sun, not when it would be enveloped in darkness. This belief matches the theme of their semi-annual exchange much better than the trials and tests that are set for Gawain on his journey by the Green Knight. Either version of this tale can very easily be incorporated into a sabbat ritual.

## LUGHNASADH/LAMMAS:

Representing a unique blending of old Celtic and Anglo-Saxon customs, this holiday evolved early on to produce two distinct themes that quickly became widespread early in Britain's formation. Here we will call them *The Games* and the *Harvest Rites*.

### The Games

Named after the god Lugh, *Lughnasadh* (*LOO-nas-ad*) was known as Lugh's wedding feast and was celebrated with a number of games of skill, all designed for good fun. This was done in celebration of Lugh's attributes as a god of many skills and would have allowed those involved to feel closer to him by engaging in activities that involved their own personal skills and talents.[137]

As a wedding feast, this was also a traditional time for handfasting ceremonies. Although today we commonly think of a handfasting as a wedding ceremony, it was originally a term for becoming engaged. The idea of this still exists in engagement terminology in the modern day. When someone says that they have promised "their hand in marriage" they are saying that they are hand fasted. As discussed previously, *handfast* literally translates from the Old English *handfæsten*, meaning to promise or pledge your hand. It is for these reasons that gifts were exchanged during such ceremonies, including the giving of a ring. The couple would have a year to decide if they wanted to make it official and become a married couple or go their separate ways.[138]

---

137 Janet and Stewart Farrar, *The Witches' God* (Phoenix Publishing, Inc. 1989).

138 Barbara L. Talcroft, *Death of the Corn King: King and Goddess in Rosemary Sutcliff's Historical Fiction for Young Adults* (Metuchen and London: The Scarecrow Press, Inc., 1995), 26-28.

## Harvest Rites

Along with these early Celtic customs, the Anglo-Saxons contributed much to the rites and ceremonies that we know today. The most prominent of these involved the harvest of the fruits which were buried upon hilltops or other significant sites to appease the gods, ensuring their favour over the tribe and protecting against blight or famine.[139]

A fun way to honour the god Lugh at home is to play games of your own choosing with your family or friends, either outside games in the garden or board games. Whatever you choose to do, start by dedicating the games to Lugh, and whoever wins gets the honour of placing the offerings on the altar. If it's just adults, then drinking games are a brilliant way of celebrating the season. Whatever game you choose, shake the rules up. For example, if someone gets the answer wrong, perhaps they have to take a sip of their drink as everyone shouts "LUGH!" If you are a solitary witch, you don't need to feel left out; do something fun that you enjoy, and don't forget to give a shout-out to Lugh.

### Autumn Equinox:

This is the time when the last of the land's crops are harvested and the iconic corn doll is made from the very last of the husks. Farmers would traditionally keep the doll in their homes over the winter months to ensure good crops for the next year. It is important to remember that despite its name, not all corn dolls appear in the form of a human being. Each region and township of Britain has its own version of the "doll," which can be widely varied in form. Some regions make animal dolls, such as horses, while other areas make wheels or spinning top-like dolls; some have flowers, while others look like elaborate wind chimes. Regardless of the doll's form, the purpose of the construction is the same: to house the fertile life-giving spirit of nature/the Earth Mother as thanks for the harvest. The doll also ensured that her spirit was safeguarded over the winter months and

---

139  Ronald Hutton, *The Stations of the Sun: A History of the Ritual Year in Britain* (New York: Oxford University Press, 1996), 327-328.

returned to the earth in spring.[140] The word "doll" itself is commonly accepted as originating from the Greek word *eidolon*, meaning an idol or spirit. In this sense, the corn doll is literally named "the spirit of the corn" or "Corn Mother."[141]

The most natural expression of this time of the year is the harvest festival which has managed to survive over the centuries as a time of gratitude for the gifts that the Earth has provided for the community. Much of Britain and Europe consider the harvest festival an important time of year in their calendars. Once the corn doll was formed, it would be housed and treated as a guest of honour for the harvest festival and receive a special toast at the beginning of the celebrations.[142] Inspiration can be taken from your local area or personal practice and used to make your own corn doll. Place it somewhere in your home and make a wish for good things to come your way and for a better year ahead. One way that I like to give thanks is to donate food to the local church to help people less fortunate than myself. It is a time to be thankful for what we have and to share with others.

The scientist in me has always loved the northern lights, and at this time of year—as well as during the spring equinox—there is a heightened change in the aurora phenomenon. According to the Russell-McPherron hypothesis, this is due to a unique alignment that occurs between the sun's solar winds and the Earth's axis at the two equinoxes. This alignment leads to an increased chance of geomagnetic electrical disturbances at twice the normal expected rate.[143] For this reason, it should come as no surprise that occultists have long found psychic disturbances around these times.

Doreen Valiente commented that hauntings tend to be more active around these times of year as well. She states that the equinoxes are

---

140 The British Museum and the BBC, A History of the World: Corn Dolly, available at: http://www.bbc.co.uk/ahistoryoftheworld/objects/JI66Kx6hSIW-MuqDN0bLQsw accessed: 14 December 2020.

141 John Lewis-Stempel, *The Running Hare: The Secret Life of Farmland*, (United Kingdom: Transworld, 2016), 256.

142 Gemma Gary, *Traditional Witchcraft: A Cornish Book of Ways—Revised Second Edition*, (United Kingdom: Troy Books Publishing, 2013), 185-186.

143 https://www.aurora-nights.co.uk/northern-lights-information/when-can-i-see-the-northern-lights/effect-equinox-northern-lights/ accessed 16 January 2021

"periods well known to occultists as being times of psychic stress."[144] I do not believe that the increased disturbances in the psychic and geomagnetic fields are unrelated. This presents a unique point in the Craft that allows space for my love of science to complement my love for the Craft.

## THEMES IN ACTION

Take time to explore these sabbat themes and use them as inspiration to create your own sabbat rituals. Draw from your local traditions and the weather patterns around you at these times, adapting the essence of the sabbat traditions. Blend them with your local customs for a unique celebration that has meaning to you. Experiment with the different ways of raising power and be sure to incorporate the methods that you find most effective into the rituals that you design.

Record your ritual experiments in your journal and review them over time. You may find that one or two methods of raising power work best for you, or you may find that different methods work better at different times of the year. As these methods can also be used to empower your spell-work, it is then that you will most likely notice whether the seasons affect the way you raise power. From there, you will be able to incorporate your findings into your sabbat rituals throughout the year.

---

144   Doreen Valiente, *An ABC of Witchcraft Past and Present* (Phoenix Publishing Inc. 1986), 185-186.

# Chapter Five

# ESBATS

## WORKING BY THE MOON

**M**agic is such a natural and undeniable aspect of any witch's path that the two cannot be separated in the cultural mind-set. As we have seen, the sabbats are important times for witches, but not for the work of magic itself. The workings of magic are reserved for those occasions that have come to be known as *esbats*. Although we tend to consider an esbat to be limited to the occasions of the full moon, the reality is that any time—other than a sabbat—can be considered an esbat. It is for this reason that the full range of the moon's phases have become important to many witches' magical timings. By harnessing the available power of a specific moon phase, the witch can ensure that the astral tides are moving in favour of their desired goal.

The prominence of the full moon in our rituals seems to have occurred due to the fact that our ancient ancestors placed such a great emphasis on them. The names of the months began as names given to the full moon that illuminated the heavens at that particular time of year. Over time, the language moved from *monaths* (from *mona* meaning "moon") to *months*, and the whole of the period—not just the full moon—acquired the name.[145] This change was largely due to

---

145    Sharon Turner, *The History of the Anglo-Saxons from the Earliest Period to the Norman Conquest*, (United Kingdom: T. Cadell and W. Davies, 1840), 138.

the influence of Julius Cesar moving the calendar observance from a lunisolar system to a solar calendar.

Despite its ancient roots, for many today, these particular lunar timings have remained relevant to the expression of their Craft. In fact, many practitioners of British Craft will favour the full moon for their esbats as it provides a spiritual link to the magico-religious practices of the past. The words *Wicca* and *witch* are largely synonymous, and for this reason, it is only logical that people would want to establish that spiritual link with those who first gave us the word. Below is a list of each of the moons' names used by the Anglo-Saxons. Many of their names came to represent our modern concept of months, so naturally, many of the names contain the word *month* in them. Each moon had a specific theme or activity associated with it, and these can be adapted to modern contexts to inspire magical workings and rituals.

## THE NAMES OF THE MOON

As the full moon began each month in the Anglo-Saxon calendar, it is important to recognise that in our modern solar-based calendar, the month in which the full moon will fall varies. For that reason, I will list its traditional month as represented on a lunar calendar and the months of our modern-day calendar in which the full moon may take place. Based on our modern calendar calculations, the full moon following the winter solstice starts the lunar calendar, meaning there are two possible months wherein each moon may fall.

If you choose to incorporate this information into your own Craft, I recommend you choose either the traditional or modern system and stick to it. Although one is called *traditional* and the other *modern*, neither is more authentic, it is just about perspective. For example, the first moon traditionally represented the start of January, but on our solar calendar, it could take place in either December or January. The first full moon after Yule is the same moon regardless of which month it falls under. The fact that we may not always call the time of this moon *January* isn't important here.

Each full moon brings a unique tide of magical power and working our magic around those tides will strengthen our Craft and help us connect with those from the past. Each full moon name and their ancient associations are compiled from the testimonies and records of Bede.[146] It is important to acknowledge that our ancestors lived very different lives than we do today. For this reason, there are aspects of the past that we cannot replicate and that are not entirely relevant to the modern world. Nevertheless, we are still able to adapt these concepts and find meaning in them that reflects our current worldview and the magic that we work. What follows are recommendations, based upon these ancient themes, that are applicable for the modern-day witch.

## After Yule
(Æfterra Gēola)

TRADITIONAL: January
MODERN: December–January

Three days after the winter solstice, the ancients would celebrate the birth of the sun by the Mother Goddess on *Modranecht* (Mother's Night) by carrying out ceremonies that were enacted all through the night. Before the changes in the calendar, these rites were held at the full moon after Yule, hence the moon's name of *After Yule*. As we turn to the Mother Goddess at this time, we can still hold her in honour and call in her many blessings. At the time of her moon, working magic for happiness, success, and love are ideal.

## Mud Month or Month of Cakes
(Sol-mōnaþ)

TRADITIONAL: February
MODERN: January–February

Making cakes as offerings to the gods was very important at this time. In our magical rites today, cake offerings can be given to our own chosen deities to show our respect and build strong ties with them. As this time concerns our personal relationship with the di-

---

146  Bede Venerabilis, trans. Faith Wallis, *Bede: The Reckoning of Time—Translated Texts for Historians*, (Liverpool: Liverpool University Press, 1999), 53-54.

vine, it is a great time for any kind of magical working. Of course, our chosen deities may have a certain magic that is more naturally geared towards them, and though it is not required, you may wish to take this into account.

## Month of (the Goddess) Rheda
(Hrēþ-mōnaþ)

TRADITIONAL: March
MODERN: February–March

During the light of this moon, people would offer sacrifices and hold rituals in honour of the goddess Rheda/Hretha. If you truly wish to connect to the ancient moon magic of the past, then calling upon Rheda in your magical rites is of great benefit at the time of this moon. As there is evidence to suggest that this ancient—and almost forgotten—goddess was concerned with new beginnings and growth; it is reasonable to work magic that harnesses these qualities at the time of her moon.[147] Spells for new ventures, manifesting long-held dreams, and wishful thinking are boosted with power at this time of the lunar year.

## Easter Month
(Ēostermōnaþ)

TRADITIONAL: April
MODERN: March–April

Feasts of celebration occurred in honour of the goddess Ēostre when this full moon was illuminating the darkened skies. There is, of course, no reason that we cannot do the same today. Most witches include a ritual meal of some kind into their esbats, so a dedication to Ēostre would be very fitting and in-keeping with the ancient traditions adapted for our modern Craft. Spells conducted in the name of Ēostre for magical fertility would be most suitable. Remember

---

147 David Raoul Wilson, *Anglo-Saxon Paganism*, (Taylor & Francis, 1992), 36.

that magical fertility does not need to refer to biological procreation, though it certainly can. Magical fertility concerns any magic that brings fresh life into a situation, such as inspiration for new ideas, reviving a business that needs a new breath of life, moving house, or healing spells (especially in serious situations when renewed life-force is needed).

## Month of Three Milkings
### (Þrimilce-mōnaþ)

TRADITIONAL: May
MODERN: April–May

For the Anglo-Saxons, the year only held two seasons: summer and winter, each representing a light and a dark half of the year. The Month of Three Milkings began the light half of the lunar year. Traditionally marking the month when the cattle were milked three times a day, most of us do not experience this need in the modern world. The ancients also used this time as a celebration of fertility and bounty, themes that are more relevant to our modern worldview and can inspire our magic. Casting spells for wealth and prosperity are appropriate to this moon's energies, as is a sense of gratitude for what we have. As this moon also marked a celebration of bounty, it is a great time to work into your esbat rites a moment of giving thanks for all that you have, especially for what you have received via the aid of magic.

## Before Midsummer/Before Litha
### (Ærra Līþa)

TRADITIONAL: June
MODERN: May–June

*Litha,* meaning "gentle," was a time of calm breezes and people would often sail on the smooth waters. The natural world started to find a quietness, and those attuned to the rhythms of nature and her forces would likewise find a gentle state within. With this came the opportunity to reflect and find inner stillness in order to make plans for the future.

As this moon and the phase that followed held the same energies, recommendations for spell-working for the modern witch will be included in the next section.

## After Midsummer/After Litha
### (Æftera Līþa)

TRADITIONAL: July
MODERN: June–July

With the gentle nature of the world around us, our magic is likewise gentle. We use these two "Litha" moons to work any type of magic, but the way we work that power should be gentle. Small changes and magical nudges in the right direction are the key to success when this moon rides high in the heavens. Avoid curses and anything which will manifest in a way that causes dramatic or sudden shifts in circumstances; this is important to ensure you avoid any unintended ripple effects.

## Weed Month
### (Þēodmōnaþ)

TRADITIONAL: August
MODERN: July–August

A time of plentiful weeds for the ancients, this was a period for hard work and "weeding out." The physical world and the spiritual world map and reflect each other well; a witch in tune with their natural surroundings can also understand the rhythm of the inner planes. When the time of physical weeding comes, we also enter a time of energetic weeding. After the gentle power of the past two moons, the Weed Month moon is the perfect time to weed things out of our lives that are no longer needed. Focus your magic on major changes and make waves. This is not the time to hold back: you have passed out of that lunar aspect and are ready to roll up your sleeves and get to work.

## Holy Month
### (Hālig̃-mōnaþ)

TRADITIONAL: September
MODERN: August–September

Holy Month marked the time of the most sacred rites and therefore provides us with the spiritual support needed to tap into what is most sacred to us and our lives. Honour your personal deities and focus on workings that are precious to you. Blessing your home and family, cleansing and empowering your working tools, and focusing on initiation are a few examples of the magic that you may choose to work at this time. Initiation focus could be expressed by carrying out our initiation rituals, performing self-dedication rites, or calling upon the gatekeepers (see Chapter 7) to find your magical path and open the ways to your spiritual advancement.

## Winter Full Moon
### (Þinterfylleþ)

TRADITIONAL: October
MODERN: September–October

Upon the Winter Full Moon, we enter the dark half of the year, the second of the lunar seasons. With the darkness comes deeper self-reflection and inward working. As the outside becomes more inhospitable, the inward focus of self and home is heightened and natural to the rhythm of the seasons. For witches today, magical work for self-discovery, inner work (mental and emotional), and ancestral work of any kind are enhanced by the pull of this month's moon.

## Blót Month/Month of Sacrifice
(Blōt-mōnaþ)

**TRADITIONAL:** November
**MODERN:** October–November

As cattle were slaughtered and sacrificed to the gods, the blood sacrifice would be used to mark the idols of the gods sustaining and renewing them. For modern witches during the housel, as discussed in Chapter Two, using red wine or other blood-like liquid is a great symbolic way of incorporating this theme into your esbat ritual. Spell-work for personal renewal, rebirth, and self-growth are particularly appropriate at this time.

## Before Yule
(Ærra Gēola)

**TRADITIONAL:** December
**MODERN:** November–December

The full moon Before Yule prepares us for the birth of the sun via the Mother Goddess and the promise of warmth ahead. Magical protections of all kinds are wonderful under the loving support of this moon's power. As the Mother Goddess is preparing to birth the sun after Yule, spells aimed at protecting the Goddess can be carried out at this time, ensuring that the warmth comes quickly and safely and that winter does not linger for too long. Spells for courage and determination—especially for the New Year to come—are also wonderful ways to spin your magic under the benevolent power of this moon.

### TRACKING THE LUNA TIDES

Although the full moon is most popular amongst witches, there are of course many other phases that the moon presents to us. Each of these phases has a pronounced effect on the astral tides of power that we harness when working magic. It is for that reason that witches often time their spellcraft by the moon, effectively using the moon as a great celestial indicator of the flow and ebb of these astral tides. Presented here is an overview of each phase and the magic that is best supported by the astral tides at that time. Some of these phases are often merged into one phase or overlooked entirely. This section is written to clarify the distinction and help provide clarity in the conversation of the magic of the moon's phases.

 ## Dark Moon

When the face of the moon is completely hidden in shadow, we call it the *dark moon*. For three nights, the moon appears to be completely absent from the sky. It is during this phase that the astral tides are most advantageous to workings in banishing, binding, cursing, restraining, breaking down, cleaning the slate, uncovering hidden truths, or hiding secrets.

When it comes to wiping the slate clean, many magical traditions use the dark moon as a great cosmic "reset button" that can be activated to repair their relationships with the Powers. If we have neglected our gods or other spirits, we can use the night of the dark moon to make amends and start over without any offense, either intentional or accidental, being held against us.

 ## New Moon

The *new moon* is when the first thin sliver of light is caught on the face of the moon and we begin to see that the abandoned night sky has a moon appearing once again. Many in the ancient world believed that the moon literally died and a brand-new moon replaced it following three nights of darkness. This is why it is called a *new moon*: it was believed that a completely new moon replaced the old one.

When the new moon makes its presence known, spellcraft geared towards new beginnings, births, planting the seeds of wishes to manifest, and opening doors to new opportunities are beneficial. If you have used the dark moon to make amends with the Powers, then the first night of the new moon is the night to invite those Powers into your home and life once again. Welcome them with offerings and flattering words to set the tone of a newly repaired relationship and they will bring their blessings into your life without hesitation.

 **Waxing Crescent**

When the moon's light forms a defined crescent, the moon has transitioned from *new* to the *waxing crescent*. The pull of this moon shapes the astral tides in such a way that offers benefits to a wide range of magical workings. Regardless of whether you seek wealth, friendship, new love, rekindling current romance, fertility, or constructive magic of any kind, this is the phase in which to act. The creative and life-giving powers of this moon bring success to any area of life that your rituals and spells are aimed at.

 **First Quarter**

At the time of the *first quarter*, the light and shadow on the surface of the moon are equally balanced. During this phase, its balanced power can be used to help us make tough decisions, such as when we feel we are stuck at one of life's crossroads. As the moon begins to move towards a greater light, we, too, are able to find more clarity in a situation that is presented at this time of the lunar cycle. Any working that is intended to bring clarity, inspiration, or uncover hidden factors in a situation will be best done under the influence of this moon phase.

Due to these factors, motivational workings can also be worked under this phase. The inspiration and illuminated opportunities will bring a greater personal drive to succeed. Clarity in divination is also particularly potent at this time. If you find that you have been struggling to get clear messages or are concerned that someone is working underhanded, now is the time to search for the truth that has been escaping your notice.

### Waxing Gibbous

As the moon moves towards her peak of power, the tides become fortuitous to workings for protection, good health, and attractive magic of all kinds. The closer we move from the waxing crescent to the full moon, the quicker the results of your spells will manifest. For this reason, any situation that requires a swift result would be greatly aided by the virtues of the waxing gibbous.

 ### Full Moon

As the moon's face becomes fully revealed, we begin to feel similar revelations within ourselves. Just as the power of the astral tides is affected by the pull of the moon, so too is the power that dwells within us. For this reason, many see this time as one of empowerment and bringing workings to completion (as we are at the apex of the time of rapid manifestation). Your tools can be cleansed and recharged during the full moon and talismans or other power objects can be made and consecrated. The full moon also offers us a chance to draw its strength into ourselves and empower us to deal with situations that we may be struggling to process and overcome.

 ### Waning Gibbous

As the shadows begin creeping over the pale face of the moon, we enter a time of release. We tend to track the cycle of the moon by its light, but consider thinking about it like this: The moon begins by waxing in light until it is fully lit, then it proceeds to wax in shadow until it is fully dark . The cycle then starts over again.

We have a time for light and a time for darkness, but they are not all that different. Just as we bring things in with the increasing light, so too do we let things go as the shadow approaches. Use this phase of the moon to let go of bad habits and outdated attachments. This time is also ideal for undoing curses and working on cleansing and binding magic.

### Third Quarter

Again, we enter a period of balance, this time drawing on the virtues of the moon to help us walk away from situations as opposed to towards them. This can mean the end of a relationship that has turned toxic (romantic, professional, or otherwise). Banishing spells are particularly potent at this time, as are spells concerning secrecy and moving past grief or traumas.

 ### Waning Crescent

Use this time to work on situations regarding forgiveness of yourself or others. Find healing in this moon phase and use it to ward against illness or bad luck. Protection workings are often reinforced at this time by cutting ties and repairing psychic damage done to your protection spells cast in the moon's lighter phases. This psychic repair will keep your shields strong and ensure they hold against magical and psychic attacks.

Knowledge is great, but wisdom is knowledge that can be applied. If you need wisdom in a given situation, or simply want help in applying your studies, use this moon phase to invite wisdom and the opportunities to use your skills.

 ### Old Moon

Harness the power of this moon phase to create major shifts in your life for the better, and eliminate the ties and forces that are holding you back from your personal happiness, dreams, aspirations, and full potential. Witches working at the second degree (or somewhere similar) can use this moon to clear out restrictions on their path of learning and help ease the effects of the equalising power of initiation. All witches can use this moon to process and integrate their personal shadows via shadow work. By facing your own self and fears, you can reclaim your lost, suppressed, or stolen powers, thus using it for positive, meaningful change.

## CONCLUSION

Regardless of how you choose to practise your Craft and which elements are important to you, one thing is likely to remain ever-present: working magic! Take time to explore and experiment with working in different ways. Do you work best by embracing the different phases of the moon? Does the Anglo-Saxon moon calendar hold a richer source of power and inspiration for you? By embracing the power of the moon in whatever form you choose, you can enhance any esbat ritual and find new and exciting ways of deepening your relationship with your own power.

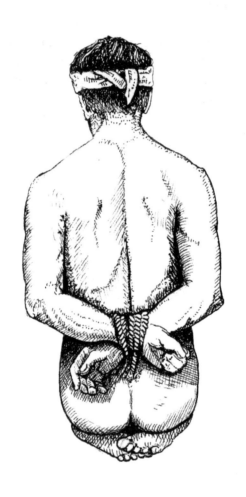

CHAPTER SIX

# INITIATION

**T**oday, a new witch can find their way into the Craft from any number of varied and diverse means. The freedom of the Information Age allows us to learn about practically any subject matter in an instant or otherwise connect with someone well-versed in the subject regardless of geographical location. Of course, this was not always the case, and when it came to Witchcraft, there was a time when only one avenue of learning was available. At that time, the only opportunity for education on the Craft was with a coven—or at the very least, an apprenticeship under an experienced practitioner. Although the times have certainly changed, we still live in a time when much remains inaccessible unless this connection with a coven or practitioner is made. Naturally, there are those who have no desire to access that knowledge and are more than happy working with what is publicly available. There is nothing wrong with that, but for some, the call runs too deep, and they are driven to take that extra step to satisfy that inner longing for something more.

When someone decides to move forward with a deeper knowledge of the Craft, there will come a time when they reach a barrier. In this event, the student can connect with a coven or experienced practitioner who is willing to assist them. They will have many conversations with that individual or group, but then the time comes when they must make a decision. Is initiation for them and are they willing to accept this step in order to proceed? If so, the initiation will be scheduled, and they will begin to learn what would otherwise remain unknown to them. Despite a large portion of our community choosing not to pursue initiation, those seeking it are at an all-time high.

Often, the subject of initiation brings up images of hierarchy and superiority in the community. Questions about validity as a witch also begin to surface, regardless of which side of the discussion you may be on. The main reason for this is often due to the unknown aspects that surround initiation which leads to assumption and misunderstanding. The aim of this chapter is to demystify these rites and practices (as far as the written word can) by exploring what initiations are, what factors come into consideration, and the culture that shapes their themes and importance. Following that, the chapter will explore the question of whether initiations are considered essential and the roles of self-dedication and self-initiation in our modern Craft history.

## WHAT IS AN INITIATION?

INITIATION:
- The action of admitting someone into a secret or obscure society or group, typically with a ritual.
- The introduction of someone to a particular activity or skill.
- The action of beginning something.[148]

For our purposes as witches, the full range of definitions for initiation are applicable, however, it is the first definition concerning ritual which will act as our focus.

### IS INITIATION NECESSARY?

Whether or not initiation is required is a frequently asked question that not only comes with a wide range of answers, but is often accompanied with a lot of bias. Some want to rebel against the perception of rules and others feel strongly that the rules exist for a reason. The truth of the matter is somewhere in the middle of these two extremes: true Witchcraft is often found in the between spaces of all dualistic expression.

---

148  Oxford University Press (OUP), "Initiation," Accessed June 1, 2020, https://www.lexico.com/definition/initiation.

Have you ever found yourself asking "do I need to be initiated to be a witch? Is it necessary?" If so, ask yourself these questions: What does being a witch mean to you? What is your personal end goal? Once you answer these, the solution to your dilemma will present itself more clearly.

If you are seeking entry into an established tradition, it is most likely that initiation will be required. The form that such an initiation rite will take largely depends on the tradition itself, and you should make sure you have all the details of what is involved and expected. This research will help you make an informed choice and know if its mysteries are truly what you are looking for. There are a large range of ritual forms practised today, but the main core of the practices—which we will explore later—is almost unanimously universal.

If you are not looking to work with an established group or you are content with an informal gathering of people, then initiation is less likely to be required for you to begin. I use the phrase "less likely" rather than "not required" as there may come a point in your journey where initiation becomes necessary in order for you to access the information or training needed in order to follow where the gods are leading you.

It should be noted that regardless of where your path takes you, serious commitment and study should be at the forefront of your journey. Regardless of whether you are in an established tradition, informal gathering, or going it alone, you are ultimately in the same situation. Only you can walk your path. Even if there are others around you, this path is always a solitary one.

## THE ROLE OF THE GODS

Regardless of whether initiation is necessary for your personal journey, it should be noted that initiation isn't for everyone. Not every witch will strictly *need* initiation in their life, even if it is something that they want. To illustrate my point, I will share a story from my Reiki training. When studying traditional Reiki, initiation is a necessary part of the process. Some people use other words such as *attunement* to describe the process, but in its earliest form (as preserved and handed down in authentic lineages), it is a ritual initiation that is received.

When completing my Master training, I came to the place where I had previously trained and when I walked in, my teacher's husband was there to greet me. "Am I the first one here?" I asked as I walked in. I was just on time due to traffic and expected everyone else to be there waiting. "It's only you," was his reply. I was confused as I knew that the class was full, but my teacher's husband (whom I had known as an occultist since my school days) had included me as a personal favour.

When my teacher came downstairs, I asked what had happened, and she said that everyone had cancelled for one reason or another; all with unavoidable coincidences that prevented them from attending. I offered to come back again as I wasn't wanting to impose on her time. "No, he [her husband] already asked if he should phone you to cancel and I told him if you come, then I will teach you."

After my initiation, my teacher revisited that comment and explained that it is all about timing: "They are not ready for initiation, that is why they couldn't come. You are spiritually prepared for any initiation beginning about two weeks prior to the event itself. If you are not ready, then you will be blocked. That is why I could not turn you away if you came in today. If you are ready for your initiation, then I cannot deny you that right."

It is worth noting that my teacher is a wise and talented witch and her words regarding initiation and timing are very relevant to the Craft. Regarding initiation, the role of the gods and the spiritual preparation that my Reiki teacher mentioned in her story is something that not many witches talk openly about. The gods do play a vital role in the initiatory process that should not, and cannot, be ignored.

If you have ever approached a coven to seek initiation, you will know that there is a formal vetting process that goes hand-in-hand with being a seeker. A coven leader will want to ensure that you are a proper person for the Craft who is seriously dedicated to the role that you are requesting to fulfil within their circle. If all goes well after a few correspondences, usually via email today, a meeting will be arranged. A number of follow-up meetings should be expected before being introduced to the other members of the group. The decision will be made as to whether you are accepted and a date for the initiation ritual is set.

If you have been through this process or read any Witchcraft books covering this application process, then the above will be very familiar to you. At this stage of the process, the key element missing is mention of the gods. Where are they in all of this? Every Craft tradition that I know of in the UK makes their final decision of whether a seeker is a "good fit" for their coven by taking the matter to the gods. Each tradition, including Gardnerian and Alexandrian Craft, has its own way of consulting with its deity to seek permission to bring the individual into their priesthood. Some traditions place greater emphasis on this process than others, as some will do this only if they are unsure, whereas other traditions will take the question to the ritual for each prospective candidate.

The gods ultimately have the final say as it is their Mysteries that initiation brings us into. If all has gone well and a coven still rejects your application, you may be wondering what went wrong. The answer is *nothing*: It isn't anyone's fault that the timing wasn't right. The gods have their reasons, and it is usually in our best interest overall. If you are rejected by a coven, it could be an incompatibility with that particular coven or this specific time in your life; it is not a bar to the Craft as a whole. It is just a sign that this exact avenue is not the one that is meant for you. Keep seeking and the right path will reveal itself. As the old saying goes: "When the student is ready, the teacher will appear."

As most initiatory traditions recognise their Craft as a religion and its initiates as a priesthood, it shouldn't be surprising that gaining clarity from the coven's gods would be part of the process. The final say in such matters is the divine prerogative. In the example of my Reiki story, spiritual preparation begins before the rite itself. In Witchcraft, it is the gods who prepare. Although the timescale of two weeks is given for initiation, this should be understood as being spiritually prepared for the change that initiation brings and not necessarily when the call to the Craft is first felt.

### Answering a Call

When I was a child, I attended a CofE (Church of England) School, which sounds far more religious than it actually is. The school itself was very multicultural for the 90s, and the only major religious element that we experienced was the assembly held by the vicar every Friday. By the time I was eight, I had already heard the vicar tell the same stories multiple times; regardless, I loved his presentation. He would tell a story and then link it to a biblical example right at the very end. It was a very easy, non-forced, approach. One particular day, the vicar came to the assembly with a new story that has stuck with me for the two decades since my eight-year-old-self first heard it. He started by telling us that he had planned to talk about something else, but on the way to the school, he was inspired to talk to us about something else: The day that he got his calling.

Although I cannot remember the exact details of the story that followed, what stuck with me was this overwhelming recognition of the feeling that he had described. "I know that feeling," I said to myself, "so that's what that is." Of course, my calling wasn't meant for the priesthood of the CofE—or any other church—but the sense of understanding that I felt that day is one that still brings a smile to my face. Whether the vicar had been inspired to talk about that story to shine a light on my own spiritual experience or whether it was for his own benefit to recall what had brought him to God, I cannot know. What I do know is that it has become an important story in my life and raises questions about the role that Fate plays in initiation.

## THE ROLE OF FATE

Fate is a funny word. The very mention of the word raises deep theological and philosophical questions. For many, the word "Fate" is rather scary, as it is taken to mean that everything is predetermined and that our choices have no bearing on the outcome of our lives. Others find the term far more reassuring and express this with phrases such as "everything happens for a reason." I would say that for the most part, I fall into the latter of the two.

My own understanding of Fate is very specific, so I will explain my perception of the word before moving forward. Imagine that you are standing on a cliff; the wind is blowing, and the sky is clear. You hear the waves of the sea crashing gently against the cliffside below and you can see the silhouette of birds gracefully flying in the distance. You take a deep breath of the clean, crisp air and…you throw yourself off the edge of the cliff. You fall, and…

The story doesn't need much of an ending, does it? We all know what happens at the end; what follows is *inevitable*. Inevitability is one of those words that I truly love. I'm sure everyone has some words that they really like for one reason or another, but I like this one because it helps me understand that thing we call *Fate*. I like to capitalise *Fate*, as I see it as a great force with a divine presence behind it. Just like in those old films where the gods would play chess with the mortals: some would throw obstacles into their paths while others would send them aid. The gods may intervene, but it was what the mortal chose to do with their circumstances that would seal their Fate.

Returning to our imaginary cliff, what would happen if you turned around and walked home instead of throwing yourself off? Would both lead to the same outcome? No! In my understanding of Fate, there is always a choice involved. Imagine Fate as a fork in a road, the road of life. When you pick a path, what unfolds then becomes inevitable—just like the cliff scenario. Fate may bring you to the cliff for whatever reason, but it is what you choose to do when you are there that determines your future.

In short: Inevitability = Fate + Choice.

## Answering the Call of Fate

What has this got to do with initiation? Everything! When I felt my call and recognised what it was, there wasn't a force on this Earth that could silence that knowing deep within me. It had always been there, and I was fortunate to have family to turn to for Craft training, but recognising a deeper call is something else; it is a question that needs an answer.

Even if you are accepted into a coven following an application period, it does not necessarily mean that the timing is right. You are the final factor in the vetting process. Fate may choose to bring you to a coven, it may be the force that has called you to the Circle's edge, however, I know of no Craft tradition in the UK that does not include an initiatory challenge. The choice is ours to make, the Craft does not rob us of our free will. Just like the gods in those old films, they may favour us and place their bet on what we will do; but just like a bet at a horse race, they can only sit back and see how events unfold. Once we accept the challenge and are exposed to that central power which is the life of the Circle, then we are set upon a path and what follows becomes inevitable.

## A Regal and Cultural Rite

It has been said in recent decades that British Witchcraft is not a cultural religion. The main hypothesis for this position is based upon Britain's colourful history. The very idea that modern Britons are somehow without a distinct culture is laughable to me. Even though our country was founded by a blend of people due to periods of invasion, it is fair to say that most other countries have similar foundations without being labelled "cultureless." Another argument used to discredit British culture in Craft is due to the fact that non-Brits can be initiated into the tradition. Vodou is founded on the understanding that all living people have a spirit, called a *Lwa Mèt Tèt*, who should be served by the individual. The very idea that anyone can be initiated into Vodou in order to serve the Master of their head (Lwa Mèt Tèt) does not invalidate the African culture present within the tradition.

As discussed in Chapter Two, many of the terms used in British Witchcraft have their origins in the culture of the people and landscape of the British Isles. I have seen non-Brit initiates accuse native Britons of "appropriating from initiates" because they used a term that was originally used in their tradition. Natives *cannot* appropriate their own culture and saying "I am a third-degree initiate of (tradition)" does not work at UK border control. Terms such as "three great events" and "comforter and consoler" are used, among many others, within our day-to-day culture. I have heard many of these—and similar terms—used on the BBC and ITV. The news reporters are not stealing or appropriating anything. *Comforter and consoler* is a title frequently given to the British Monarch: Queen Elizabeth II wasn't stealing from initiates either.[149]

The most popular branches of British Witchcraft include initiation rites that all have very similar themes. Initiation is a cultural rite that is steeped in our nation's history and ceremonial symbolism. The act

---

149  This section was originally written under the reign of Queen Elizabeth II, Monarch of the United Kingdom from 1952 until her death in 2022. While at the time of this publication, Charles III holds the throne, the historical significance of Queen Elizabeth's coronation ceremony in 1953 remains unparalleled as a comparative event to initiation ritual.

of Coronation of the British Monarch follows all the same hallmark themes of a witch's initiation—correction: a witch's initiation follows all the hallmark themes of a Royal Coronation. The coronation ritual itself is an old rite of pre-Christian origins, much of which was completely transferred into the Christian rite. Surprisingly, even the Sacred Marriage to the Earth-Goddess survived into the Christian ceremony. Only the helmet was left abandoned, being replaced with a crown in 966 CE.[150]

## The Parallels

The ritual of coronation, as previously discussed, holds all the same themes that are found in traditional (UK) initiation rites. As the most commonly available public rites are those used by Gerald Gardner, they will be used to highlight the parallels. It should also be noted that the three-degree initiations together hold the themes that are combined with one coronation. Those unfamiliar with the Gardnerian form will be easily able to find them online.

### Disrobe

During the ritual of coronation, the Monarch is disrobed of their prior status. In the ritual used for Queen Elisabeth II, her tiara, robes, and jewellery were removed, leaving her in a simple white ritual gown. In many Witchcraft initiation rites, the candidate is also required to be disrobed, either of their worldly persona, as with the Monarch, or of their clothing in its entirety (skyclad).

### Challenge

The Monarch is challenged at the beginning of the ritual wherein they must state who they are and why they have come. This parallels the practice found in British initiation rites. The new witch-to-be is challenged before entering the Circle (or similar ritual space) to ensure that they are prepared to accept the position that they will

---

150   Roy Strong, *Coronation: From the 8th to the 21st Century,* (London: Harper Collins UK, 2013), 28-29.

soon be granted within the coven and are prepared to accept its relevant duties.

## Presentation

Within both rituals, the four directions are called to witness the rites. Witnessing is an important aspect as it confirms the rite in the same way that human witnesses legitimise marriages and legal documents. For witches, this part of the process carries extra significance. The powers of the directions as elemental guardians act as keepers of the Mysteries. As such, they will guard and preserve certain magic from those that are not seen as "proper persons." By having these spirits witness the rites, you effectively have your name placed on the metaphorical list that gets you through the door.

## Oath

The formalising of the process with an oath is typically the first aspect of both rituals where the candidate is the one bringing something to the table. By pledging a commitment in such a way, the candidate freely gives themselves to the role and duties that the ritual confers. For a Monarch, the oath binds their life to their country and its people, and within the Craft, initiation brings one into the priesthood, or in some traditions, the religion. For the witch, this oath binds their life in service, faith, and commitment to the religion, its gods, and its magic.

## Anointing

Anointing a candidate with consecration oil helps to bring blessings upon them and invests them with spiritual support. The anointing is performed within both the Craft and Royal rites to elevate the candidate to the position that they are now claiming. Within the coronation, the Monarch is covered with a canopy to allow them a private moment with God that cannot be witnessed by anyone nor questioned later. This action echoes aspects of the Sacred Marriage, discussed in the eighth point of this list, which is found within Witchcraft and may represent a more subtle aspect of the Great Rite (a *private moment* with God).

## Name

It isn't often known that the British Royal Family, in a sense, have no names. Their last names fluctuate depending on whether they are Dukes or Duchesses of an area, in which case that area name is their "name." First names for a Monarch are also just as flexible. Before the coronation of a new Monarch, they are required to inform the Archbishop of Canterbury of their new name.

When the Prince or Princess title is discarded for King or Queen, so is the whole name. A Monarch may choose to retain their original name, as was the case of Queen Elizabeth II, but it is not required. While the people of the UK had long suspected that Prince Charles would take the name George VII at his coronation, the decision was formally made to use the name *King Charles III*. The Queen's own father, King George VI, formally Prince Albert, was the last British Monarch to take a new name at his 1937 coronation.

Within the Craft, there comes a time when a witch will choose their own name. This name is the one that will be used within Circle and acts as a seal upon the initiation and all that has so far taken place. By being effectively reborn, it is only fitting that the new witch would choose a name for themselves. Each tradition has its own way of choosing a name as well as how it is formally bestowed. Titles are also bestowed at this time, such as Witch-Queen, Witch, and Priest(ess). Just as the Monarch is bestowed with a new title to accompany their new status, so too is the witch.

## Weapons of Power

Both witches and Monarchs wield Weapons of Power. It is worth noting that the four primary tools, which are the four suits of the tarot, share a royal connection all their own. The Arthurian myth cycle naturally has *the Sword in the Stone* and *Excalibur of the Lady of the Lake* as two examples of magical blades, *the Holy Grail of the Fisher King* parallels the Chalice, and the *Shield of Sir Gawain*, which bears a large pentalpha (pentagram), is hard to miss. Wands are more subtle in these tales, however, can anyone really imagine Merlin without a staff in hand?

These tools or instruments represent aspects of the individual's newfound power within the role that they have received. Within both rites, a token use of each weapon is carried out by the individual upon instruction of each weapon's symbolic powers or properties. By wielding these instruments, the candidate demonstrates their ability to carry out the office into which they have just been sworn. This act also demonstrates to the witnesses that the candidate now embodies the full power and authority that each item represents.

## Sacred Marriage

The Sacred Marriage, commonly known today as the *Great Rite*, often poses a number of controversial conversations within our community. Whether symbolic or actual, the rite itself often comes back to one main question: "Is it really necessary?" From a cultural standpoint, it can be argued that, in fact, it is. Although this subject will be revisited in greater detail in the chapter *Sacred Sexuality*, for the purposes of the present subject, we will explore the power that comes from marrying a goddess.

As previously discussed, the coronation ritual used today retains all elements of the original rites used by Britain's Anglo-Saxon ancestors, including the Sacred Marriage to the Earth-Goddess. Following the ritual anointing, the Monarch is crowned and then receives the Coronation Ring, also known as the Wedding Ring of England.[151] This ring is placed onto the fourth finger of the Monarch's right hand to seal the Sacred Marriage and consecrates them as "… head and prince of this kingdom and people."[152] It is interesting to note that the use of the titles *Prince* and *King* are used during this section of the ritual, regardless of the gender of the Monarch. This echoes the need for polarity that is often found within Craft practices.[153] Although it is fair to say that initiations

---

151 Royal UK, "50 facts about The Queen's Coronation", Accessed June 16, 2020. https://www.royal.uk/50-facts-about-queens-coronation-0

152 Royal Collection Trust, "Coronation ring", Accessed June 16, 2020. https://www.rct.uk/collection/441925/coronation-ring.

153 Oremus, "The Form and Order of Service that is to be performed and the Ceremonies that are to be observed in The Coronation of Her Majesty Queen Elizabeth II in the Abbey Church of St. Peter, Westminster, on Tuesday, the second day of June 1953." Accessed June 16, 2020. http://www.oremus.org/liturgy/coronation/cor1953b.html

often take the form of ritual that confers power and authority, it is the marriage or connection created between the gods and their priesthood that places the ultimate consecration upon an initiate.

## THE BOOK

Finally, the ritual concludes with an exchange of knowledge. If you have ever seen an old woodcut from the period of the witch trials, then you are likely familiar with the image of the devil handing a book over to the newly initiated witch.

Priests in many faiths receive a book of rituals and liturgy upon completion of the rite, and the same goes for witches and Royals.

When a Monarch has been officially crowned, the Archbishop will present them with a copy of the King James Bible. This receiving of the knowledge of the Church of England only seems fitting after receiving the Wedding Ring of England. Likewise, witches will receive tuition within the tradition that they are now part of, and in many instances, this involves the careful copying of the coven's materials—such as the *Book of Shadows*.

Gone is the notion that British Craft is devoid of culture or that its initiation rites are merely an imitation of freemasonry. By comparing these nine key themes, I hope that you are better able to see that the rituals of initiation, used in all branches of British Witchcraft, are richly filled with the culture of this nation. These rituals represent long-held traditions that are both important and sacred to the people of Britain.

## HOW DOES IT WORK?

Now that we have examined what initiations mean to different people, the role that the gods and Fate play in calling a candidate, and the British cultural themes and influences that shape the rite; it is important to establish how the rites actually work. What is it about these themes, which are considered so essential, that they have been preserved within a culture since its earliest foundations?

It should be noted here that some branches of British Craft have differing numbers of initiation rites. All contain the complete set of themes previously discussed dispersed across its number. In this example, references may be made to the three-degree system that is most commonly understood within our community, however, I wish to make it abundantly clear that I am speaking generally about all forms of *British* Craft. A degree of generalisation is given to cover such a broad band of traditional ideas and beliefs, such as those that have been presented throughout this book.

### THE GREAT EQUALISER

To me, initiation is the great equaliser, especially the first two degrees. The first brings someone into the priesthood, coven, or Craft, signifying that they are a new witch ready for instruction. There is no judgement here, as everyone must start somewhere. The second acts as an equaliser in a slightly more judgemental manner—because of this, I personally find it to be the most amusing. In short, whether or not you have prepared yourself for this stage of initiation, the rite will take you there. For those who are prepared and have put the work in, this should be plain sailing, and for those who haven't bothered … you're in for a bumpy ride.

The analogy that I often give for this initiation is that of a *tidal wave*. The student that does the work moves to a certain point on their path (imagine this as a physical path) and they have reached the right place for the ritual to take place. The current of power is passed through them and they are fine. The student who has not done the work finds that they are not as far along the path as their peers. When that tidal wave comes crashing down (the current of power), instead of standing in the safe zone where their feet may get lightly splashed, they experience that primal force of nature slam into them at full force. As they flap and splash around frantically, trying to escape the inescapable, they are carried full force by the raging waters (magical power) until, at last, it settles down and dumps them next to their more prepared peers.

This is why there is always a statement made that follows along the lines of "are you willing to suffer to learn?" in all branches of Craft. The work must be done, but how you get there is a circumstance of your own making. The final grade, as previously discussed, comes from establishing that Sacred Marriage with the gods. The equalising factor here is that the gods, not their flawed human representatives, seal the consecration of your power and authority. Just as the Kings of old and Monarchs today may only rule by the grace of the Goddess, so too do her chosen people ultimately "rule" over covens by divine authority.

*"A Witch is born, not made; or if one is to be made, then tears must be spilt before the moon can be drawn. For the Lady chooses whom she wills to be Her LOVER, and those She loves the most, She rends apart and makes them Wise."*

– Robert Cochrane[154]

### Current of Power

Much of this equalising comes from the power of the rite itself. It is not true to suggest that one gets their power from another person, as this would be misunderstanding the process entirely. When seeking initiation, a good initiator is looking for someone who already has that spark of magic within their soul. The current of power is something that comes through, not from, the initiator. It is the gods, elemental guardians, and the spirits of witches past who reach through the initiator, acting as an open conduit to place their hands upon the initiate. By doing so, they are able to pass the current associated with that particular branch of Witchcraft. This

---

154 Robert Cochrane, quoted in Christopher Penczak, *The Living Temple of Witch-craft*, (Woodbury, MN: Llewellyn, 2008), 34.

confers their blessings, guidance, power, and protection upon the newly consecrated witch. The Circle and its gods and guardians all have a power that is innately their own. When someone is brought into a tradition, they are brought into alignment with these forces so that they can become true servants to the power and work of the Circle.

Personal power (or magic) is latent within us, yet just like a car battery, we sometimes need exposure to another's power in order to have a jump-start effect. The power of the Circle is something else, something which we seek out because we are deeply called to find it; this is the power that is passed at initiation. Witchcraft has no messiah, nor does it need one, so the concept of a Witchcraft apostolic succession is somewhat redundant. As discussed in previous chapters, the concept of lineage is here to stay (and I am not complaining), however, it wasn't always there, nor was it always important. Gerald Gardner was initiated by Dorothy Clutterbuck, but who initiated her? Gerald certainly never knew, and why should he? The power that Gerald received didn't come from him anyway, it came from communion with the Circle and its inner plane contacts.

## BORN OR MADE?

A somewhat controversial and very divisive question that often arises within the subject of initiation is this: Are witches born or made? Today, the question is often overlooked, with simple answers such as: "Does it really matter?" or "Are labels that important?" being given. If we think about these answers logically, we will begin to notice that they aren't actually answers at all—they are questions. Answering a question with another question is impractical. Not only does this not provide any meaningful insight into the original question, but it leaves the serious practitioner with far more unanswered questions than they started with.

Although controversial, the question is important. As stated in the introduction of this book, Witchcraft is provocative. If we are afraid to ask the difficult questions, then the world of the occult is not a place to be. The occult is literally the hidden knowledge. If occultists are unnerved by shining a light on the unknown should it reveal an uncomfortable truth, then they are truly missing the point.

As witches of the twenty-first century, we are very fortunate. There is so much information available to us from the past. This means that most of these seemingly difficult questions have already largely been answered. Thomas Rudd, a little-acknowledged yet influential contemporary of Elizabethan magician Dr. John Dee, beautifully answered the question of whether magical skill is something you are born with or acquire:

> *"He that is a true Magician, is brought forth a Magician from his Mother's Womb; and whoso is otherwise, ought to recompense that defect of Nature by Education."*

—Thomas Rudd, *The Nine Celestial Keys*[155]

Although I wouldn't go as far as to describe being born without magical skill as a "defect of Nature," the balance in Rudd's philosophy is striking and worth inspection. Despite the fact that this quotation is tapping into the notion that magical skill is a birthright, Rudd's statement that education is its equal shows that being *born* or *made* makes no real difference. This was a radical way of thinking, even in its day. Other occultists more strongly held to the notion of born ability, believing that those who perused the magical arts otherwise would have unhappy lives.[156] Frances Barrett, author of the influential classic *The Magus*, lays down similar examples of natural ability while simultaneously offering initiation and training for those serious seekers who would wish to build and refine magical power.[157]

Looking at the broad history of this ubiquitous question, it is natural to assume that the truth is that witches and other occultists are a mixed bag of born and made. Some people can have a natural talent for art, dancing, singing, or athletics, while others have a greater need for training to strengthen those abilities. It would seem that history

---

155  Thomas Rudd, quoted in Philip Carr-Gomm & Richard Heygate, *The Book of English Magic*, (London: John Murry, 2010), 254.

156  *The Astrologer's Magazine, and Philosophical Miscellany*, Volume 1, (London: W. Locke, 1791), 345.

157  Frances Barrett, *The Magus*, (London: Lackington, Allen, and Company, 1801), 140.

tells us that magic is no different. When I am asked if I think witches are born or made, my go-to answer is this: "All witches are born, but some are made." This may sound like a contradiction, but please allow me to explain. Whether a person is born from nature or by the spiritual rebirth of initiation makes no difference to me. Many witches have arisen from both instances (nature and initiation). Alex Sanders recorded audio in 1970 of the initiation rites called *A Witch Is Born,* echoing the occult philosophy that initiation is understood as a type of "birth."[158]

## SELF-INITIATION AND SELF-DEDICATION

Within the sub-section of initiation is the much debated question of what makes an initiation valid or legitimate. For some, self-initiation is perfectly valid and offers a viable option when no other alternative is readily available, while for others, only a witch can make a witch. In all honesty, the answers, like the others we have discussed, are not as cut and dry as that and usually sit between the two extremes of the debate. The main reason that this is a widely debated issue usually stems from a lack of understanding the terminology. There is a distinct difference between self-initiation and self-dedication, as you will see. Neither option is better than the other, it is about using correct terminology so that you aren't perceived to be making false claims—that is when things usually start to get heated.

At the beginning of this chapter, we looked at the definition of the word *initiation.* The main emphasis of this definition was on bringing someone into an established group or body of practices. This is why the term *self-initiation* can be a difficult term to navigate, however, this section aims to clear up that matter. If initiation is defined by a shared body of philosophy, practices, beliefs, or skills, then determining whether something is a "valid" self-initiation can only be done based upon its context. In the Farrars' classic *A Witches' Bible* and Doreen Valiente's *Witchcraft for Tomorrow,* self-initiation rituals can be readily found. Within the context of these two examples, these are completely valid initiations. Not only do they follow the basic pattern of themes previously discussed, but they also follow a clearly

---

158    Alex Sanders, *A Witch Is Born,* (London: A & M Records), 1970.

explained body of teaching and practices. Neither claim to be an entry into a *specific* tradition, but that does not in any way lessen or invalidate what they do represent.

Self-dedication is somewhat different. When an individual chooses to go it alone and find their own path, they are taking a huge step that requires great determination and deep dedication. A rite of self-dedication is therefore a more accurate term for this chosen path, as it can (though not always) be more eclectic in nature and is not directly related to an organised *group* practice. Raymond Buckland in his book *Buckland's Book of Saxon Witchcraft* provides a complete system of Witchcraft in its entirety. Within this text is found a self-dedication rite as well as an initiation ritual.[159]

The self-dedication is designed for those who are working Seax-Wica in a solitary capacity or who are founding a new coven within the tradition. Buckland's use of the term *self-dedication* in both instances is correct. In the former example, there is no group—the practitioner is solitary, while in the latter example, the founders of the new coven have not yet formed their group—they are still technically solitary. The initiation ritual is then used to bring others into the group, newly formed or long established, along with its determined beliefs and practices.

Britain is full of places in which people can go to "self-enter" Witchcraft. These places include specific stone circles, the Logan stone of Cornwall, and even some churches that have local traditions of Witchcraft rites attached to them. In many ways, these represent Britain's oldest, longest, and unbroken Craft traditions. What makes these rites an initiation or dedication is the presence of a body of lore, other people, and power. Power must be present in all forms of ritual designed for entry into the Craft: initiation, self-initiation, or self-dedication. It is that inner plane contact, that current of power, which makes it valid. Although the term "self" is used in two of these contexts, it is only because you are carrying out the rites *yourself*; always remember it is "self" and not "solo" initiation/dedication. True ritual of any kind is never really solitary, as there must be that meeting of souls; that communion with the otherworld. If our rites

---

159   Raymond Buckland, *Buckland's Book of Saxon Witchcraft*, (Boston, MA: Red Wheeler/Weiser, LLC. 2005), 42-44, 45-49.

fail to make contact with the unseen, then it is no more valid than TV Witchcraft. True Witchcraft has a spirit and a spark of magic that cannot be denied.

## DEDICATION

Anyone who has read my first book *Aradia* will know that I am not a fan of dedication rituals in books. It isn't that they are not useful, it is that they are only useful to the right people. When it comes to dedication rituals, you are making a statement expressing that you are *already* dedicated to that which the ritual represents. Dedication should come *before* the ritual, not after. The ritual should act as a seal on the work the individual has put into their development within a particular system or tradition. It is supposed to actually mean something—all rituals should. If you are wishing to dedicate yourself to Witchcraft, you should create your own ritual. That way it will legitimately be your very own beautiful, meaningful, and truly dedicated ritual. That level of personalisation will be a product of the dedication that comes before the ritual itself and will be a demonstration of your study and resolve to follow the witches' path.

### TIPS:

Is this something you want to be dedicated to? What part of Witchcraft is it that you are actually dedicating yourself to? Write it down in as much detail as possible and then read it back over. Is this everything? Is this what you really want?

Review information on the gods of this Witchcraft perspective (if applicable) as well as the underpinning cosmology that informs the method of practice. Do you still want to be dedicated to *this* specific path?

Check-in with yourself. Does this resonate with you? Do you actually believe in it? There is no point in empty rituals or paths; they don't lead anywhere.

Think about what you know. Do you understand enough about this specific path to claim to be dedicated? If not, what do you need to learn, and are you willing to find out *before* committing to it in ritual?

If you said "YES!" to all the above, then it is time to craft your very own dedication ritual. Make sure you have done other rituals in this system first. You must know the system inside and out before claiming to be dedicated to it.

## CONCLUSION

At the start of this chapter, we looked at the most frequently asked question regarding initiation: "Do I need to be initiated to be a witch? Is it necessary?" The only way to truly answer these questions is to ask yourself what being a witch means to you and what you consider your personal end goals to be. It is my hope that by looking at these various aspects and components of initiation, you will be able to answer these very personal questions for yourself. Regardless of where your path takes you, I wish you well.

CHAPTER SEVEN

# GATEKEEPING

**T**oday, we like to reminisce about the old days and speak of the ancient Celts or some other civilisation. When talking about the modern revival, we speak about many of those whose names were covered in Chapter One. All in all, we talk about our community like it is both romantically antiquated and freshly renewed by the Revival, remaining the same with the passage of time. The truth is that the Craft evolves at an almost alarming rate and it can become difficult to keep track of the latest trends; things that the people we recall from history would never have encountered in their lifetime. With a rapidly expanding community, this is bound to happen. When people who are at different parts of their Witchcraft journey all gather in one place it can be chaotic, fun, informative, and everything that you would expect any community to be—diverse.

Part of that diversity is in reference to dialogue. When I first started my journey into the Craft, the popular terminology of today just didn't exist within the community. We had a certain dialogue of course, but most of the popular terms used today are quite new. One of these terms that come to mind is *gatekeeping*. Like Witchcraft, it is an odd little word that can be either empowering or provocative, depending on the scenario. In recent years, the scenario has definitely been provocative.

The Oxford English dictionary defines gatekeeping as "the activity of controlling, and usually limiting, general access to something."[160]

This can be either unhelpful or practical depending on the motivation or rationale behind the action.

In the past few years, gatekeeping has become a reference to anyone who seeks to correct someone else's understanding of Witchcraft. Before then, the term was used to describe those who were unwilling to share their knowledge with others as they didn't consider them to be valid witches. This change in the use of the term often leaves some individuals feeling confused when they are labelled a "gatekeeper" for sharing their insights. It is for this reason that the two sides of gatekeeping must be clarified. By creating clarity, the intention of this chapter is that people will be better able to understand another's perspective and appreciate that, at times, "gatekeepers" may have something of value to impart. After looking at these opposing sides, the following chapter will examine some of the divine gatekeepers and the important role that they can play in expanding our Craft, providing us with focus and guidance.

## UNHELPFUL GATEKEEPING

Some of the most frequent examples of unhelpful gatekeeping include statements such as: "If you think that it is a religion then you are a Wiccan, not a witch" or "Wicca is the religion, Witchcraft is a practice." As discussed previously, these are contradictory statements and prove to be unhelpful when someone, usually a complete stranger, tells someone what it is that they are doing in a private setting.

The Craft has no centralised authority that decides how you practise or exactly what you can or cannot call yourself. This is true even within the most popular traditions. This type of gatekeeping or label policing is generally unhelpful in all its forms. I call this "unhelpful" as I have found that in most instances, the people themselves mean well. They tend to fall short of hitting their intended mark due to the fact that they are usually inserting their opinion

---

160    Oxford University Press (OUP), "Gatekeeping", Accessed Jan 13, 2020, https://www.lexico.com/definition/gatekeeping

where it was not asked for nor required. That is the part that makes it unhelpful and causes friction.

Some initiates are also guilty of this type of gatekeeping. I have seen those who, to paraphrase, make statements such as: "That tradition does something different than our tradition, so they aren't practising real (or true or proper) Witchcraft" or "That tradition does something different than our tradition, so they will never know the *real* secrets." These types of statements are unhelpful for different reasons.

The former statement suggests a "one true faith mentality" that does not, and never has, had a place in the Craft. As discussed in Chapter One, the history of Witchcraft, there was a time when Witchcraft was considered to be one Craft that had many differences—and to a certain extent, it is still this way today. Although traditions are here to stay, they only represent a lens or system of accessing the true essence of the Craft. The Mysteries themselves are eternal and will reveal themselves to anyone who makes those inner plane contacts. The systems themselves are man-made as the Craft has no prophets, and they aren't needed. It is the connection that is important and there are many paths to the centre.

The latter of these gatekeeping statements leads away from the former. It implies that the individual has failed to understand their connection to Mystery within their chosen tradition or path and feels that they have a god (or goddess) given religion which is the only true way. Witchcraft is not that restrictive. It should be free and liberating and statements like this are an example of one of the most unseemly words in the Craft: proselytising.

One of the universal qualities that connect all systems and expressions of Witchcraft, both today and in the past, is a clear rule that forbids any form of proselytising. The active recruitment of others to the faith is a big no-no yet statements like: "That tradition does something different than our tradition, so they will never know the *real* secrets" are perfect examples of it. By suggesting that the "*real* secrets" can only be found in one place, the person is (knowingly or unknowingly) partaking in proselytising behaviour. I would still consider this unhelpful as it seems that although the offenders are usually those who should know better, there is a disconnect in their training somewhere that makes this more of a mistake than an attempt to actively recruit.

The truth of the matter is that no witch knows the complete ins and outs of every system of Witchcraft and, therefore, really doesn't know what another practitioner knows. I was once in a conversation with a Gardnerian High Priestess here in the UK, and during the course of the conversation, she said, "How do you know oath-bound material? Only those of the third degree should know that." I was honestly stunned. The subject that we were discussing was actually from my own Craft background. Although it may have seemed that I had openly discussed a "secret," as far as I was concerned, I had lightly mentioned something while keeping the private elements of the practice quiet. Gatekeeping upon where the "real" secrets are is, therefore, nonsensical. Many would probably be surprised at exactly what other witches *do* know that they themselves consider a well-kept secret. It just goes to show that witches probably have far more in common than the presence of different traditions would appear to suggest. This does make sense though, after all, there was a time when there were no traditions at all—just plain old Witchcraft.

## PRACTICAL GATEKEEPING

As with most things in the occult world, there is always another side to the coin, and this is no different. Although gatekeeping can be unhelpful in some instances, it also has its practical aspects that should not be ignored or disregarded. One of the first examples that come to mind is in the form of guarding tradition. In this context, the limitation and restricted-access side of gatekeeping is paramount. Not only is it correct for people within established traditions to state when a teaching, practice, or historical point is inaccurate, it is also their "job" as representatives of that tradition to ensure that correct information is available.

This form of internal regulation of traditions in the public arena also occurs if someone falsely claims lineage to a tradition. It is fully acceptable for people to bar access to knowledge (or coven information) from someone who is lying to them. Coven leaders especially have a duty of care to their coven mates, ensuring that their private matters remain private. Formalised access to the Mysteries through an established initiatory system is not for everyone, as mentioned earlier. Even when the initiation is valid there are important gatekeeping issues that arise, most prominently that lineage and initiation are not automatically transferable. Yes, there are those traditions that will accept initiations from other branches as it is accepted that the Craft traditions all come, ultimately, from a common origin. However, there are those that would require someone to be initiated in their system in order to Circle with them.

This is not casting any negative light on the lineage that they already hold, but simply states that the form of said initiation does not reflect the focus of the Mysteries that are equivalent within the new branch of Craft. These forms of gatekeeping are not an issue in other religions, including those that are part of our wider community; but in the Craft, it seems that the preservation of truth is undermined.

## DIVINE GATEKEEPERS

### WHO ARE THE GATEKEEPERS?

Practical gatekeeping primarily takes the form of the human agent, usually coven leaders, acting in the physical world—just like the High Priestess of the tarot is both Guardian and Revealer of the Mysteries hidden behind the veil. The human aspect is not the only form of gatekeeping that comes into play: the Divine Gatekeepers must also be acknowledged, as they play such a prominent role in spirituality and religion from all over the world. Whether explicit or implicit, the gods (or honoured spirits) have held a prominent place in traditional practices as gatekeepers and form some of the most loved and respected bands of powers, both in the classic era and today.

Most gatekeeping powers are honoured first in their rites, as they need to be addressed before other powers can be brought forward. In this sense, the gatekeeper is literally controlling access to the wider "pantheon" of the tradition and, therefore, acts as a gatekeeper for the religion or system as a whole. Those who follow these traditions are usually on more regular speaking terms with these powers than any other. This is due to the fact that they are the ones who need to respect human practitioners the most. Otherwise, they will simply keep the gates barred to them and effectively shut them out of the tradition, cutting them off from its Mysteries.

Within Witchcraft, the gods are the most apparent gatekeepers. They choose with whom they wish to work and build connections via our rites. Although we can reach out to any of the many gods and goddesses that we choose, they do not have to respond. In fact, they usually don't. When a deity chooses you, you do not have to respond, but it is usually advisable as they will make their presence felt. If a deity approaches you and you are not comfortable with them or their demands, then politely explain and either end the connection or negotiate the nature of the relationship. Within a tradition, this is slightly different. The gods of that tradition are firmly predetermined and there is usually little flexibility in what they expect from their initiated priesthood.

The gods are not the only ones who gatekeep within the Craft. The spirits that gather at the edge of the Circle, the powers of the four directions, and sometimes the spirits who walk with members of the coven can also work in this capacity. An example of a gatekeeping spirit can be found in a footnote in Stewart Farrar's *What Witches Do*, where additions to the invocations of the watchtowers are given.[161] Two examples are given here, one for the North and one for the West:

> *"... to the north, 'Boreas, thou gardian [sic] of the northern portal, open the gate that the powerful God and gentle Goddess may enter in'—a favourite of Alex's."*

And:

> *"This summoning, too, is flexible. For example, to the west may be added 'Lords of the realm of death and of initiation.'"*

In these two examples, it is clearly demonstrated that Boreas is opening a gate, allowing the coven deities to enter the Circle. He is quite literally a gatekeeper in every sense of the word. In the second example, the gatekeeping is more subtle. As Lords of Death and Initia-

---

161  Stewart Farrar, *What Witches Do*, (David & Charles fw media, 2012), Loc. 4722, Kindle.

tion, these spirits are controlling such forces. Initiation and death hold a common thread—both require a call and an acceptance. What else is that if not gatekeeping?

What follows are some examples of gatekeepers from around the world. The list is in no way complete regarding the categories that each Divine Gatekeeper is listed under, nor are the categories, in themselves, complete with every culture's gatekeepers. These are merely illustrative of the divine powers and honoured spirits that can be found most frequently (as well as some which are a little more obscure).

## GREEK

### Aphrodite

As previously discussed, Aphrodite is a goddess who blurs boundaries, yet despite her apparent freedom from limitations, she does hold a gatekeeping quality. As the goddess whom the Romans would give sacrifice to before battles, Aphrodite is a goddess of death; the goddess in control of the threshold between the worlds and a guardian of the veil that stands between them.[162]

### Dionysus

Dionysus, like most gatekeeper gods, crosses freely over boundaries that appear to separate things in the world. *He* is sometimes *she*, a local (yet also foreign) ruler of death, and a bringer of life. The gate that Dionysus is most frequently considered patron of is the Internal Gate to Ecstasy. As Dionysus Psilax (who gives men's minds wings), Dionysus is opening the doorway within the human body to allow the spirit, or mind, to enter an ecstatic state, thus experiencing direct exposure of the Mysteries.[163] Dionysus gatekeeps in this capacity by regulating the difference between what is *toxic* and what is *ecstatic* intoxication.

---

162 Bettany Hughes, *Venus Uncovered: Ancient Goddess of Love*, Produced by: Sandstone Global Productions Ltd, First aired on BBC Four: November 15, 2017.

163 Bettany Hughes, *Bacchus Uncovered: Ancient God of Ecstasy*, Produced by: Sandstone Global Productions Ltd, First aired on BBC Four: April 11 2018.

## Hecate

Hecate is a goddess of Witchcraft whose popularity has risen in recent years and has prominent gatekeeping qualities. As a goddess of the crossroads and thresholds, as well as the holder of the keys to the various realms or worlds, she is the ultimate authority when it comes to free movement across boundaries.

## Hermes

As the messenger of the gods, Hermes represents the movement between worlds and carries the prayers of humans up to the ears of those petitioned. In this respect, if Hermes, as a member of a magical system's pantheon, were to be offended, he could bar access to free communication with the gods completely.

### ROMAN

### Cardea, Forculus, and Limentinus

Cardea (Goddess of Hinges), Forculus (God of Doors), and Limentinus (God of Thresholds) are a unique trinity of gods who ensure the proper function of their respective roles and thereby ensure physical safety and protection. Gatekeeping against home invaders definitely fits into their agenda.

St. Augustine attacked this belief in a divine trinity, rather ironically, in an attempt to promote the power of the Christian God:

> *"Evidently, Forculus can't watch the hinge and the threshold at the same time."*[164]

Cardea, as a lover of Janus (introduced later), was given powers to guard against malevolent magic being worked upon a household—especially when directed towards children—which suggests that this

---

164   Maijastina Kahlos, *Debate and Dialogue: Christian and Pagan Cultures c. 360—430*, (Ashgate, 2007), 139.

trinity of deities held powers between them that watched over more than just the physical entryways of a space.[165]

## Janus

*Janus*, whose name literally means "gate," is responsible for many gatekeeping roles within the Roman pantheon. Although, in our modern community, he is remembered for ruling over the threshold between one year and the next. This is preserved in the first month of the year, January, having been named after him. Janus does, however, have more impact than most would realise regarding gatekeeping, and his role affects both gods and men.

Ovid wrote in his classical work, *Fasti:*

> *"Why Janus,' I asked next, 'though I worship the power of other divinities, do I first offer incense and wine to you?*
>
> *'So that through me' says he, 'the guardian of the threshold, you can have access to whichever gods you want.'"*[166]

## Portunes

God of keys and ports who was conflated with—or considered to be a manifestation of—Janus.

## Terminus

A god who protects the physical boundaries of a place. Worship to him was given with sacrifice at the boundary stones of a place to ensure protection from invasion.[167]

---

165 Kathleen N. Daly, Marian Rengel, *Greek and Roman Mythology, A to Z*, (Infobase Publishing, 2009), 31.

166 Ovid, *Fasti*, (OUP Oxford, 2013) n.p.

167 Ibid.

## VODOU

### Baron Samedi and Maman Brigitte

As father and mother of the Gédé (the dead), respectively, these two Lwa (spirits) are gatekeepers of the cemeteries and the realms of the dead. If contact with an ancestor is needed, then it is the Baron who is called to open the way to that deceased spirit. Without his blessing, contact cannot be made. It is also held that if the Baron refuses to "dig the grave" of a person then they will not die, even if they are on the brink of death.

Likewise, Maman Brigitte, the wife of the Baron, is called upon to help those in need, usually children, from a serious illness. As the mother of the dead, she has great influence over who enters the realm of the dead and when. This can be by her own power or by persuading her husband not to dig the person's grave.[168]

### Legba

Papa Legba is far from the caricature featured in *American Horror Story*. He is the recognised gatekeeper of the Vodou Religion, for, without his permission, no Lwa can be present at a Vodou ritual. Legba is a gatekeeper in the truest sense of the word: the activity of controlling, and usually limiting, general access to something.[169] In this instance, that something is the Lwa.[170]

### Kalfou

Literally meaning "crossroads," Kalfou is seen as the "darker" aspect of Legba. Kalfou is viewed as Legba's opposite: if Legba stands for order, then Kalfou is chaos. Although this aspect of the Lwa is responsible for opening the way to more malevolent forces when

---

168   Shannon R. Turlington, *The complete idiot's guide to Voodoo*, (Alpha Books, 2002), 97-99.

169   Oxford University Press (OUP), "Gatekeeping", Accessed Jan 13, 2020, https://www.lexico.com/definition/gatekeeping

170   Shannon R. Turlington, *The complete idiot's guide to Voodoo* (Alpha Books, 2002), 85.

called upon by practitioners who work with curses, this is not the only work Kalfou offers his blessings to.

For those practitioners who wish to protect others from curses or spiritual harm, Kalfou offers them a "closing of the door." In this role, those harmful forces that he lets loose can be restrained if approaching someone who has been placed under his protection. Kalfou can be perceived, therefore, as a useful ally to practitioners regardless of the intentions of their work.[171]

## Lebat

Serving a similar function to Papa Legba, this Lwa found his way into New Orleans Voodoo in a rather unconventional way. In the gatekeeping sense that most think of today, the missionary Father Jean Baptiste Lebat was responsible for trying to stamp out the practice of Voodoo in the seventeenth and eighteenth centuries. Despite his role in life, Voodoo sees the spirit world as being from the other side of a mirror, therefore the disruptor of Voodoo rituals is now petitioned as a doorman who opens the ways and keeps out those who would disrupt the rites.[172]

## EUROPEAN

## Arianrhod

An unusual divine gatekeeper, Arianrhod takes on the role of stating who *is* and who *is not*; who *can* and who *cannot*. At the birth of her son, she vowed that he shall have no name, bear no arms (weapons), nor have a wife of a race that is on Earth without her permission. Here she keeps initiatory experiences and important life phases from being obtained.[173] Her name, which is Welsh for *Silver Wheel* (*arian* meaning "silver" and *rhod* meaning "wheel"), is believed to derive

---

171  Ibid. 86.

172  Lilith Dorsey, *Voodoo and Afro-Caribbean Paganism*, (Citadel Press Books, 2005), 61-62, 197.

173  Michelle Skye, *Goddess Afoot!: Practicing Magic with Celtic & Norse Goddesses*, (Llewellyn Worldwide, 2008), 24-28.

from the constellation *Northern Crown* (Corona Borealis) which, in Welsh, shares the name of her palace, *Caer Arainrhod.*[174]

## Lleu Llaw Gyffes

Lleu Llaw Gyffes, the cursed son of Arianrhod, was able to overcome his mother's three curses, however, her influence made him a liminal figure that is worth its own entry. From the gatekeeping of his mother, Lleu was left in a state between all boundaries and thus could not be killed by conventional means.

> *"He cannot be killed inside a house, nor outside one, on horseback, or on foot. Blodeuwedd tricks him into revealing that [he] can be killed only by a spear which must be a year in the making, but he must be standing with one foot on a trough built on the side of a river with a roof over it, with the other foot on the back of a billy goat."*[175]

From being cursed, he has become a gatekeeper in his own right and acts as a guardian of all that lies betwixt and between worlds. Lleu can also be called upon to help overcome any obstacles that you may encounter.

## Brigantia

Throughout the UK and Ireland, this goddess is known by a variety of names including Bride, Brede, and Brigit. With a repeated theme that is found with such divine beings, Brigantia is no exception when it comes to crossing boundaries. Primarily a goddess dedicated to sacred wells (wherever a variation of her name is known), she is also Goddess of the Fires of the Forge.

As a gatekeeper, she is the goddess who oversees the role of the priesthood and is therefore the exclusive authority to operate within

---

174 James MacKillop, *Oxford Dictonary of Celtic Mythology*, (Oxford University Press, 2004), 24.

175 BBC: Welsh history, "Mabinogion: fourth branch", Accessed Jan 22 2020. https://www.bbc.co.uk/wales/history/sites/themes/society/myths_mabinogion_04.shtml

aspects of the sacred. So important was her position as gatekeeper to the priestly office that when Christianity took dominance in Ireland, she was made into a Saint who gave patronage to the Christian priesthood.[176] Later, the Saint that she would become would be known as a *Bishop of the Church*. This begins a shift that implies that her authority within the priesthood comes from the Church and sets a precedence for a shift of who gatekeeps the priesthood; a shift from the Goddess to their own God.[177] It would seem that this was a power move, enacted to ensure that the locals would accept the new priests as legitimate. Without it, they would not have been accepted as having the authority to replace the pre-existing caste.

## Cernunnos

Similar to the Baron in Vodou, Cernunnos is the keeper of the doorway between the land of the living and that of the dead. It is for this reason that he is attributed with qualities of divination via seeing beyond the veil and communing with spirits in the ancient world. He is also heavily attributed to healing powers. This makes sense, as the one who controls life and death can show favour and give newfound life to those who seek his blessings.[178]

## CALLING THE GATEKEEPERS

The following ritual is something that can be used by anyone but is specifically designed for those who are new to the Craft. Many times, I have seen people asking for advice on which path they should explore, with questions usually along the lines of "Hi, I'm new and not sure what type of witch I am. I am drawn to X, Y, and Z. What should I be looking at? What should I be practising?" People will

---

176  Patrick Weston Joyce. *A Smaller Social History of Ancient Ireland,* (Longmans, Green and Company, 1906).

177  Gary Macy, *The Hidden History of Women's Ordination: Female Clergy in the Medieval West,* (Oxford University Press, 2012), 87.

178  Janet Farrar and Gavin Bone, *Lifting the Veil: A Witches' Guide to Trance-Prophecy, Drawing Down the Moon, and Ecstatic Ritual* (Acorn Guild Press, 2016), 95; Craig Spencer, Aradia (Llewellyn Worldwide, 2020), 214-216.

often respond, all with the best of intentions, with a definite answer. Usually, the seeker thanks them and then goes off to learn everything they can about that one suggestion.

Is this actually the right path for them? How are we to know? The answer is that we're not!

Following is a simple ritual used to call upon the various Divine Gatekeepers, asking them to guide the serious seeker to the tradition, practice, or form of magical work that is best for them. By having a gatekeeping spirit open the way, the seeker will be able to receive signs, guidance, and be given the confidence that they are where they are supposed to be. Although this ritual names specific Divine Gatekeepers, the working itself will only bring you into contact with the spirit (or spirits) that are aligned with your best interests, both spiritually and physically. Be open to any possibility, as we don't decide who presents the path. We only get to decide whether we are willing to walk the path that has been made available to us.

## THE RITUAL

You will need:
- Wand
- Altar
- White cloth
- Bowl
- An offering of your choice for the spirits: Alcohol such as rum or vodka works well, as will sweets or anything considered "bad" for you.

Prepare a sacred space and a simple altar in your own preferred manner. If you are very new and do not have a preferred method, then set up a simple altar on a small table or another clear and convenient surface, if that is all that is available. Cover this altar surface with a simple white cloth. If you are stuck for getting hold of a cloth, then postponing the ritual would be ideal; however, if you wish to proceed, a white pillow case will work.

Clear the space that will be used to form the Circle of any clutter and unnecessary items. If possible, move furniture and other items to create a clear working space. Once the space is cleared, place the working altar facing North in the centre of what will form the Circle's bounds.

*Note about facing: I'm frequently asked what "altar facing a direction" means, so let me add this note for clarity. When an altar is described as facing a direction, it means that when you are in front of your altar, you are facing that direction while your back faces the opposite direction. In this case, you will be on the South-facing side of the altar with your back to the South. When you look over your altar, you will be facing North.*

If you already have an altar set up, you can use this for the ritual but be mindful to keep it stripped back to its most basic form. The guidance of the Divine Gatekeepers may require changing the altar anyway. If you don't have a preferred method for conjuring the Circle, you can use the steps provided here.

### 1. CONJURE THE CIRCLE AND CALL THE ELEMENTAL GUARDIANS.

Take your wand and starting in the East, move clockwise in the Northern Hemisphere (or anti-clockwise in the Southern Hemisphere) and begin conjuring the Circle. As you walk the perimeter, take your time, and focus on the action that you are carrying out. Where your wand is directed, visualise a blue flame forming the boundary of the Circle on the ground. If you are concerned that your visualisation is not strong, don't worry. Take a moment to recall a memory, any memory at all. How did you "see" the playback of this event? Use that as the starting point for how your mind recalls images, and instead of recalling something already seen, use those mental processes to create an image that you want to "see." Remember, the seeing does not have to be exceedingly "real" in the sense that you are almost hallucinating. You should be simultaneously aware of the image you wish to project and the actual scene (which isn't catching on fire at all) that you are literally seeing with your eyes. It takes practice to focus on both but have faith and it will pay off in the long term.

While taking your time and "seeing" the blue fire form the Circle, speak the words:

*"I conjure now the Circle round,*
*Between the worlds, it shall be bound,*
*A meeting place of love and peace,*
*The power raised and then released.*
*My sacred space: sealed, protected,*
*To work the rite I have selected,*
*Forged of Mighty Astral flames,*
*Hallowed by the Sacred Names:*
*[Deity names here]."*

Once you have returned to the East, completing the conjuration of the Circle, it is time to call upon the power of the elements. The powers called upon here are actually the Elemental Guardians, not the raw power of the elements themselves. The job of the Elemental Guardians is to regulate the flow of power from the element to the Circle so that it is balanced and usable to those working within it. Just as a transformer steps down electrical power from the main grid before flowing it into your home, so too do the Elemental Guardians step down the elemental power before flowing it into the Circle—so that we don't get fried.

As it is the Guardian that is being called, they should be specifically visualised at each direction with something behind them representing the elemental power that they guard. You are free to use whatever visual imagery you like. Following is a list of examples of imagery that you may use:

**Angels:**
- East with Raphael
- South with Michael
- West with Gabriel
- North with Uriel

**Elemental Beings:**
The Guardian may appear as a "person" or being made out of the element that they Guard.

- East with Air
- South with Fire
- West with Water
- North with Earth

**Devoted Spirits:**
They may appear as unnamed and unknowable robed and hooded human-like silhouettes, representing Inner Contacts who are dedicated to the work of that direction and its power. Robes will be in various colours, such as:

- East in Black
- South in Red
- West in White
- North in Grey

Do not forget to visualise the elemental power behind them, such as:

- **East:** a tornado or windswept trees.
- **South:** a wall of fire or a desert with visible heatwave.
- **West:** a waterfall or the Guardian standing before a well.
- **North:** the Guardian standing on a rocky space, mountain, or fertile field.

*Note about directions: The examples given here are for the Northern Hemisphere. Please remember that in the southern hemisphere, the North and South examples will be reversed, but the East and West examples will remain the same.*

## The Call:

Whatever visual you use for the contact is fine. Select one before you begin and stick with it, though don't be surprised if you find the image changes from your initial plan. This can be a result of the contact responding and causing a psychic insight that is more in tune with their nature. If this happens, use this visual in the future and it will act as a direct line of communication to the Guardian itself.

Focus on your visual and take a brief moment to feel your desire to establish contact with the Guardian of that direction. Once you have this feeling and while holding the visual, draw the corresponding pentagram with your wand.

| FIRE | WATER | AIR | EARTH |

When you have finished, point at the centre of the pentagram to project your inner call and visualisation to the direction and speak:

*"Guardian of the East and the powers of Air, I call you forth to empower this Circle and witness my rite of the Divine Gatekeepers."*

Repeat the call in like fashion for the remaining directions, moving clockwise in the Northern Hemisphere (NH), or anti-clockwise in the Southern Hemisphere (SH):

*"Guardian of the South (NH)/North (SH) and the powers of Fire, I call you forth to empower this Circle and witness my rite of the Divine Gatekeepers."*

*"Guardian of the West and the powers of Water, I call you forth to empower this Circle and witness my rite of the Divine Gatekeepers."*

*"Guardian of the North (NH)/South (SH) and the powers of Earth, I call you forth to empower this Circle and witness my rite of the Divine Gatekeepers."*

Once you have completed all the relevant calls, walk the Circle three times (in the appropriate direction for your hemisphere) to stir up the power and make it ready for use in the ritual.

## 2. CALL THE GATEKEEPERS

Lift your offering with both hands above the altar—either your usual space or your simple for-this-moment version—and say:

> *"I come before this altar to commune with the Divine Gatekeeper who guards the way to the path that is calling to me. I call back in reply so that I may seek guidance and offer this (chosen offering) with honour and respect."*

Place the offering onto your altar and take a moment to breathe, allowing your mind to slow down and prepare for the next part of the ritual.

If you are new to ritual, calling to such a powerful being can be exciting or cause some nerves. This is fine, it's not too different from when you go for an interview. You want to be received well and want to make a positive first impression. It's only natural, just take the time you need to steady yourself before progressing.

When you are ready, get yourself into a comfortable sitting position. Take up your instrument—or just clap a steady rhythm—and begin to chant. You may want to read this chant over first to find the natural rhythm within it before you start the ritual.

> *"I call upon the Gatekeepers to come this day,*
> *Guide and enlighten me on my way.*
> *I call upon the Gatekeepers to open the door,*
> *Show me what I need to know.*
>
> *Legba, Maman, Baron Samedhi,*
> *Dionysus, Mercury, Aphrodite,*
> *Lugh, and Cernunnos, Arianrhod,*
> *Goddess of the Crossroads and All-seeing God.*

*I call upon the Gatekeepers, one and all,*
*Hear my words, to you I call.*
*Open my mind and help me see,*
*The way to the path that is right for me."*

Repeat the last two lines three more times, then follow back by chanting the names of the Divine Gatekeepers through to the end. Now close your eyes and repeat the final line *"The way to the path that is right for me,"* playing with the rhythm and tempo until the words start to blur into one another. When you notice that you have started to feel relaxed by the rhythm, allow your voice and instrument (or clapping hands) to fall silent.

Be still in the silence and allow yourself to experience whatever is necessary. Once you feel your experience is over, write everything down in your journal, no matter how minor or irrelevant a detail may seem. Record as much as you possibly can about this ritual experience, then put it away for at least three days before reading it back. This allows you enough distance from the experience so that you can return to it with fresh eyes. You may want to record any dreams that you have over the next three days, as these could also hold clues that you would have otherwise missed.

### 3. CLOSE THE RITUAL

To close the ritual, go to your altar and place both hands on its surface on either side of the offering and say:

*"I give thanks to the Divine Gatekeeper for hearing my call and*
*sharing this space with me. I am open to your guidance and all that*
*you have to show to me."*

Bow your head briefly at the altar, then banish the Circle:
Starting in the East and working in the opposite direction from the way the Circle was conjured, use your wand to banish the Circle.

## Thank the Elemental Guardians:

*"I give my thanks to the Guardian of the East and the powers of Air for answering my call to empower this Circle and witness my rite of the Divine Gatekeepers. I now release you with gratitude and respect."*

| FIRE | WATER | AIR | EARTH |

Draw the relevant pentagram and point to its centre while taking a moment to project your thanks, gratitude, and respect.

Repeat in like fashion for the remaining directions:

*"I give my thanks to the Guardian of the North (NH)/South (SH) and the powers of Earth for answering my call to empower this Circle and witness my rite of the Divine Gatekeepers. I now release you with gratitude and respect."*

*"I give my thanks to the Guardian of the West and the powers of Water for answering my call to empower this Circle and witness my rite of the Divine Gatekeepers. I now release you with gratitude and respect."*

*"I give my thanks to the Guardian of the South (NH)/North (SH) and the powers of Fire, for answering my call to empower this Circle and witness my rite of the Divine Gatekeepers. I now release you with gratitude and respect."*

## Banish the Circle:

Continue by walking the boundary of the Circle, visualising the fire that forms it disappearing as you pass over it with your wand:

*"I banish now the Circle round,*
*Between the worlds no longer bound,*
*This meeting place of love and peace,*
*With due respect, I now release.*
*Extinguished are your boundaries flames*
*By the hallowed sacred names [names here]."*

Go about your day remaining passively open to any further experiences that you may have. Again, it is best to record these without initial analysis and contemplate them again at another time. Leave the offering on the altar for a couple of hours before disposal.

CHAPTER EIGHT

# THE WITCHES' QABALAH

**The** history of the Qabalah in British occultism is very old, and for many, it has become deeply rooted in the fabric of British Craft. Owing its origins to more distant lands, there are some people in Britain who feel that this wisdom does not have a place in the Craft at all. Much of this comes from people referencing different *forms* of the system. In this chapter, we will discuss the different forms that this system has taken over the centuries and how Kabbalah and Qabalah are very different things. Discussion on the subject of the Qabalah within the Craft has always been controversial. There are those who fully embrace its presence as a system of spiritual development and personal growth, usually known as the *Greater Mysteries*. Others feel that the presence of any form of Kabbalistic philosophy within the Craft is a watering down of the "pure" witches' Craft.

Regardless of your stance on the subject, this chapter has been included to acknowledge and explore the legitimate historical ties between Qabalah and Witchcraft in Britain; a tie that still subtly influences its practice and those that have evolved from it to this day. In no way is the intent of this section to change people's minds about their personal position. It is intended as a presentation of the material as-is, allowing you to come to your own decision of whether this system has a useful place within *your* Craft practices.

## DIFFERING FORMS

Kabbalah, Cabala, Qabalah; all pronounced exactly the same but each representing distinct systems and forms. Literally meaning "that which is revealed,"each system represents a development of these revelations over time.[179] Although their origins lie in Jewish mysticism, the natural development of its forms led to revelations that became foundational to many non-Jewish people as well. Understanding the evolution of each is important if any sensible conversation is to be had on the subject, especially in relation to the Craft. So, what are the differences? Below you will find, in brief, a breakdown of the three core branches of kabbalah and its sub-branches as they were formed and developed over time.

### JUDAIC KABBALAH

This branch exists in two distinct forms:

**Kabbalah:** The original philosophies of the Jewish people, influenced by the sacred text, the *Zohar.* The Kabbalah teaches Jewish mysticism in respect to the Jewish people's relationship with their god. Later becoming known as *Classic Kabbalah,* this form is the oldest known system.[180]

**Lurianic Kabbalah:** Evolving out of Classic Kabbalah came this interpretation of the core teachings as proposed by Rabbi Isaac Luria. The principles of Lurianic Kabbalah have formed the foundation for all major branches of Kabbalistic mysticism that exist today. For this reason, Lurianic Kabbalah is considered by the largest part of the Jewish community worldwide as representing the truest interpretations of the *Zohar.*[181]

---

179   Rabbi Ted Falcon, Ph.D. and David Blatner, *Judaism for Dummies 2nd Edition,* (New Jersey: John Wiley & Sons, Inc. 2013), 70.

180   Arthur Kurzweil, *Kabbalah for Dummies,* (New Jersey: John Wiley & Sons, Inc. 2007), 23, 42.

181   George Robinson, *Essential Judaism: A Complete Guide to Beliefs, Customs & Rituals,* (Simon and Schuster, 2016) Quoted at: https://www.myjewishlearning.com/article/isaac-luria-kabbalah-in-safed/ accessed: 29 June 2020.

## Cabala

The Cabala is a later development of Judaic Kabbalah as understood by Christians, incorporating their philosophies concerning Jesus.[182] If *Judaic Kabbalah* demonstrates the Jewish relationship with God, then *Cabala* can be seen as a Christian understanding of their relationship with the Holy Trinity.

## Qabalah

This branch exists in two distinct forms:

**Hermetic Qabalah:** Developing out of Judaic Kabbalah, this form of Qabalistic teaching and philosophy was highly syncretic, blending many cultures and philosophies together. The strongest syncretic influences came from Paganism and Neoplatonism, stressing that humanity and divinity were not separate—a concept based on monotheistic thinking.[183] The philosophy surrounding the Sefirot [184] (spheres) of the Tree of Life also changed. The limitless light passed through three key stages prior to creation and the Sefirot, previously believed to be ways of understanding God, became the result of this light becoming differentiated and manifest.[185]

**English Qabalah:** First mentioned in writing in 1899 as *English Cabala*, this branch represents an evolution of Hermetic Qabalah which better reflected the occult traditions found in Britain.[186] It would seem that although Hermetic Qabalah was popular, its all-inclusive syncretic nature meant that it had become cluttered. We don't like

---

182   Ibid. 71.

183   Dion Fortune, *The Mystical Qabalah*, (Aquarian Press, 1987), 37-42.

184   This word is spelled "Sephirot" when used in reference to the Qabalah but spelled "Sefirot" in use with the Kabbalah. For consistency, the spelling "Sefirot" will be used throughout this book.

185   Dion Fortune, *The Mystical Qabalah,* (Aquarian Press, 1987), 29-36; Israel Regardie, The Golden Dawn, (Llewellyn, 2000), 51.

186   Willis F. Whitehead, *The Mystic Thesaurus,* (Chicago: Willis F. Whitehead, 1899) 62-63.

clutter over here (take it from a Brit). The logical development would then be to refine that system, making it more practical.

There is no universal form of English Qabalah. It is popular in a number of occult practices, but different traditions teach different versions.[187] Aleister Crowley would later contribute to this growing form of Qabalistic knowledge with his *Book of the Law* and *Liber 777*, amongst other works.[188]

Many mistake this branch of Qabalah as a form of English *gematria* (basically an alphanumerical-based system). However, English gematria was developed independently of English Qabalah by Michael Stifel in 1532 and does not represent a system of English Qabalah (though the two may be used together).[189]

Having looked at the different forms of Kabbalistic philosophy, the question still remains: What has any of it got to do with Witchcraft? The answer is simple!

In the Middle Ages, Britain was well aware of the concept of Witchcraft. Much archaeological evidence can be found throughout Britain—and England, in particular—of the Qabalah being present within the philosophy and practices of Witchcraft during that time.[190] It would, therefore, appear to be the case that English Qabalah owes its core origins to the practitioners of this time period. Blending local Paganism, Lurianic Kabbalah, and aspects of Hermetic philosophy together creates a truly perfect combination of ideology and tradition for British Craft.

As previously stated, British Craft evolved differently from the rest of European Craft, making its practical application a unique strand of occult philosophy. The most popularly used form of Qabalah found in Witchcraft today (the 60s onward) owes much to that

---

187   Nema, *Maat Magick: A Guide to Self-Initiation,* (York Beach: Weiser, 1995) 24-25.

188   Aleister Crowley ed. Israel Regardie, *777 & other Qabalistic Writings of Aleister Crowley,* (York Beach: Weiser, 1993)

189   Underwood Dudley, *Numerology, Or, What Pythagoras Wrought,* (Cambridge: Cambridge University Press, 1997), 50.

190   Clive Anderson & Mary-Ann Ochota, *Mystic Britain: Witches and Demons,* (Smithsonian Channel), Originally aired 23 April 2019.

created by Aleister Crowley. This can prove problematic as Crowley was a Ceremonial Magician, not a witch. As the philosophies of Ceremonial Magick and Witchcraft are fundamentally different, it stands to reason that the application of Qabalistic knowledge would also be different. Within British Craft, the main expression of this knowledge comes in the form of the training process, usually performed via a system of initiation that the witch goes through to deeply connect with their chosen path.

## THE RELATIONSHIP BETWEEN QABALAH AND INITIATION

The Tree of Life in this branch of English Qabalah also reflects the system of initiation. Within the Craft, three symbols have become prominent representations of levels or stages of training: the inverted triangle, the inverted pentagram, and the crowned pentagram. Each symbol is marked out on the Tree of Life, therefore representing a stage or level of the Tree as it is "climbed" by the initiate.

The first symbol, the inverted triangle, not only represents the knowledge and skills developed during training, but also the old occult motto "*know thyself.*" It is at this initial stage that the initiate, or any new witch, learns to interact with the natural forces around them in order to work magic. The witch, by engaging with these forces, gains a better understanding of their place *within* those forces, thus better understanding themselves.

The second symbol, the inverted pentagram also represents knowledge and skills developed, as well as the occult motto "*nothing in excess.*" As mentioned in the previous chapter, the level of the inverted pentagram acts as the great equaliser because it forces you to do the work. Today, the work mentioned here is most commonly referred to as *Shadow Work*. There have been many greats among the ranks of Ceremonialists, but they often share the same flaw: they go mad. This is the mistake so often made by Ceremonial Magicians. Initiation, when forced, can be literally maddening to the individual. *Forced* is used here to mean that there is resistance to the unfolding process, either from the Inner planes or from the individual themselves. Too many Magicians seek that level of Ipsissimus (utmost self-ness) where they believe that they can become like the gods.

While the Ceremonial Magician seeks to stay at the heights of the Tree, the witch knows better. Following the climb to the top, a secret pathway is revealed known as the *Path of Return*, which leads down to the bottom of the Tree once again. This is not the same as climbing back down; it is an entirely new pathway that must be followed to anchor us and prevent delusions of grandeur from setting in. The process of following this Path of Return reflects the myth of Prometheus stealing fire from the heavens. The gods feared what humanity could do with this heavenly fire and punished Prometheus for retrieving it for us.

Within the witches' training, this same process occurs. We climb to touch the infinite but must remain mindful that if we truly seek to use it for our benefit, then we must carry it back to our community. From there, we can show others the way of finding that knowledge and power for themselves. Some Ceremonial Magicians, seek to stay with the fire and become one with it. They find that they are instead consumed by its power, and it is here that the maddening effect of the initiate's journey occurs.

## THE WITCHES' QABALAH

As will be discussed shortly, the Craft Revival movement was clearly founded on the form of English Qabalah as seen in the Middle Ages. This is most strongly apparent due to the use of Lurianic Kabbalah as opposed to Classic Kabbalah at the core of its symbolism.[191] The only "flaw" with this method, however, is that its pattern of interaction between the God and Goddess is not balanced. As a system that has its origins in a patriarchal monotheistic faith, this is hardly surprising. As Witchcraft respects the Divine Feminine as equal to the Divine Masculine, this section will discuss reversing the Tree to produce a Witches' Qabalah that works for our various streams of practices and traditions today. This reversal is quite common in initiatory British occult traditions (though not all of them) in order to balance the two polar aspects of divinity. Some aspects of the lore as presented below are also revised. It should

---

191   Ibid.

be understood that the information that follows is only an overview. Although it will hint at some deeper teachings that are found within some Initiatory Craft lines, it must not be considered a representation of the complete lore that is found within these practices.

## THE WITCHES' TREE

### The Material World

### Malkuth
### *(Kingdom)*

**Spiritual action:** Magic in action, the Powers of Nature harnessed to shape Creation.
**Spiritual experience:** The experience of faith.
**Symbol or tool:** The altar.

This is the world in which we live out our day-to-day lives; the place of our usual interactions and what we most readily think of as home. Although all parts of the Tree are equally important, this level is often overlooked by occultists because it is the level of the Tree where we all coexist—occultist and non-occultist alike.

Within the context of magic, this level is where the power of magic becomes action. When the forces of Nature are employed to give shape and substance (life), the power is grounded into Creation, making the desire manifest. Without this level being engaged, the magic simply would not work. Too often, we hear the phrase, "You are a spirit having a human experience." This has always felt like an early Christian sentiment. The idea of the human (or earthly manifestation) not truly being part of ourselves and showing favour to the soul just screams of early teachings about rejecting the natural world as evil. This type of philosophy has no place in Witchcraft.

On the witches' journey, this is the starting point, the level that everyone has reached by virtue of being born. From here, we can look at the Tree and see the various levels that we need to climb. The Material World is, therefore, our place of personal perspective, and like the Fool in the tarot, we must take a leap of faith for personal progress to develop.

## The Inverted Triangle—Know Thyself

### Yesod
*(Foundation)*

**Spiritual action:** Astral counterpart to Malkuth, place of the Divine Covenant.
**Spiritual experience:** The Four Powers, the Mystery of Initiation.
**Symbol or tool:** Incense.

This level of the Tree can be best interpreted as the etheric or astral double of the Material World. It is on this level that the spiritual aspect of every physical thing in existence resides and is the place where our personal power (magic) is housed and generated. Although it is often easier to think of our power as being within our body, these two concepts are not contradictory. The power *is* within your own body, but the body in which it is held is the astral counterpart to the physical body. Our ability to move an object on Earth is based upon the power (or strength) of our physical body. Our magical power, on the other hand, is based upon the power or strength of our spiritual muscles—the power of our soul.

### Hod
*(Splendour)*

**Spiritual action:** Giving direction to power, the true essence of magic.
**Spiritual experience:** Working the magic.
**Symbol or tool:** Names and words of power.

Hod is the Sefira of all magical workings where the natural forces provided by Netzach (the following Sefira) are taken to ensoul the thought forms created here. As the sphere of intellect and thought, it is the teaching of this level that provides the focus necessary to give magical power direction and purpose. In short, without a focused image for the power to flow into (ensoul), the power remains directionless and without purpose like a battery disconnected from an appliance.

## Netzach
### *(Endurance)*

SPIRITUAL ACTION: The drive and determination to attain your goal.
SPIRITUAL EXPERIENCE: Raising the power.
SYMBOL OR TOOL: Candles, lanterns, or a cauldron.

The emotional heart space of the Tree and the seat of the witch's will-power. The magical discipline of Netzach is to harness the power of our emotions as fuel for our magical work. By using focused emotion within your spell-work, you will find that the forces of Nature become far more compliant or sympathetic to your needs and desires. Taking advantage of this source of power provides the perfect circumstances for successful magic to occur.

### INTERACTION

Sometimes referred to as *The Triangle of Magic*, these three Sefirot teach the new witch the foundational processes necessary for the successful practise of magic. In brief, all magical applications can be broken down into a simple formula: *Heart + Mind + Spirit = Magical results.*

All spells start with an emotional drive, not a rational one. A healing spell starts with the feeling of love or compassion while a protection spell begins with anxiety or fear of danger. Likewise, a curse begins with anger, rage, or a sense of vengeance. All magic has its origin in emotion. Following the initial emotional drive, that impulse needs somewhere to go. Without direction, that emotion has no magical purpose. This can be as simple as holding a mental picture that represents the end result of your desire in either a literal or symbolic sense.

The final step is to unite the Heart and Mind with the essence of Spirit to complete the Triangle of Magic. The Spirit mentioned in this formula is the expression of your own personal power via a symbolic action. This could be anything as simple as lighting a candle to something more ritualised. The important thing is that the action should make you feel powerful; in fact, it should be an expression of the power that you feel within yourself.

By holding a mental focus (image) into which you pour your emotions and expressing them in the outer world via the language of spirit (symbolism), you are ensuring that your Heart, Mind, and Spirit are joined together as a single, focused unit. Returning to our simple formula: *Heart + Mind + Spirit = Magical results,* we are better able to see the teaching of the lowest three Sefirot. When thought and feeling are united in action, our personal power has a mechanism that allows the power to flow and manifest itself in the physical world.

It is for these reasons that the first teaching, the teaching of the Inverted Triangle, is to *know thyself.* Magic within Witchcraft requires the ability of each individual to understand and utilise their emotions, thoughts, and the very essence of their being. It is only when this level of self-knowledge is achieved that true magic is attained; for the first thing that magic changes is the self.

## THE INVERTED PENTAGRAM—NOTHING IN EXCESS

### Tiphareth
*(Beauty)*

SPIRITUAL ACTION: Doorway to the Mysteries, Guardian of the Mysteries, The Great Equaliser, Connection to all Sefirot/Mysteries.
SPIRITUAL EXPERIENCE: The Mystery of Love.
SYMBOL OR TOOL: Necklace/pendant.

Here is the place of the Divine Gatekeeper or the Guardian of the Mysteries, for it is at this level of the Tree that the initiatory attribute of the Great Equaliser is found. Regardless of how a witch gets to this stage, the process is much the same: the inner work (which is commonly referred to today as *Shadow Work*) is initiated.

The Guardian of the Mysteries will not allow anyone to be brought or pass beyond the Veil of the Mysteries if they are unprepared for what lies ahead. In many ways, this part of the Tree can be seen as the emergency cut-off switch that stops the curious (yet unprepared) from being fried by the power that lies beyond.

Tiphareth is also the natural harmonising point of the Tree where all the other Sefirot are allowed to flow and find a balance within paradox. This is what makes this part of the Tree the most suitable to act as Guardian: it is the one point that knows the essence of all other parts of the Tree.

## Geburah
### (Strength)

Spiritual action: Release of hindering forces, reclaiming personal power.
Spiritual experience: Communion with the Goddess, the Mystery of Death/Release.
Symbol or tool: Pentagram

Geburah is the necessary force of breaking down and that which is being unmade; the power to break down in order to be made anew. The power of Geburah is the first example of the second lesson: the lesson of the Inverted Pentagram—*nothing in excess*. By learning to accept the impermanence of all things within our lives, we are better able to experience the world without obsessively clinging to anything or become mentally or emotionally imbalanced by loss or change.

The higher points of the Tree, those that exist beyond the Veil of the Mysteries which are guarded at Tiphareth, are concerned with the evolution of the soul as well as building a relationship with the divine. It becomes paramount that you integrate the teachings of accepting change early on in your journey up the Tree. Failing to do so will quickly lead to you becoming consumed by an inner conflict where you try to evolve while also attempting to cling onto who you thought you were.

## Chesed
### (Lovingkindness)

Spiritual action: Allow inspiration to flow, remove the burden of control/responsibility. The Draw/Lifting the Veil.
Spiritual experience: Communion with the God, The Mystery of Life/Rebirth.
Symbol or tool: Wand.

The natural and necessary polar opposite of Geburah, Chesed represents that which is being made manifest or that which is coming into being. As the source of transforming that which *isn't* into that which *is*, Chesed acts as the centre for all activities involving inspiration. To the witch, this is not only the insights gleaned via methods of divination but also the insights that are communicated to us by spirit contact and communication.

When Chesed is properly polarised with Geburah, the witch develops a healthy scepticism whereby there is no need to become hung up on inspiration and prophecy to the extent that it becomes a distraction or burden. This also feeds into the second teaching of *nothing in excess*. The trap is far too easy to fall into where every feather, number, or tea leaf can become something that is trying to communicate with us. A world where every waking moment becomes a sign that needs to be interpreted is a road to madness for the reason that it has no end.

Once a person gets caught up in this pattern and then falls asleep, every dream becomes something to interpret as well. This isn't to suggest that these things can't be omens, it is a gentle reminder that inspiration must be balanced with the complementary force that teaches us not to hold onto everything. If the witch can achieve a healthy balance of the two, then, and *only* then, are they on the right path to attaining the experience of the true Mysteries.

## Binah
### *(Understanding)*

SPIRITUAL ACTION: Communion with the God, giving form without hindering the flow of inspiration (connection to Chesed).
SPIRITUAL EXPERIENCE: Union with the Goddess, leading the coven.
SYMBOL OR TOOL: Cup/chalice.

*Binah* is the Divine Feminine—pure and undiluted. The initiating or "birthing" power of all creation in a state of full potential, it is a force without form or direction. It is the natural polar opposite of *Chokmah* (the following Sefira), balanced and stable but without interaction—which occurs at *Da'ath* (another Sefira described later).

For the witch, Binah is the location at which we connect with the Mysteries of the Goddess in their totality. When the *Charge of the Goddess* states that the Goddess can be found when we seek within, this message being conveyed is the Mystery of Binah. When we turn within and trust that the Goddess is ever present, then the restraints that prevent total union with the Goddess are removed. From this state, direct experience of Her can be known. This is most evident when a coven leader brings the Goddess into their own body to allow the coven time to have a direct encounter with their Divine Mother.

As Binah is balanced by Chokmah, so too is the Goddess balanced by the God. Through this harmonious relationship between the two, devotees of the Goddess can experience communion with the God. It should be noted that *communion* is not the same as *union*. The former speaks of the ability to reach out to the gods and build a relationship that is somewhat ethereal in nature. Union with the gods is more direct; physical, and yet transcendental at the same time. They have a greater physical presence, and we get to touch the ecstatic and ethereal nature of their world; it can be summed up as an exchange of experiences and point-of-view between a deity and their devotee.

## Chokmah
### *(Wisdom)*

SPIRITUAL ACTION: Communion with the Goddess, freedom tempered
    by limitation (connection to Geburah).
SPIRITUAL EXPERIENCE: Union with the God, leading the coven.
SYMBOL OR TOOL: Magical blade.

Chokmah is the Divine Masculine—pure and undiluted. The shaping power of the force provided by Binah; it is a force provided with direction that it can become form. As the natural polar opposite of Binah, Chokmah is balanced and stable but without interaction— which occurs at Da'ath.

Just as Binah allows us to experience union with the Goddess and communion with the God, so Chokmah allows union with the God and communion with the Goddess. The Tree provides a perfect balance between their two complementary forces and an experience of either will lead to the experience of the other. It is these interactions between the levels of the Tree that allow us to develop and continue to push us forward. Each Mystery feeds into the experience of the next, and so on. This continues until you have made connections between the different experiences that were not otherwise apparent.

The information provided for each level of the Tree so far is complex and is only scratching the surface of its many lessons. What has been provided to you here is enough to set you on the right track. With each experience that you have, you will begin to find greater clarity concerning the brief outlines provided in this chapter.

## BETWEEN THE WORLDS

### Da'ath
*(Knowledge)*

SPIRITUAL ACTION: Culmination, Mystery in action, magic in priest-hood and worship in magic, third degree in principle/experience.
SPIRITUAL EXPERIENCE: Walking between the worlds, natural magic/Witchcraft.
SYMBOL OR TOOL: The Magic Circle.

For the witch, the position of Da'ath is the place where the Circle exists on the levels of the Tree. Yes, it is true that the Magician will employ *a* circle, but it cannot be considered to be the *same* Circle that is found in the witches' Craft. The circle of the Magician is employed to *separate* the practitioner from the spirits and forces raised in their ceremonies, effectively acting as a magical border control that doesn't let anything inside. The Circle employed by the witch, however, is more of a magical boundary than a border, in so much as it is used to indicate the working space for the Craft rites. Unlike the Magician, the witch at no time attempts to be separated from the forces and spirits that are called by the rites. The witch *shares* the Circle with them. It is this difference in approach that makes the concept of Da'ath as a place of caution incompatible with the Craft. Witches can, and often do, work in a Circle of one kind or another without experiencing any psychological damage from the experience.

Unlike other forms, Da'ath is classified as a Sefira within Lurianic Kabbalah. This is because Da'ath takes the place of Kether, which is also a useful working model in Witchcraft. Once the Supernal Mother (Binah) and Supernal Father (Chokmah)—understood in Craft to be the Goddess and God—came into being from the potential of the limitless light represented by Kether,[192] they were then united in love at Da'ath. This union, which took place off of the Tree, is to be understood as a space between the worlds from which the gods' interaction and love created all things. By understanding that the Circle exists within this between place, it is easier to understand why this is a suitable location for witches to work. When the witch wishes to create new scenarios in their lives or redirect the unfolding of events within the physical world, what better place is there? By going directly to the space from which all life began and introducing changes, the witch is able to shape and reshape the very essence of creation.

## A New Perspective and the Path of Return

### Kether
*(Crown)*

**Spiritual action:** Revelation, Mystery expressed as experience, expanse of consciousness, third degree in action/sovereignty through inspiration.

**Spiritual experience:** Union with the divine, The Mystery of Mysteries.

**Symbol or tool:** Ring.

Just as the Material World (expressed by Malkuth) is our natural vantage point at the start of our journey, so Kether is the viewpoint of the gods. Before anything came into being, all was one and in a state of potential. Then the forces that we know as the gods came into being and from them, all creation was formed. Until all things end and the universe collapses back on itself, there is no Kether in the most literal sense. As long as there is a "you" and a "me," then all is not one. The oneness of Kether is to be understood as a non-differentiated reality. As long as there is an ability to identify two separate things, then all is no longer "one."

Within the model used here, Kether is the raw collective power of creation that flows through the gods, i.e., the raw essence of divinity.

---

192 Within Lurianic Kabbalah and some branches of Western Occult Qabalah only.

Many see this as the end goal of the journey up the Tree, an error that often leads to delusion. Instead, Kether should be understood as a bird's eye view used to look back at your journey before returning to Malkuth. When we look down the Tree, we no longer see the Inverted Triangle and Pentagram that was first visible on the climb. Instead, we see the complete picture—a Crowned Pentagram, the symbol of the highest grade of training.

Once here, if you are in an initiatory practice, you will undergo a rite that opens the Path of Return. This Path is the middle column of the Tree and acts as a "shortcut" back down the Tree to the Material World. The climb *should* teach people that we require balance. The Crowned Pentagram combines the teachings of "*know thyself*" and "*nothing in excess,*" ensuring that we know that we must be grounded in the physical world. At this point of the journey, the witch knows not to excessively cling to the spiritual Mysteries that we encounter.

Once we walk the Path of Return, we are back at the place we started but are deeply changed by the experience. The Path will remain open permanently so that everything that you have learned can be drawn upon again. This open connection also means that the gods and the witch have a more direct line of communication and unity. The opening of the Path of Return should be done *only* after deep training in the Craft. This is because the experience of the "downloads" that come through this open channel can be highly disorienting, even for the well-prepared.

Speaking from experience, I can tell you that these "downloads"— there is no better description—can occur at the most unusual times. I once woke up in the middle of the night knowing that I was completely still and yet also feeling like my mind was rushing at a speed fit for a rollercoaster. I was also acutely aware of my thoughts existing both within my head and yet simultaneously existing external to my body. All the while, new information was inexplicably appearing in my mind and I was *very* aware that this new information was creating connections to things I already knew. These connections were like knocking over dominos in the sense that the new information had a direct impact on other thoughts and knowledge that I had.

Once it was over, I felt a little spaced out, but still managed to go back to sleep. It was the next morning that it really hit me. I was amazed by all this new understanding that I had, and I walked around, occasionally slipping into a slight daze (for about fifteen minutes at a time) throughout the day before snapping out of it. This is the reason that the Path of Return is so well-protected and the method of opening it is guarded within the branches of Craft that employ it, not all traditions use this. Could you imagine dumping that burden on someone who isn't prepared to handle the impact?

## SELF-ASSESS YOUR CRAFT

Using the Tree of the Witches' Qabalah, take the following self-assessment of your own Craft knowledge and practices.

- What aspects of the Tree are already part of your regular practice?
- What do you feel needs to be made stronger?
- What parts aren't actually there at all?

Create a list of areas to strengthen (or introduce for the first time) along with how you plan on achieving this. Some of those gaps can be filled by exploring this book. Others may require you to experiment with ritual, work with others, commune with the gods, or read other types of Craft-related books that you wouldn't usually buy.

You may find that you have something strong at a high point on the Tree but have weaker or missing points below it. If this is the case, once you have strengthened those lower points (or introduced the missing element into your Craft), take time to look back at that strong higher point. With newfound knowledge and experience from one of the lower branches of the Tree, you may find that the higher point was not as strong as you thought. Use the insights from your newly expanded knowledge of the lower branches to improve your understanding of the higher branches. The information will start to present itself to you, as this is how the Tree works. The pathways connecting the different parts act as *interaction points* with lessons to be learned. As each part is in some way connected to the other parts, it is important to con-stantly review and never underestimate the power of going back to the basics.

## SUMMARY

Within the history of the Craft, Qabalah has held a long and enduring legacy as a model for understanding the complexities of training and the initiatory journey as a whole. Though it is by no means essential to incorporate the Qabalah into your own Craft, its historical context and influence should not go uncredited. Of course, there may be some who feel that the use of this model is a form of cultural appropriation, however, I hope that this chapter has been able to rest those concerns. As we have discussed, Witchcraft from the Middle Ages onwards has incorporated a form of Qabalistic wisdom and symbolism which continue to be relevant to many branches and traditions of the Craft today. This should not be surprising, as we have seen that the Kabbalah blended early on with British Paganism, folk magic, and Craft teachings to co-parent a new form of Craft that has endured, in essence, to the present day. The offspring philosophies of today's Craft therefore cannot be considered appropriation as their roots are owed to their parentage. It would be a greater disservice to ignore these influences than it would be to actively embrace them.

# Chapter Nine

# SACRED SEXUALITY

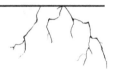

**It's** a generally safe assumption that witches today, and those of past decades, would support the belief that sex and sexuality are sacred. This belief is often among the first things about Witchcraft that attracts new practitioners and seekers who wish to explore the subject in greater depth. Many have previously been denied the ability to explore their sexuality without feelings of guilt, shame, or sin. This can leave people feeling both isolated from the physical community as well as disconnected from the spiritual. Yet, despite the freedoms that Witchcraft brings to such people, it must be asked: *Where has the sacredness gone?*

The ritualised practice that epitomises this underpinning belief in the sacredness of our own sexuality is often referred to as the *Great Rite*. Often perceived as a modern invention, this time-honoured magical act is possibly one of the most misunderstood. Most of the misinformation is a result of oversimplifying the concept and it would take an entire chapter to cover its complex history and theory, which is the intention of this section.

Most literature that explores the concepts of sexual magic comes from occult traditions that exist outside of Witchcraft. This means that many witches are left with a methodology that does not *relate* to the witches' worldview surrounding the sacredness of sex. This is not to suggest that other occultists reject the concept of sacred sexuality, it is to highlight that we are often speaking a similar, but not identical, language when it comes to *application*. When witches seek to have a greater understanding of the subject of sacred sexuality and sex magic, they are usually left with few options. The most detailed discussions on the subject are from Ceremonial and Chaos Magic and can usually be summarised as complex instructions on masturbating over a post-it note. That is not to say that such methods are without merit—on the contrary, many magical practitioners the world over find great use in such methods and practices. What this chapter aims to explore are the practices that are most relevant to today's witches and how they can be applied regardless of path or tradition.

## WHAT IT IS AND ISN'T

Sacred sexuality within the context of Witchcraft usually takes the form of a ritual known as the *Great Rite.* More accurately, it usually takes the form of a *series* of practices that are known collectively as the Great Rite. The word "collective" is used here because that is the most honest and accurate definition of the term. There is not one ritual, set of words, or standardised form for a Great Rite to take. Even those within the Revivalist traditions use variations, additional material, or complete rewrites of the version that is believed to be the "standard."

What made the Great Rite so great in the first place was the fact that it was such a diverse and multi-purpose ritual, with each varying context using a different name to describe the act. Examples include "going a-maying" at Beltane or the "Sacred Marriage" at a Monarch's coronation, as previously explored in Chapter Six. Over time, the fact that each context used the same ritual, either literally or symbolically, led to the use of the blanket term "Great Rite" that we are so familiar with today. The fact still remains that the term describes a multitude of scenarios and contexts—each as perfectly valid as the next—and this should not go unnoticed.

It is also important to emphasise the fact that the sex component of sacred sexuality does not need to be our own. In the context of a symbolic union, the "sex" component is the interaction between the forces invoked and not necessarily the participants of the ritual themselves. This means that such rites can be performed by anyone without hindering or limiting anyone's ability to provide or withdraw their consent. A symbolic rite is just as valid and legitimate as its literal counterpart.

Knowing these facts about the Great Rite and sex magic within the Craft is important for understanding what the Great Rite *isn't*. Many people like to label these ritual actions as predatory and that is a major problem. This is not to say that predatory behaviour has not attempted to masquerade itself as a Great Rite, as it most certainly has. What is problematic with the label is that we are projecting an image in which we should *expect* it to be predatory—and that is not OK! When we say things like "the Great Rite is predatory," we appear to blame victims who have been abused from a position of naivety as if to say "well, what did you expect?"

Instead, we should be educating people, especially those new to the Craft, so that they know what is and isn't part of the Rite. By educating those less informed than ourselves, we are teaching them that they have just as much right to say "NO" in a spiritual context as in any other. Being spiritual does not detract from the fact that people are people and not all of us are decent human beings.

## THE GREAT RITE—ALREADY AN INCLUSIVE PRACTICE

The Great Rite, known in some British circles as the "Great Act," has quickly developed into a rather controversial topic. Of course, the rite was always controversial to people outside of the Craft as they tend not to see anything remotely hinting at sex being sacred or spiritual. For many witches today, these views are also becoming more popular. This is most likely due to a new initiate entering the Craft and bringing older beliefs with them. For those witches, these old beliefs tend to fall away rather quickly, or if failing to do that, the Craft falls away from them. In either scenario, the two ideals naturally repel each other over time.

The main concern surrounding the rite among witches is the view that it is in some way "heteronormative" in nature. This is simply not the case. What I find most concerning about this is *not* the fact that people believe that it is heteronormative, but rather that there are those who publicly speak out about the subject, with few exceptions, allowing this misinformation to stand. By refusing to correct this common error, the Craft is becoming an unwelcome place for those that it naturally embraces. When people are allowed to *believe* they have no place in the Craft, how are they possibly going to find their way?

I believe that this idea has come about from a misunderstanding of the ritual. Usually, such misunderstandings come from the fact that many try to describe such a complex topic in simple terms. The oversimplification has led many to gaining the false impression that the ritual can only be done between a man and a woman. It is my hope that by breaking down the ritual's components, people will clearly understand that this is not always the case.

The truth of the matter is that the rite has *always* been, and still is, an inclusive practice. Much of this misinformation—and perception of heteronormative behaviour—stems largely from the fact that two *separate types* of ritual activity are assumed to be founded on the same magical principles. The rite takes the form of either a symbolic or literal variation, each of which is governed by similar yet separate underpinning magical principles. Simply put, the symbolic version is a ritual of *polarity,* and the literal form is a ritual of *sexuality.* Though I will break down these two approaches in more detail, I hope that you are already aware of the significant difference between the two.

Some covens and traditions may choose to apply these principles in different ways than how I present them here. It is important to remember that most of you reading this will not belong to these covens or traditions. Why tie yourself down with practices that are part of something you don't even belong to? It really is an unnecessary restriction to apply to your Craft. Don't do it!

### Symbolic Principle

The symbolic principle that underpins the rite is polarity. In order to understand the inclusive nature of the rite, it is first important to establish what polarity actually refers to. Polarity is a product of otherness. There must be something that is other than yourself, or whatever is being polarised, in order for the power to be generated. If you were making a cup of tea, you would need (at the very least) a cup of hot water and a tea bag. Now imagine you have just added hot water to hot water, or you have mashed the tea leaves from two bags together. This would either produce a cup of hot water or a pile of tea leaves—exactly what you started with. The absence of "other" means that you create no change and you have exactly what you started with. Put simply, that is how the principle of polarity works.

It's important to remember that there is a place for members of the LGBTQ+ community within the concept of polarity. Though many have argued that polarity is discriminatory against LGBTQ+ people, I have to disagree. By its nature, divinity is all inclusive and anyone is capable of working ritual with anyone else, no matter their identity.

Some may argue that the binary nature of polarity excludes non-binary and trans people, but again, I disagree. The binary poles are used to generate power and that power is a third entity in the equation. In essence, if you are combining opposing poles together, then the third component produced will, by its very nature, exist in a non-binary state. Using the terms "male and female" or any other gender labels does not exclude trans people. Trans-men are men and trans-women are women. Where is the exclusion other than within the minds of those who are trying to use polarity to create division? The nature of polarity is inclusive as it calls us to accept everything, human or otherwise, for exactly what it truly is. Polarity also helps us understand that what is different from ourselves is just as valid.

## Applied Polarity

Now that polarity has been defined, what is the best way to apply it in your Craft? Many know that the joining of a chalice and a magical blade is the most common symbolic action of polarity within modern Craft. For that reason, this will be used as an example to describe how it can be applied to your own magic. The consecration of wine, or any liquid in a chalice for that matter, utilises polarity on all levels of reality— "all levels" meaning the physical, astral, mental, and spiritual planes. The act works at all levels simultaneously, where *every* binary and non-binary force in existence is called upon to generate power and seal the act of consecration. Much like the backward and forward movement of strands of DNA, active and receptive poles alternate as they move up the planes of reality. Though the terms "male and female" will be used here, it must be remembered that the joining of the forces invoked represents the non-binary forces of existence on all levels of reality.

|  | MALE | FEMALE |
|---|---|---|
| PHYSICAL | Active | Receptive |
| ASTRAL | Receptive | Active |
| MENTAL | Active | Receptive |
| SPIRITUAL | Receptive | Active |

|  | BINARY | NON-BINARY |
|---|---|---|
| PHYSICAL | Male and female of all existence—human, animal, plant. | Non-binary of all existence—human, animal, plant. |
| ASTRAL | Cup and blade. | The content of the chalice—in contact with both the chalice and the blade. Participants' hearts—the way they approach the ritual action. |
| MENTAL | The spoken words—words of consecration. | Participants' minds—the way they approach the ritual action. |
| SPIRITUAL | God and Goddess. | The Mysteries expressed and contained within the content of the chalice. |

Although the application of the levels of reality is by far the most complete form of practice, it is only applicable if the participants make it so in their own minds and hearts. If you choose not to take this approach yet remain inclusive, then I recommend applying the Astral and Spiritual levels of the ritual. By using this method, you can remove human identity from the equation completely. The ritual becomes solely about the gods and the polarity between the magical tools—which have absolutely no bearing on human affairs or those who are performing the ritual.

## A CONSECRATION RITUAL

The following words can be used or adapted should you decide to use a symbolic union on all levels by joining a chalice and a magical blade together in your practice. Remember that the poles switch as they move up the levels and that the non-binary reality is in the final product of the consecration—where the inner alchemy occurs and all paradox is resolved.

If working in a male-female pair, the man should hold the chalice and the woman, the blade. This demonstrates the weaving of the poles up the ladder of reality (physical and astral). If you are working in another scenario, be it same-sex, non-binary, or even solitary, then use the information provided for each level of reality and find a balance that works for you.

In this rite, the chalice should be raised halfway and the blade lowered halfway so that neither is left unengaged from the symbolic union. The words spoken should come from the person holding the chalice. Again, this is to demonstrate the weaving of the poles up the ladder of reality. Starting with the active force at each level, the words themselves should demonstrate an upward weave, such as:

*"Binary to Non-binary*
*Self to Other*
*We gather now to unite the forces of all creation."*

Raise the chalice and lower the blade then continue, weaving the levels together:

*"Male to Female*
*Cup to Blade*
*Mind to Heart*
*Goddess to God*
*We invoke and unite the forces of all creation*
*To impart their blessing upon those gathered here!"*

Take a few moments to hold the position. You will feel a noticeable shift of power—wait until it passes its peak, then separate the chalice and blade. Regardless of sexuality or gender expression, everyone has a place in such a ritual.

LITERAL PRINCIPLE

### A Heteronormative Rite?

Just as the symbolic form is a *rite of polarity*, the literal form is a *rite of sexuality*. This has always been the case in Witchcraft—at least as far as it is practised in the UK. Gerald Gardner is the best account of this prior to the repeal of the Witchcraft Act. In his novel, *High Magic's Aid*, Morven the witch states the two requirements for the performance of the Great Rite:

> *"There is no oath, and all who have taken the second degree are qualified to work it, but 'tis the quintessence of Magic, and 'tis not to be used lightly, and then only with one whom you love, and are loved by, may it be done, all else were sin. To misuse it were the greater death, in this world, as in the next."[193]*

From this statement, two things become apparent:

This is a ritual of sexuality. Nothing states that this should be heterosexual. Love doesn't only express itself that way and love is clearly the key here.

Within the context given here, only a second-degree witch may perform the rite, largely due to practical reasons. The first-degree witch has little use for the ritual within the context of a coven and likely lacks a certain degree of training.

For context, it should be stated that Gardner intended this to mean the full range of the rite's applications. This is due to the fact that many covens require their first-degree witches to demonstrate

---

193    Gerald B. Gardner, *High Magic's Aid*, (Aurina Books: UK, 2010), 247.

an ability to successfully work magic using all methods of raising power—of which this is one such way.

From this summary of the Great Rite, I fail to see why the term "heteronormative" has ever been applied to the practice. The position is clear: The ritual requires a love that is reciprocated and requires a witch who is well-studied because the rite represents "the quintessence of Magic, and 'tis not to be used lightly." Some practitioners believe that the reason for this requirement is due to a unique and literal bond on the soul level that doesn't occur in the symbolic/polarity-based form of the rite. In short, if the rite is to be performed in the context of a sexuality-based ritual, then the participants should be mature enough to take into account the magical and metaphysical consequences of their actions. The soul experiences many lifetimes, and therefore is beyond the limitations of present-life gender identity. The ramifications of such a bond on the soul level will have ripples throughout those lifetimes.

Have you ever been in a situation where someone comes to you with the remnants of a strong spiritual bond with their ex? Sometimes these are simply energetic cords attaching the two—cords that are easily broken, but this is not always the case. In some instances, the two souls share a bond which may be due to similar practices performed in another lifetime. Souls progress, not regress, as they move from life to life. If a bonded couple are incompatible now, then they were before. They hadn't, and still haven't, addressed their issues or learned the lessons needed in order to break this cycle.

Love, on the other hand, transcends the levels of reality. Souls will be drawn to each other, and on some level, remember each other time and again. This is why strict criteria are in place for the literal form of the rite. It takes awareness of these facts and a healthy level of discernment to assess whether such a *lasting* bond *truly* exists between the two.

To further understand the distinction between this form of the rite and its symbolic counterpart, some important history on its deeper symbolism must be explored.

## Woman as the Altar

From Great Rite to Black Mass, as discussed later in this chapter, the image of a (usually naked) woman acting as the altar is one of the most notable and controversial elements of ceremonial imagery found in connection to Witchcraft. It should hardly be surprising that this image has lingered, as the Goddess herself has ensured that her customs and traditions have survived throughout the centuries. Just as the image of the Triple Goddess has continued to reappear and make her presence known to the world, so too has the image of the sacred altar that is Woman. Though the Black Mass that we most readily think of today is a parody of the Christian Mass, the origins of these themes are far older and go "back to the days of the ancient worship of the Great Goddess of Nature, in whom all things were one, under the image of Woman."[194]

The establishment of the Roman Catholic Church saw much of the older religion absorbed into its doctrine to ensure ease of conversion. Even the full official title of the Pope, Pontifex Maximus, comes from his pre-Christian predecessor whose religious position was taken over during the Church's rise to power—so the same is found with the altar. Around 270 CE, Pope Felix I ordered the mass to be performed "over the tombs of the martyrs." When more churches existed than martyrs, their remains were broken up and "transferred from their place of burial and placed in the interior of newly erected altars" to act as relics.[195] In short, a body was, and still is, essential for an altar within the act of worship.

Thought about with any degree of logic, it only makes sense that this is Pagan-based thinking. The Church generally turns away from the physical world in favour of securing its place in heaven. To think of the human form as a sacred or holy vessel used as an altar in the most sacred ceremonial action of the faith doesn't speak of Christianity at all. Pre-Christian faith, however, is far more compatible with this line of thinking, viewing the natural world as a sacred and necessary complementary force with the spiritual—as

---

194   Doreen Valiente, *An ABC of Witchcraft*, (USA: Phoenix Publishing, 1986), 44.

195   Nikolaus Gihr, *Holy Sacrifice of the Mass: Dogmatically, Liturgically and Ascetically Explained*, (United States: B. Herder, 1908), 370.

opposed to something that is in conflict with the spirit. Even today, the altar is treated as if it is a person within Church practices. The consecration of an altar is given as a form of initiation rite where the "bishop uses holy oils to bless the altar and vests it with a white garment after the prayers have been completed."[196]

Within such ceremonies of Pagan origin, the focus in ritual is given to either the lower back or the region just above the pubic bone, depending on whether the Woman is depicted face-up or face-down. The reason that the focus of the rite, usually with the aid of a chalice, was at this region of the body is due to the fact that it is the location of the sacrum bone. The sacrum, meaning "sacred bone," was at one time offered to the gods following animal sacrifice or used in other religious ceremony as it was believed to house sacred power.[197]

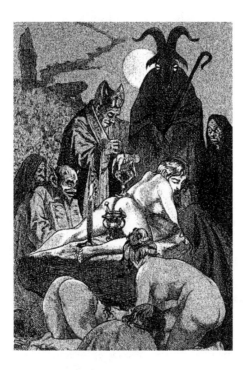

---

196    Aleteia, "This is why the priest kisses the altar at Mass", Accessed October 20, 2020.
       https://aleteia.org/2017/07/26/this-is-why-the-priest-kisses-the-altar-at-mass/

197    Etymonline, "Sacrum," Accessed October 22, 2020. https://www.etymonline.
       com/word/sacrum

When a person is offering their body as a living altar, it only stands to reason that this "sacred point" would be used as a sort of altar stone for the act of consecration. Many narratives and illustrations from the trial days depict a witch kissing the backside of the Devil. This act is usually labelled today as the "Kiss of Shame," and may have actually been centred on an acknowledgement of the sacrum. The Latin phrase *osculum infame* does not mean "kiss of shame," it actually means "the infamous kiss." Although the *osculum infame* gained a widespread reputation as being central to Witchcraft, it was not presented in such a black-and-white manner.

In the earliest records, the concept was used as part of an initiatory experience, as the Great Rite is today, within the witch-cult. In such rituals, the kiss was said to be given to one of three parts of the body: the feet, genitalia, or "under the tail."[198] All three of these locations have some connection with the sacrum: the back being the bone itself, above the genitalia (i.e., sacral region) being opposite the sacrum, and the sciatic nerve, a pathway which starts in the sacrum bone and runs to the soles of the feet. It is therefore difficult to conclude that this kiss is pure fiction, especially when we know that the pre-Christian forms of these rites not only existed but profoundly influenced the development of the Church.

## Only Women?

Of course, both historically and today, women are not the only ones who can fulfil the role of the sacred altar. It was recorded in some earlier records that the kiss was used by the Devil to honour his witches—both male and female.[199] It stands to reason that anyone can take on the position of the altar within modern sexual or symbolic rites as every-one has a human skeleton. Records that describe a Pagan form of the ritual show that it may have centred around the worship of a God and

---

198  Jonathan Durrant, "The Osculum Infame," in Karen Harvey (ed.), *The Kiss in History*, (Manchester University Press, 2005), 38.

199  Ibid. 34.

Goddess celebrated on the first of May. The kiss would take the form of an exchanged between priest and priestess as an act of consecration to ready them both for the ritual.[200] Here, the sinister and diabolical tone of later centuries is removed, and the basis of a ritual far more familiar to modern-day witches appears to reveal itself from antiquity.

The goddess celebrated in these earlier accounts of sexual rites is identified as Dianom, presented as the Triple Goddess: Diana-Luna-Hecaté, and the god identified with Pan, presented as a triple god: Priapus-Bacchus-Sabasius.[201] Interestingly, the epithets (titles) given to Pan are all associated with the god Dionysus. The first and last name are those of his offspring—God of Garden Fertility and God of Wine and Vegetation, respectively. The name *Bacchus* was a cult name of Dionysus and represented him as God of Sexual Ecstasy.[202] The three together cover a full range of sexual and fertile power, so it is understandable that Pan should be a natural syncretic form for their worship as a trinity. Furthermore, the triple nature of Dianom is strikingly close to that of Diana found in the *Gospel of the Witches,* where, in my previous book *Aradia,* I explained that the name of her daughter, Aradia, could be translated to mean "Altar of the Goddess."[203] If this is echoed here, it demonstrates that either priest or priestess can act as representatives of the gods on Earth. The woman is more commonly found to be called, though not exclusively, to act as the sacred altar. These accounts also demonstrate that a public symbolic form of the ritual immediately follows a literal and private form of the ritual act; something that is also commonly found within modern Craft.[204]

---

200  Jules Michelet, *The Sorceress* (1862) translated by Alfred Richard Allinson as Satanism and Witchcraft, (New York: Citadel Press, 1939), 104-105.

201  Ibid. 99.

202  Aaron J. Atsma, "Dionysos Family" Accessed October 23, 2020. https://www.theoi.com/Olympios/DionysosFamily.html

203  Craig Spencer, *Aradia,* (Llewellyn Worldwide Ltd. 2020), 15, 109.

204  Jules Michelet, *The Sorceress* (1862) translated by Alfred Richard Allinson as Satanism and Witchcraft, (New York: Citadel Press, 1939), 99.

## The Black, or Witches, Mass

As we have seen, the image of a person as an altar has permeated world religion from Pagan religious forms to the rise and spread of the Catholic Church. This is a difficult fact to ignore. When presented with images of a Black Mass, occasionally referred to as a *Witches Mass*, it should come as no surprise that the "holy vessel" used to consecrate the rite was the body of a living person. The fact that this was usually a woman is most likely due to the fact that the priest officiating the rite, usually depicted as Catholic, was a man. As such, the balance of polarity takes precedence here as the Black Mass has always been symbolic in nature.

Following the rite, the participants were often depicted as participating in a wild orgy, thereby participating in a literal and sexual rite. It is interesting to note that all expressions of sexuality were represented in these scenes and tend to linger, seductively or horrifically, within the minds and imaginings of people and Hollywood movies. We know that these themes genuinely existed in the rites of European Paganism and were later absorbed into the Church as it attempted to convert the masses. We also know from our previous exploration of the sabbats that sex rites observing both symbolic and literal expression existed and continued to exist during the dominant era of the Church. To think that these themes do not continue to be relevant today would be rather narrow-minded and unnecessarily pessimistic.

### The Kiss in Ritual

Many of you will be familiar with the concept of the fivefold kiss that is found in some branches of Initiatory Craft. What many don't realise is that these five points of the body, which are acknowledged during such an act, hold prominent ritual significance in other Craft traditions, occult traditions, and the ancient world. These traditions may be tapping into ancient occult symbolism that is beneficial, but they aren't the only traditions doing so. It should also be remembered that their interpretations are not the only valid examples. What follows are explanations and expressions that are not drawn from Revivalist Craft, though there will be some degree of overlap. What is presented here represents a framework that can be used by all.

Though the term is usually known as the *Fivefold Kiss,* some branches of Craft call it the *Fivefold Salute.* This is due to the fact that the "kiss" is not literal, but a symbolic breath that has been known for centuries as a symbolic "kiss."[205] As this method of salute can be adopted or adapted to suit your own personal needs within either a symbolic or literal ritual act, it is for you and those involved to conclude whether a literal or symbolic kiss is appropriate. Neither is more powerful, better, or more authentic than the other. Never allow someone to suggest otherwise, as the Craft never removes your ability to give or deny personal consent.

## Feet

The English language is full of expressive symbolism, each referring to an older truth that, for the majority, has lost its meaning and importance. Yet, its preservation demonstrates that the human spirit is persistent and does not easily let go of what is important to remember. When we look at the symbolism of the feet, we are presented with the symbol of our own ability to utilise our personal power in the world.

Consider sayings such as "I'm putting my foot down," or that something abhorrent to society needs to be "stamped out!" These expressions show that we hold the power to shape the world within our feet. We also stand to show respect but may not "stand for it" if something is undeserving of respect. We even say that people need to learn to "stand on their own two feet" when they don't claim their personal power but expect others to help them get by in life.

For these reasons, feet are a symbol of power. Rulers, gods, and religious leaders held large groups of people under their control by having them bow or grovel at their feet. It can be said that these people are kept "underfoot." Within the context of ritual, it would be beneficial to acknowledge the power of the person receiving the salute. Doing so demonstrates their spiritual power and their ability to "walk their own path" and shape their own reality.

---

205 Encyclopaedia Britannica, "Religious Symbols: Gestural and Physical Movements," Accessed November 4, 2020. https://www.britannica.com/topic/religious-symbolism/Gestural-and-physical-movements#ref399228

## Knees

Many kneel in prayer, usually in devotion or moments of despair, to win the favour and mercy of the gods. The knees are the seat of mercy, and in the ancient world, the devoted would pray while touching the knees of the gods' statues to acquire the favour of their more merciful nature.[206] Within the English language, we have the phrase that a situation or outcome is "in the lap of the gods," indicating that the situation or outcome is at their mercy. I have always liked this expression, particularly due to the fact that it has never changed from "gods" to "God." The old idea of a divine pantheon still lingers in day-to-day expression.

Prior to being a symbol of mercy, the knees—or kneeling, specifically—were understood as an aspect of ritual directed to chthonic or underworld gods and spirits. The hands raised with palms to the sky was understood as ritual directed to the heavens and its gods and spirits.[207] Within the context of a ritual salute, the knees should be acknowledged as a place where the powers of the feet are tempered by mercy through knowledge and discipline—for it is from self-control (discipline) and the lack of ignorance (knowledge) that mercy is made possible.

## Sacral (Aligned to the Sacred Bone)

As we have already discussed in our exploration of the Black Mass, this part of the body holds a prominent place within the acts of sacred sexuality. With its location considered, this should come as no surprise. Through the sacred bone, this area becomes an expression of the human power of magic and fertility. It should be remembered that the salute is of the human expression as a whole and not of the circumstances of any specific individual. As such, the ability—or

---

206 Thomas Dudley Fosbroke, Dionysius Lardner, *A Treatise on the Arts, Manufactures, Manners, and Institutions of the Greeks and Romans, Volume 1*, (Longman, Rees, Orme, Brown, Green & Longman, and John Taylor, 1833), 298.

207 Encyclopaedia Britannica, "Religious Symbols: Gestural and Physical Movements," Accessed November 4, 2020. https://www.britannica.com/topic/religious-symbolism/Gestural-and-physical-movements#ref399228

lack thereof—of a person to experience physical fertility is wholly irrelevant, as far as the ritual symbolism expressed here is concerned.

Due to the association with fertility, this location of the body represents the power to create on the physical level. Just like reproductive fertility, the power of fertility allows an individual to manifest something material that takes form on the physical plane of existence. As we have already described, the sacrum and the feet share a common connection via the sciatic nerve. This means that the raw power of a person, as expressed within their feet, takes on a creative action and direction via the sacral region of the body. Within the context of a ritual salute, this connection should be honoured along with its inherent fertile powers by layering these connections. As you go through the salute, you are actively reinforcing the belief that the human form is divinely perfect.

## Breast/Chest

This part of the body is a place of comfort and nurture. People are often brought in close to the breast or chest when embraced, showing comfort or affection. Sometimes we need to get something "off our chest" when we need someone to talk to so we can process what is uncomfortable. The most logical rationale for the associations here is that this area is close to the heart, and therefore, the seat of our emotions.

Within the context of the ancient world, the heart did symbolise emotion, but not exclusively. Along with emotional processes, the heart was also the source of our memory, intelligence, and that which ensured our ability to remain in harmony with the world and the spiritual and divine inhabitants of the otherworld.[208] Emotion, memory, intelligence, and harmony seem to speak of the four chambers of the heart, but the fact that two are cognitive processes while the others are feeling-driven seems curious. The hint of the two sides of the heart, each with two chambers, echoes these ancient beliefs within physical form. These qualities can all be acknowledged within the context of a ritual salute. Bringing our cognitive and feeling-driven

---

208   Ziskind B, Halioua B. "La Conception Du Coeur Dans l'Egypte Ancienne [Concepts of the heart in Ancient Egypt]." Med Sci (Paris). 2004 Mar;20(3):367-73. French. doi: 10.1051/medsci/2004203367. PMID: 15067585.

processes into alignment with the previously saluted powers makes for a perfect foundation upon which potent magic can be built.

## Lips

The lips are the place of creation on a non-physical level. A natural counterbalance to the physically creative sacral, here we create by expression of the intangible—thoughts, feelings, a sigh of frustration or relief, etc. Effectively, our lips are the place where we breathe life into those processes that are symbolised by the heart, giving them a vehicle by which they can become externalised. The connection of the lips to the breast/chest should be apparent when we consider that our lungs use our mouth (and nose) to draw breath into the chest and then release it again via the same point from which it entered.

Within the ritual salute, each bodily location has been "kissed" with the breath of the working partner. This fact within itself expresses the lips' symbolism of "infusing life into non-physical qualities" so that they can express themselves actively within the world. Just as a poppet may have life breathed into it so it can heal or harm at a distance, so too is the breath given here to allow internal human powers to become active within the context of ritual.

Of course, if the ritual is to take the form of a literal sexual act, then there is no reason why the kisses should be symbolic breaths. However, if you wish to maintain the tradition of breath-work within the context of sex magic, then the following should be considered. If the rite is symbolic, then the breaths given should be cold. Blow on your hand and you will notice that the breath is cold. This is the appropriate breath for symbolic work. Now open your mouth wider and breathe on your hand, noticing that the breath is warm. This breath can raise sexual energy within the body so should be reserved for when sexual magic is literally performed. When working with the warm breath, you may also wish to add a slow continuous breath up your partner's spine from the base to the top of their neck. Do this three times in total to ensure an overall even flow of sexual energy once the five points have been saluted properly. This will allow the sexual energy to flow evenly and unhindered during the active part of this rite.

The more observant reader will have noticed that these five points form the pattern of the pentagram and triangle. Effectively, this ritual pattern and its powers map the Tree of Life upon the human form. It represents the weaving of the levels, the truth that the path is within, and acknowledges that our physical form is sacred because of what it is, not in spite of it. The ritual action therefore expresses the truth that we have a right to walk the sacred path because the map is literally encoded into the very fabric of who we are in the world.

## WORKING THE RITE

Now that we have properly addressed the theory of the two forms of ritual, dispelled the notion that the rites are restricted to heteronormative expression, and restored the historical context that connects sex (symbolic and literal) to the witches' Craft, we can learn how to actively apply this knowledge. The version of the Great Rite that is presented here is made of six distinct parts, the final part being that which will change depending upon whether the ritual is symbolic or literal. The former of the two is an act of polarity and most often uses a male and female pairing while the latter is an act of sexuality that is as diverse as sexual expression. I have opted to use non-specific placeholder names for the participants below. The person who will take up the position of the Altar will be identified as such in the ritual instructions while their partner will be simply identified as "the Witch."

You will need:
- Wand
- Chalice/Cup
- Wine or other suitable liquid for the chalice
- Working knife/athame
- Black candle
- White candle
- Two candle holders
- Something to light the candles with

- A small *working altar* (in addition to the person acting as the Altar)—decorated to personal preference with emphasis on deities being called upon.

- An appropriate anointing oil—a plain carrier oil such as a vegetable oil will work well for this purpose. Do not use mineral-based oils as they are harsh on the skin, making them unsuitable for this purpose. If the rite is to be literal and contraceptive protection will be used, keep in mind that mineral-based oils will destroy a condom, making it ineffective and unsafe.

### 1. CONJURING THE CIRCLE AND CALLING THE ELEMENTAL GUARDIANS

Clear the space that will be used to form the Circle of any clutter and unnecessary items. If possible, move furniture and other items to create a clear working space. Once the space is cleared, place the *working altar* (not the person acting as the Altar) in the Northeast of what will form the Circle's bounds; all other items should be placed in the Southwest. The Witch (the ritual partner) will take their wand and, starting in the East, move clockwise in the Northern Hemisphere, or anti-clockwise in the Southern Hemisphere to conjure the Circle.

As the Witch walks the perimeter, they should take their time and focus on the action that is being carried out. The Witch should visualise a blue flame forming the boundary of the Circle at the place where their wand is directed.

Taking their time and "seeing" the blue fire form the Circle, the Witch speaks the words:

> *"I conjure now the Circle round,*
> *Between the worlds, it shall be bound,*
> *A meeting place of love and peace,*
> *The power raised and then released.*
> *Our sacred space: sealed, protected,*
> *To work the rite we have selected,*
> *Forged of Mighty Astral-flames,*
> *Hallowed by the Sacred Names:*
> *[Deity names here]."*

Once the Witch has returned to the East, completing the conjuration of the Circle, it is time to call upon the power of the elements. The powers called here are the Elemental Guardians, not the raw power of the elements themselves. The job of the Elemental Guardians is to regulate the flow of power from the element to the Circle so that it is balanced and usable to those working within it.

| FIRE | WATER | AIR | EARTH |

Because it is the Guardians that are being called, they should be specifically visualised in each direction with something representing their respective elemental power behind them. As previously discussed, you are free to use whatever visual imagery you'd like. Do not forget to visualise their elemental powers, such as:

- East—A tornado or windswept trees.
- South—A wall of fire or a desert with visible heatwave.
- West—A waterfall or the Guardian standing before a well.
- North—The Guardian standing on a rocky space, mountain, or fertile field.

## The Call:

The Witch focuses on their visualisation and takes a moment to feel their desire to establish contact with the Guardian of the direction. Once they have this feeling, and while holding the visual, the Witch will draw the corresponding pentagram with their wand. Pointing at the centre of the pentagram after having projected their inner call and visualisation, the Witch will speak the relevant call:

*"Guardian of the East and the powers of Air, I call you forth to empower this Circle and witness our Great Rite."*

The Witch will repeat the call in like fashion for the remaining directions, moving clockwise in the Northern Hemisphere (NH), or anti-clockwise in the Southern Hemisphere (SH):

*"Guardian of the South (NH)/North (SH) and the powers of Fire, I call you forth to empower this Circle and witness our Great Rite."*

*"Guardian of the West and the powers of Water, I call you forth to empower this Circle and witness our Great Rite."*

*"Guardian of the North (NH)/South (SH) and the powers of Earth, I call you forth to empower this Circle and witness our Great Rite."*

Once all of the relevant calls have been made, the Witch will walk the Circle three times in the appropriate direction to stir up the power and prepare it for use in the ritual.

## 2. Fivefold Kiss Exchange

The Witch will salute the Altar first and the Altar will follow suit—the process is exactly the same regardless of which working partner is carrying out the action.

The Altar stands facing the Witch and both will take a moment to contemplate their reason for choosing to perform the rite—be it for healing, general blessings, fertility etc. Once the Witch feels ready, they will lower themselves to the ground so that they are kneeling, their head lowered toward the Altar's feet. Unless the salute will take the form of a literal kiss, there is no need for the participants to be too close to one another.

**The Witch to the Altar:**

*"[Name], I salute your feet, the source of your power ..."*

The Witch salutes the right foot, then continues:

*"... and independence."*

The Witch salutes the left foot.

The Witch then raises their back slightly so that they are in the region of the Altar's knees. Saluting the right knee first, then the left, and the Witch continues:

*"I salute your knees as an expression of your discipline ..."*

The Witch salutes the right knee, then continues:

*"... and knowledge ..."*

The Witch salutes the left knee, then concludes:

*"... gained from devotion."*

Straightening their back, the Witch will now salute the sacral region of the Altar, being mindful of the sacrum bone, while saying:

*"I salute your fertile sacral power ..."*

The Witch salutes the sacral area, then concludes:

*"... where your creativity is grounded into material form."*

The Witch now rises to their feet and speaks the salute of the breast/ chest, again acknowledging the right side of the Altar first, followed by the left:

*"I salute your breasts/chest, where feeling ..."*

The Witch salutes the right side first, then continues:

*"... and thinking ..."*

The Witch salutes the left side, then concludes:

*"... are united as one to nurture and bring harmony."*

Finally, the Witch concludes their salute at the lips:

*"And I salute your lips that express and give life to the intangible."*

The Witch then salutes the lips.

It should be noted that the breaths of these salutes should be easy, not forceful; there is no need to harshly blow into your working partner's face. In fact, if done correctly, they should barely notice the breath at all. Once the Witch has finished and before the Altar repeats these actions, both should return to a moment of contemplation on the reason that they have chosen to perform this rite. Once the final salute has been given, the Witch will then anoint the Altar, consecrating their body to the sacred work.

If the ritual is to be performed in a literal sense and the "hot breath" method was used as previously discussed, the Witch should remember to add a slow continuous breath up their partner's spine from base to the top of their neck before the Altar salutes the Witch. This is done three times in total to ensure an overall even flow of sexual energy once the five points have been saluted properly. It will allow the sexual energy to flow evenly and unhindered during the active part of the rite.

### 3. Anoint the Body as the Altar

The Witch transforms their working partner into the Altar proper by consecrating them as such. The Altar must hold a predetermined mental image of the outcome of the ritual throughout the anointing process while pouring as much of their emotional energy and faith that the magic will work into that image as possible. This links the mind, heart, and spirit—the three essentials of the magic triangle of the Qabalah—into the ritual, giving it life.

The Witch also focuses on the predetermined mental image during the anointing to help focus the mental aspect of the Altar's work, but the Altar infuses the heart and spirit into the image alone at this stage. The Witch speaks the words of anointment while applying oil with their thumb to the Altar's body in a dot or X on the relevant places.

When speaking the word, "mind," the forehead will be anointed. The Altar's heart will be anointed when they say "heart" and the space between the belly button and pubic bone when they say, "spirit."

*"I anoint this body as a living altar by mind, heart, and spirit in the name of [deity] and as the altar, you are consecrated to [state purpose of the altar/function for the rite]."*

The reason for using this method of raising ritual power will depend on the function of the rite. The participants will speak their intentions for the magic as plainly and concisely as possible without too much flowery language—which can often pull focus from the ritual intention and disturb the outcome of the magic.

### 4. GREAT RITE

The Altar now lays on the ground facing upwards, holding their body in a pentagram position with their arms outstretched and their legs apart. The Altar's head should be facing the Northeast of the ritual Circle and the space between their feet, where the Witch will kneel, in the Southwest. Position the black candle in the empty space between the Altar's right hand and foot and a white candle on their left. Position a chalice near the Altar's right foot and the magical blade near their left. The actual *working altar* (not the person) at the very edge of the Circle in the Northeast will be used only in the next step (step 5) of the ritual.

The Altar continues to hold the image of the ritual goal in their mind as the Witch continues the ritual:

*"I light these pillars, black and white...*

The Witch will briefly pause their chant to do so before continuing:

*...to invoke the power of the Great Rite.*
*I call upon the worlds unseen,*
*to open up the way between,*
*and bid the Goddess enter in,*

*to fill this shrine of bone and skin.*
*Unite the forces dark and light,*
*and give their power to our rite."*

The words "the Goddess" given here should be replaced with the name of the deity—female, male, or other, that was used during the anointing and conjuring of the Circle. If you only use generic titles such as "God and Goddess" or "Lord and Lady" in your practice, feel free to retain the wording as-is.

The Witch should focus their power on the deity being called down throughout this section from the moment just prior to lighting the candles to the end of the spoken words. The Altar will signal when they feel the divine presence has fully merged with them. How the signal is given will depend on whether the ritual is literal or symbolic. If literal, then the Altar is free to move and begin having sex with their partner. If the ritual is symbolic, the Altar will raise their right hand to indicate to the Witch that they are ready to receive the chalice.

### 5. CONCLUDE THE RITE

This part of the ritual will vary depending upon whether the ritual is enacted in a symbolic or literal expression.

**Literal:**

If the rite is literal, then the couple may break away from all formality and enjoy each other freely without fear of judgement or shame. Sex is sacred *because* of its authentic expression of love, passion, and desire—not in spite of it. Feel free to move around, move the candles further to the edge of the Circle if required, and change positions as desired. If you wish to practice safe sex or incorporate any items/toys during intercourse, these should be placed at the base of, but not on, the working altar before the ritual begins.

People are often taught that they must fix the image of their intentions in their minds while engaging in sex magic, especially at orgasm. This is not at all necessary in this ritual—in fact, it is strongly advised against. During the consecration of the Altar, these mental images were actively projected onto the rite in just the same way that having a picture on any *working altar* would provide the same ritual focus in other workings. The act of literal sex is now used to raise the power necessary to send that image and its intentions up to the gods so that it may receive their blessing. As this step of the ritual—the anointing—has already taken place, the need to focus on the image during sex is unnecessary and is more likely to distract from the experience. For that reason, the sex itself should be allowed to play out authentically without being restrained by ritual etiquette; it is the ability to fully immerse oneself in the experience that leads to the true ecstatic state that is essential for tapping magical power from sex in the first place.

**Symbolic:**

When the Witch sees the Altar raise their right hand slightly, they will hand them the chalice which is then placed by the Altar—now holding it with both hands—over their sacral region. The Witch takes up their magical blade and holds it, pointing down, over the chalice—which is already filled with wine or another predetermined drink as appropriate for the participants involved (alcohol is not essential).

Unlike in the consecration of wine previously given in this chapter in which the words are spoken by the one holding the chalice, in the context of a Great Rite, the words will be spoken by the Witch. This maintains the flow of power created by the weaving of the poles up the ladder of reality. The Witch should remain mindful that the words also demonstrate that weaving by starting with the active force at each level:

*"Binary to non-binary*
*Self to Other*
*We gather now to unite the forces of all creation."*

Raise the chalice and lower the blade halfway in so that neither is left un-engaged from the symbolic union. Continue, weaving the levels together:

> *"Male to Female*
> *Cup to Blade*
> *Mind to Heart*
> *Goddess to God*
> *We invoke and unite the forces of all creation*
> *To impart their blessing upon those gathered here!"*

Take a few moments to hold the position. There should be a noticeable shift of power; wait until it passes its peak, then separate the chalice and blade.

Once the wine has been blessed by the rite, the Altar is helped up and takes the first drink, followed by the Witch. If others are present, then the chalice can either be passed around to share or the contents of the chalice can be poured into other cups to be shared before the Altar takes their first drink. This action completes the cycle of magic which has passed up the levels of reality to the gods, down again to the astral level in the wine (or other drink), and finally, to the physical level by being consumed. This completes the cycle of manifestation by projecting and re-anchoring the power into the material world.

**Literal and Symbolic:**

As the final action to be taken, regardless of the expression that the rite takes, the Altar now goes to the *working altar* and lays both their hands—palms down—onto the altar's surface. This grounds the power back into the sacred items and ends their role as the Living Altar. This step is vital and should be completed as soon as possible following intercourse or consumption of the consecrated wine. Failure to do so can cause disorientation to Altar mentally, emotionally (heart), and in their sense of self (spirit). If for any reason this action is forgotten, it should be completed as soon as possible to reverse the side effects. If a large amount of time has passed since the conclusion of the ritual, these effects may take time to completely disappear.

### 6. CLOSING THE RITE

Once the rite has concluded, the person who acted as the Altar will banish the Circle. They will blow or snuff out the candles as they prefer, white first followed by black, while giving a silent thanks to the gods who were called upon for the ritual.

The Altar will use their wand to banish the Circle, starting in the East and working in the opposite direction from how it was conjured.

**Thank the Elemental Guardians:**

| FIRE | WATER | AIR | EARTH |

*"We give our thanks to the Guardian of the East and the powers of Air for answering our call to empower this Circle and witness our Great Rite. We now release you with gratitude and respect."*

Draw the relevant pentagram and point to its centre while taking a moment to project thanks, gratitude, and respect from yourself and those present.

Repeat in like fashion for the remaining directions:

*"We give our thanks to the Guardian of the North (NH)/South (SH) and the powers of Earth for answering our call to empower this Circle and witness our Great Rite. We now release you with gratitude and respect."*

*"We give our thanks to the Guardian of the West and the powers of Water for answering our call to empower this Circle and witness our Great Rite. We now release you with gratitude and respect."*

*"We give our thanks to the Guardian of the South (NH)/North (SH) and the powers of Fire for answering our call to empower*

*this Circle and witness our Great Rite. We now release you with*
*gratitude and respect."*

**Banish the Circle:**

Once all the directions have been duly thanked, the Altar will continue
by walking the boundary of the Circle, visualising the fire that forms it
disappearing as they pass over it with the wand:

> *"I banish now the Circle round,*
> *Between the worlds, no longer bound,*
> *This meeting place of love and peace,*
> *With due respect, I now release.*
> *Extinguished are your boundaries flames*
> *By the hallowed sacred names [names here]."*

## SUMMARY

For witches, sexuality is a manifestation of the sacred. As we tend to
readily embrace the wonders of life into our Craft, it is no wonder
that rituals surrounding and celebrating sexuality are part of our
work. Despite common misinformation insisting that such rituals are
heteronormative, it is my hope that readers will now better be able to
make the distinction between rituals of polarity and sexuality. While
it is often believed that there is only one way for certain rituals to
be followed and performed, this is not strictly the case. Although
the underpinning theories behind the rites are time-honoured, the
application is often adaptable and, most importantly, it always has
been. Dogma is practically an alien notion to the Craft as a whole.
As was seen throughout this chapter, even accounts where the "Devil"
presided over such rites, different sexual orientations and expressions
were freely accepted throughout, and today's Craft should be no
different.

Even in the 1980s, there were instances in which initiations via
Great Rite were performed literally between an established couple
according to *sexuality*, not polarity. This was not just among fringe

groups, but something that was practised in both Britain and America alike—and likely in many other countries as well.[209] The witches then knew the clear distinction between one version of the rite and another and accepted their equal validity—and rightly so. It is for the witches of today to ensure that this precious and necessary distinction is not lost, ensuring that the Craft remains the inclusive and accepting path that it always has been.

---

209   Quoted interviews with a diverse number of witches from various traditions and countries available in: Janet and Stewart Farrar, *The Life and Times of a Modern Witch*, (Great Britain: Judy Piatkus (Publishers) Limited, 1987), 82.

# CLOSING WORDS

**In** the introduction, I stated that there are few words in the English language that are more empowering, offensive, and provocative than the word "witch." You may have come across things in this book that have challenged your views or given you something to reflect on—this is a good thing! Whether you are new to the Craft or have been practising for a while, I hope that you have enjoyed exploring and reconnecting with our history. There is something we all can gain from history if we are willing to open our eyes and look with a new perspective. The journaling and questions that I have posed throughout are specifically designed to help you document your exploration of the history of British Witchcraft and how this relates to your own practice. Once you have found *your* answers, you can make a simple shift in yourself and remove anything that has become a limitation upon your own expression of power.

It is not my intention to tell you which path to follow—that is a decision that only you can make. My sincere hope is that by having the history that is quickly being lost restored, you will be able to embrace and weave it into your own practice. Learning our history in no way discredits our modern expressions of the Craft but provides a strong foundation upon which it can be built. Just like when building a house, it doesn't matter what type you want, how many bedrooms you need, or how you decorate it. Those are all based on personal choice, however, all houses will have one unifying feature if they are going to be practical, stand strong, and endure: a solid foundation to build upon. Witchcraft is no different! Your practice—whether solitary or in a group—and how you choose to dress or decorate your altar is based on personal taste. Your Craft will always be stronger, and you as a witch will be more confident, with the knowledge that your path is built on a solid foundation. No matter how different our practices are, it is our history that unites us as witches throughout time and regardless of location.

Preserve our history, love your Craft, and grow into the Elders of tomorrow—today!

# BIBLIOGRAPHY

"50 Facts About the Queen's Coronation." *50 Facts About the Queen's Coronation*, 2003, https://www.royal.uk/50-facts-about-queens-coronation-0.

"Apocalypse Then." *American Horror Story*, created by Brad Falchuk and Ryan Murphy, season 8, episode 10, FX Network, 2018

Atsma, Aaron J. "Dionysus Family—Greek Mythology." *Theoi Greek Mythology—Exploring Mythology in Classical Literature & Art*, https://www.theoi.com/Olympios/DionysosFamily.html. Accessed 23 Oct. 2020.

"Athanasian | Etymology, Origin, and Meaning of the Name Athanasian by Etymonline." *Etymonline—Online Etymology Dictionary*, https://www.etymonline.com/word/Athanasian#etymonline_v_18011. Accessed 07 Jun. 2021.

"Aurora Nights Explains How Equinox Effects the Northern Lights." *Aurora Nights*, https://www.aurora-nights.co.uk/northern-lights-information/when-can-i-see-the-northern-lights/effect- equinox-northern-lights/. Accessed 16 Jan. 2021.

Balch, William Ralston. *The Complete Compendium of Universal Knowledge*. Franklin Square Bible House, 1891.

Barrett, Frances. *The Magus*. Lackington, Allen, and Company, 1801.

"BBC—A History of the World—Object: Corn Dolly." *BBC*, 2014, http://www.bbc.co.uk/ahistoryoftheworld/objects/JI66Kx6hSI-WMuqDN0bLQsw.

"BBC Inside Out—Sybil Leek; White Witch." *BBC*, 2014, https://www.bbc.co.uk/insideout/south/series1/sybil-leek.shtml. Accessed 1 Jul. 2021.

"BBC Wales—History—Themes—Mabinogion: Fourth Branch." *BBC*, 2014 https://www.bbc.co.uk/wales/history/sites/themes/society/myths_mabinogion_04.shtml. Accessed 22 Jan. 2020.

"Before Gardner—What?" *Pentagram*, Nov. 1964.

"Berserkers." *National Museum of Denmark*, https://en.natmus.dk/historical-knowledge/denmark/prehistoric-period-until-1050-ad/the-viking-age/weapons/berserkers/. Accessed 3 Feb. 2020.

Bosworth, Joseph. *A Dictionary of the Anglo-Saxon Language*. Longman, Rees, Orme, Brown, Green, and Longman, 1838.

Buckland, Raymond. *Buckland's Book of Saxon Witchcraft*. Red Wheeler/Weiser Books, LLC., 2005.

Carr-Gomm, Philip, and Richard Heygate. *The Book of English Magic*. Harry N. Abrams, 2012.

"Cecil Williamson Another MI6 Dabbler in the Black Arts—Maier Files Series." *Maier Files Series*, 1 Feb. 2019, https://www.maier-files.com/cecil-williamson-another-mi6-dabbler-in-the-black-arts/. Accessed 10 Sep. 2020.

Chisholm, Hugh. "All Saints, Festival Of." *Encyclopedia Britannica 11th Ed.*, Cambridge University Press, 1911.

Chlup, Radek. *Proclus*. Cambridge University Press, 2012.

"Conjure Etymology, Origin and Meaning of Conjure by Etymonline." *Etymonline—Online Etymology Dictionary*, https://www.etymonline.com/word/conjure#etymonline_v_18215. Accessed 22 Jul. 2021.

Crowley, Aleister. *777 And Other Qabalistic Writings of Aleister Crowley: Including Gematria & Sepher Sephiroth.* Edited by Israel Regardie, Weiser Books, 1993.

—. *Moonchild.* Mandrake Press, 1929.

Crowther, Patricia. *Witch Blood! The Diary of a Witch High Priestess.* House of Collectibles, 1974.

Daly, Kathleen N., and Marian Rengel. *Greek and Roman Mythology, A to Z.* Infobase Publishing, 2009.

Daneau, Lambert. *A Dialogue of Witches.* Translated by Thomas Twyne, R.W. Watkins, 1575, https://quod.lib.umich.edu/e/eebo/A19798. 0001.001/1:1?rgn=div1;view=fulltext. Accessed 9 Jan. 2020.

Day, Sharon, and Maxine Sanders. *Maxine Sanders on Missing Digits & Disabilities—Oct '16.* YouTube, 7 Feb. 2018, https://www.youtube.com/watch?v=_PPqG2SJ0HQ.

Dorsey, Lilith. *Voodoo and Afro-Caribbean Paganism.* Citadel Press, 2005.

Dudley, Underwood. *Numerology Or What Pythagoras Wrought.* Cambridge University Press, 1997.

Eliade, Mircea. *Patterns in Comparative Religion.* U of Nebraska Press, 1996.

"England—Coronation Ring." *Royal Collection Trust,* https://www. rct.uk/collection/441925/coronation-ring. Accessed 16 Jun. 2020.

Etheredge, Laura. "Heka." *Encyclopedia Britannica,* 2008, https:// www.britannica.com/topic/heka. Accessed 10 Jan. 2020.

Falcon Ph.D., Rabi Ted, and David Blatner. *Judaism for Dummies.* Second Edition, John Wiley & Sons, Inc, 2013.

Farmer, John Stephen, and William Ernest Henley. *Slang and Its Analogues Past and Present: A Dictionary, Historical and Comparative, of the Heterodox Speech of All Classes of Society for More Than Three Hundred Years.* 1891.

Farrar, Janet, and Gavin Bone. *Lifting the Veil: A Witches' Guide to Trance-Prophesy, Drawing Down the Moon, and Ecstatic Ritual.* Acorn Guild Press, 2016.

—. *The Inner Mysteries.* Acord Guild Press, 2012.

Farrar, Janet, and Stewart Farrar. *A Witches' Bible: The Complete Witches' Handbook.* The Crowood Press Ltd., 2017.

—. *The Life & Times of a Modern Witch.* Piatkus Books, 1987.

—. *The Witches' God.* Phoenix Publishing Inc, 1989.

—. *The Witches' Goddess.* David & Charles, 2012.

Farrar, Stewart. *What Witches Do.* David & Charles, 2012.

Forlong, James George Roche. *Rivers of Life, or Sources and Streams of the Faiths of Man in All Lands; Showing the Evolution of Faiths from the Rudest Symbolisms to the Latest Spiritual Developments.* Quaritch, 1883.

Fortune, Dion. *The Mystical Qabalah.* Aquarian Press, 1987.

Fosbroke, Thomas Dudley, and Dionysius Lardner. *A Treatise on the Arts, Manufactures, Manners, and Institutions of the Greeks and Romans.* Longman, Rees, Orme, Brown, Green & Longman, and John Taylor, 1833.

Freud, Sigmund. *The Complete Psychological Works of Sigmund Freud.* Translated by James Strachey, The Hogarth Press, 1958.

Gardner, Gerald B. *High Magic's Aid.* Aurinia Books, 2010.

—. *The Meaning of Witchcraft*. Red Wheeler/Weiser Books, LLC., 2004.

—. *Witchcraft Today*. The Citadel Press, 2004.

Gary, Gemma. *Silent as the Trees: Devonshire Witchcraft, Folklore & Magic*. Troy Books Publishing, 2017.

—. *Traditional Witchcraft: A Cornish Book of Ways*. Revised Second ed., Troy Books Publishing, 2013.

Gary, Macy. *The Hidden History of Women's Ordination: Female Clergy In The Medieval West*. Oxford University Press, 2012.

*Gatekeeping*. https://www.lexico.com/definition/gatekeeping. Accessed 13 Jan. 2020.

Gihr, Nikolaus. *Holy Sacrifice of the Mass: Dogmatically, Liturgically, and Ascetically Explained*. B. Herder, 1908.

Gomme, George Laurence. *The Gentleman's Library Magazine: Popular Superstitions*. Elliot Stock, 1884.

Grillot de Givry, Emile. *Witchcraft, Magic and Alchemy*. George G. Harrap & Co. Ltd., 1931.

Guerra, Elizabeth, and Janet Farrar. *Stewart Farrar: Writer on a Broomstick*. Skylight Press, 2013.

Guiley, Rosemary Ellen. *The Encyclopedia of Witches, Witchcraft, and Wicca*. Third Edition, Facts on File, Inc., 2008.

"Hag Etymology, Origin and Meaning of Hag by Etymonline." *Etymonline—Online Etymology Dictionary*, https://www.etymonline.com/word/hag?ref=etymonline_crossreference. Accessed 2 Jun. 2021.

Hand, Lynne. "May Day—British Culture—British Customs and Traditions in May." *Learn English Free—English Learning Online*, https://www.learnenglish.de/culture/mayday.html. Accessed 12 Nov. 2020.

Harrison, Jane Ellen. *Prolegomena to the Study of Greek Religion.* Cambridge University Press, 1908.

Harvey, Karen. *The Kiss in History.* Manchester University Press, 2005.

"Helmets." *National Museum of Denmark,* https://en.natmus.dk/historical-knowledge/denmark/prehistoric-period-until-1050-ad/the-viking-age/weapons/helmets/. Accessed 3 Feb. 2020.

Heselton, Philip. *Wiccan Roots: Gerald Gardner and the Modern Witchcraft Revival.* Capall Bann Pub, 2000.

House, Zondervan Publishing, and Zondervan. *Holy Bible.* 2013.

"Housel Definition & Meaning Dictionary.Com." *www.dictionary.com,* https://www.dictionary.com/browse/housel. Accessed 2 Jun. 2021.

Howard, Michael. *Modern Wicca.* Llewellyn Worldwide, 2009.

Hughes, Bettany. *Bacchus Uncovered: Ancient God of Ecstasy.* Sandstone Global Productions Ltd., 2018.

—. *Venus Uncovered: Ancient God of Love.* Sandstone Global Productions Ltd., 2017.

Hutton, Ronald. *Stations of the Sun: A History of the Ritual Year in Britain.* Oxford University Press, 1996.

*Initiation. https://www.lexico.com/definition/initiation. Accessed 1 Jun. 2020.*

Jamieson, John. *An Etymological Dictionary of the Scottish Language.* Albernethy & Walker, 1818.

Johnston, Sarah Iles. *Religions of the Ancient World: A Guide*. Harvard University Press, 2004.

Jones, Pollyanna. "Understanding the Fylgjur of Norse Mythology—Exemplore." *Exemplore*, Exemplore, 14 Nov. 2014, https://exemplore.com/magic/Understanding-the-Fylgjur.

Joyce, Patrick Weston. *A Smaller Social History of Ancient Ireland*. Longmans, Green and Co., 1906.

Kahlos, Maijastina. *Debate and Dialogue: Christian and Pagan Cultures c. 360–430*. Ashgate Publishing, Ltd., 2007.

"Key of Solomon, Book II." *Esoteric Archives*, http://www.esotericarchives.com/solomon/ksol2.htm. Accessed 7 Jun. 2021.

Kipling, Rudyard. "A Tree Song." *Poetry Lovers' Page*, https://www.poetryloverspage.com/poets/kipling/tree_song.html. Accessed 17 Dec. 2020.

Knowles, George. "Raymond Buckland." *Controverscial.Com*, 2007, https://controverscial.com/Raymond%20Buckland.htm. Accessed 7 Sep. 2020.

Koloski-Ostrow, Ann Olga, Claire L. Lyons, Natalie Boymel Kampen. *Naked Truths: Women, Sexuality, and Gender in Classical Art and Archaeology*. Routledge, 2000.

Kurzweil, Arthur. *Kabbalah For Dummies*. John Wiley & Sons, 2011.

Lévi, Éliphas. *Transcendental Magic Part 1*. Rider & Company, 1896.

Lewis-Stempel, John. *The Running Hare: The Secret Life of Farmland*. Random House, 2016.

Liguori, Saint Alfonso Maria. *The Glories of Mary*. 1868.

MacKillop, James. *A Dictionary of Celtic Mythology*. Oxford University Press, 2016.

Macy, Gary. *The Hidden History of Women's Ordination*. Oxford University Press, 2012.

Marks, Joshua J. "The Negative Confession." *World History Encyclopedia*, 2017, https://www.worldhistory.org/The_Negative_Confession/. Accessed 10 Jan. 2020.

Mathers, S. L. MacGregor. *The Key of Solomon the King*. Book Tree, 1999.

"Maurus Servius Honoratus, Commentary on the Aeneid of Vergil, Servii Grammatici In Vergilii Aeneidos Librvm Quartvm, Line 511." *Perseus Digital Library*, http://www.perseus.tufts.edu/hopper/text?doc=Perseus%3Atext%3A1999.02.0053%3Abook%3D4%3Acommline%3D511. Accessed 30 Jan. 2019.

McNeill, Florence Marian. *The Silver Bough, Vol. 2: A Calendar of Scottish National Festivals, Candlemas to Harvest Home*. William MacLellan, 1959.

Mellinkoff, Ruth W. *The Horned Moses in Medieval Art and Thought*. Wipf and Stock Publishers, 1997.

Meyer, Kuno, editor. *Hibernica Minora*. Translated by Kenneth Jackson, Clarendon Press, 1894.

Michelet, Jules. *Satanism and Witchcraft*. Translated by Alfred Richard Allinson, Citadel Press, 1939.

Miravalle, Mark I. *Introduction to Mary: The Heart of Marian Doctrine and Devotion*. Queenship Publishing, 2006.

Moritz Artur Goldammer, Kurt. "Religious Symbols: Gestural and Physical Movements." *Encyclopedia Britannica*, 1999, https://www.

britannica.com/topic/religious-symbolism/Gestural-and-physical-movements#ref399228. Accessed 4 Nov. 2020.

Murray, Margaret Alice. *The God of the Witches*. Oxford University Press on Demand, 1970.

Naydler, Jeremy. *Temple of the Cosmos: The Ancient Egyptian Experience of the Sacred*. Inner Traditions / Bear & Co, 1996.

Nema. *Maat Magick: A Guide to Self-Initiation*. Weiser Books, 1995.

Opie, Iona Archibald, and Peter Opie. *The Oxford Dictionary of Nursery Rhymes*. Second Edition, Oxford University Press, 1997.

Ovid. *Ovid Volume 1*. Translated by Brookes More, M. Jones, 1978.

—. *Ovid's Fasti: Roman Holidays*. Translated by Betty Rose Nagle, Indiana University Press, 1995.

Parkinson, Richard. "Exorcists, Conjurors & Cunning Men in Post-Reformation England." *Serpent Songs: An Anthology of Traditional Craft*. Scarlet Imprint, 2013.

Passavanti, Jacopo. *Lo Specchio Della Vera Penitenza*. Poligrafia Italiana, 1354.

Patterson, Steve. *Cecil Williamson's Book of Witchcraft: A Grimoire of the Museum of Witchcraft*. Llewellyn Publications, 2020.

Paxson, Diana L. *The Essential Guide to Possession, Depossession, and Divine Relationships*. Red Wheel/Weiser, 2015.

Peacock, Thomas Love. *Rhododaphne: Or The Thessalian Spell: A Poem*. M. Carey & Son, 1818.

Pearson, Nigel G. *The Devil's Plantation: East Anglican Lore, Witchcraft & Folk-Magic*. Troy Books Publishing, 2016.

Penczak, Christopher. *The Living Temple of Witchcraft Volume One*. Llewellyn Worldwide, 2008.

—. *The Mighty Dead*. Copper Cauldron Publishing, LLC, 2013.

"Pentacle." *Etymonline—Online Etymology Dictionary*, https://www.etymonline.com/search?q=pentacle. Accessed 2 Jun. 2021.

Porphyry. *On Images*. Translated by Edwin Hamilton Gifford, http://classics.mit.edu/Porphyry/images.html. Accessed 30 Jan. 2020.

Regardie, Israel, and John Michael Greer. *The Golden Dawn*. Llewellyn Publications, 2015.

Robinson, George. *Essential Judaism: A Complete Guide to Beliefs, Customs & Rituals*. Simon and Schuster, 2016.

Römer, Thomas. "The Horns of Moses. Setting the Bible in Its Historical Context" *OpenEdition Books*, translated by Liz Libbrecht, https://books.openedition.org/cdf/3048?lang=en. Accessed 3 Jan. 2020.

Rose, Elliot. *A Razor for a Goat: A Discussion of Certain Problems in the History of Witchcraft and Diabolism*. University of Toronto Press, 1989.

"Sacrum Etymology, Origin, and Meaning of Sacrum by Etymonline." *Etymonline—Online Etymology Dictionary*, https://www.etymonline.com/word/sacrum. Accessed 22 Oct. 2020.

Sanders, Alex. *A Witch is Born*, A&M Records, 1970.

Sanders, Maxine. *Fire Child: The Life & Magic of Maxine Sanders "Witch Queen"*. Kindle ed., Mandrake of Oxford, 2007.

Shaw, Philip A. *Pagan Goddesses in the Early Germanic World*. Bristol Classical Press, 2011.

Skye, Michelle. *Goddess Afoot! Practicing Magic with Celtic & Norse Goddesses*. Llewellyn Worldwide, 2008.

Spencer, Craig. *Aradia*. Llewellyn Worldwide, 2020.

Strong, Roy. *Coronation: From the 8th to the 21st Century*. HarperCollins UK, 2013.

Talcroft, Barbara L. *Death of the Corn King: King and Goddess in Rosemary Sutcliff's Historical Fiction for Young Adults*. Scarecrow Press, 1995.

Taliesin. "Ancients and Moderns." *Pentagram Magazin*, Mar. 1965.

Taylor, Thomas, translator. "Orphic Hymns 1-40—Theoi Classical Texts Library." *Theoi Greek Mythology—Exploring Mythology in Classical Literature & Art*, https://www.theoi.com/Text/OrphicHymns1.html#31. Accessed 21 Mar. 2021.

*The Astrologers' Magazine and Philosophical Miscellany*. Vol. 1, W. Locke, 1791.

"The Coronation of Queen Elizabeth II." *Oremus*, http://www.oremus.org/liturgy/coronation/cor1953b.html. Accessed 16 Jun. 2022.

"This Is Why the Priest Kisses the Altar at Mass." *Aleteia — Catholic Spirituality, Lifestyle, World News, and Culture*, https://www.facebook.com/AleteiaEn/, 26 July 2017, https://aleteia.org/2017/07/26/this-is-why-the-priest-kisses-the-altar-at-mass/.

Turlington, Shannon. *The Complete Idiot's Guide to Voodoo*. Alpha, 2001.

Turner, Sharon. *The History of the Anglo-Saxons from the Earliest Period to the Norman Conquest*. Cadell & Davies, 1840.

Turville-Petre, Gabriel. *Nine Norse Studies*. Volume 5. Viking Society for Northern Research, University College London, 1972.

Valiente, Doreen. *An ABC of Witchcraft Past and Present*. Phoenix Pub, 1988.

—. "Doreen Valiente: A Witch Speaks." Beltane Edition. *Pagan Dawn*, 1998.

—. *The Rebirth of Witchcraft*. Robert Hale, 2008.

—. *Where Witchcraft Lives*. Fourth Edition, The Doreen Valiente Foundation, The Centre for Pagan Studies, 2014.

—. "Working with Gerald and Robert Cochrane, Magister." *The Paganism Reader*, Routledge, 2004.

Venerabilis, Beda. *Bede, The Reckoning of Time-Tanslated Texts for Historians*. Translated by Faith Wallis, Liverpool University Press, 1999.

"Weapon Etymology, Origin, and Meaning of Weapon by Etymonline." *Etymonline—Online Etymology Dictionary*, https://www.etymonline.com/word/weapon#etymonline_v_4873. Accessed 08 Jun. 2021.

Whitehead, Willis F. *The Mystic Thesaurus, Or Initiation in the Theoretical and Practical Secrets of Astral Truth and Occult Art*. Willis F. Whitehead, 1899.

Whiterig, John. *Christ Crucified and Other Meditations of a Durham Hermit*. Gracewing Publishing, 1994.

Wilson, David Raoul. *Anglo-Saxon Paganism*. Taylor & Francis, 1992.

"Witch Etymology, Origin and Meaning of Witch by Etymonline." *Etymonline—Online Etymology Dictionary*, https://www.etymonline.com/word/witch. Accessed 4 Sep. 2020.

"Witches and Demons," *Mystic Britain*, Clive Anderson and Mary-Ann Ochota, Blink Films, 2019.

Wright, Brian. *Brigid: Goddess, Druidess and Saint.* The History Press, 2011.

Ziskind, Bernard, and Bruno Halioua. "La Conception Du Cœur Dans l'Égypte Ancienne." *Médecine/Sciences*, no. 3, EDP Sciences, Mar. 2004, pp. 367–73. *Crossref*, doi:10.1051/medsci/2004203367.

# INDEX

# OTHER TITLES FROM CROSSED CROW BOOKS

*Wiccan Mysteries* by Raven Grimassi
*The Bones Fall in a Spiral* by Mortellus
*Your Star Sign* by Per Henrik Gullfoss
*The Complete Book of Spiritual Astrology* by Per Henrik Gullfoss
*Icelandic Plant Magic* by Albert Bjorn
*The Black Book of Johnathan Knotbristle* by Chris Allaun
*A Witch's Book of Terribles* by Wycke Malliway
*In the Shadow of Thirteen Moons* by Kimberly Sherman-Cook
*Merlin: Master of Magick* by Gordon Strong
*Sun God & Moon Maiden* by Gordon Strong
*Wiccan Mysteries* by Raven Grimassi
*The Way of Four* by Deborah Lipp
*Celtic Tree Mysteries* by Steve Blamires
*Star Magic* by Sandra Kynes
*Witches' Sabbats and Esbats* by Sandra Kynes
*A Spirit Work Primer* by Naag Loki Shivanaath
*A Witch's Shadow Magick Compendium* by Raven Digitalis
*Flight of the Firebird* by Kenneth Johnson
*Witchcraft and the Shamanic Journey* by Kenneth Johnson
*Travels Through Middle Earth* by Alaric Albertsson
*Craft of the Hedge Witch* by Geraldine Smythe
*Be Careful What You Wish For* by Laetitia Latham-Jones
*Death's Head* by Blake Malliway
*The Wildwood Way* by Cliff Seruntine

LEARN MORE AT
WWW.CROSSEDCROWBOOKS.COM